Screen dreams

MANCHESTER
UNIVERSITY PRESS

Screen dreams

Fantasising lesbians in film

CLARE WHATLING

MANCHESTER UNIVERSITY PRESS   Manchester and New York

distributed exclusively in the USA by St. Martin's Press

Copyright © Clare Whatling 1997

Published by Manchester University Press
Oxford Road, Manchester M13 9NR, UK
and Room 400, 175 Fifth Avenue, New York, NY 10010, USA

Distributed exclusively in the USA
by St. Martin's Press, Inc., 175 Fifth Avenue, New York, NY 10010, USA

British Library Cataloguing-in-Publication Data
A catalogue record is available from the British Library

Library of Congress Cataloging-in-Publication Data
Whatling, Clare.
  Screen dreams: fantasising lesbians in film/Clare Whatling.
    p. cm.
  Includes bibliographical references and index.
  ISBN 0–7190–5066–9 (hb). — ISBN 0–7190–5067–7 (pb)
  1. Lesbianism in motion pictures. I. Title.
PN1995.S.L48W53   1997
791.43'6529206643—DC21   97–6973

ISBN 0–7190–5066–9 *hardback*
ISBN 0–7190–5067–7 *paperback*

First published 1997
01 00 99 98 97   10 9 8 7 6 5 4 3 2 1

Typeset in Photina with Frutiger
by Northern Phototypesetting Co Ltd, Bolton
Printed in Great Britain
by Biddles Ltd, Guildford and King's Lynn

Contents

List of figures	*page* vi
Acknowledgements	vii
Introduction: (In)appropriate(d) others or how Vanessa Redgrave turned me lesbian	1
1 The appropriateness of appropriation	11
2 Psychoanalysis and the lesbian supplement	35
3 Fantastic desires	53
4 'In the good old days when times were bad': The nostalgia for abjection in lesbian cinema spectatorship.	79
5 Stars and their proclivities	116
6 Fostering the illusion	134
Afterword: The persistence of the specular	160
Bibliography	167
Index	177

Figures

1. *Heavenly Creatures*, Wingnut/Fontana/GMBH, 1994 99
2. *Butterfly Kiss*, Electric pictures, British Screen, The Merseyside Production Fund, Dan Films Ltd Productions, 1994 101
3. *Silkwood*, Twentieth Century Fox, 1983 107
4. *Walk on the Wild Side*, Columbia Pictures, 1962 109
5. *Sommersby*, WB/Regency Enterprises, V.O.F. and Le Studio Canal, 1993 138
6. *Hotel New Hampshire*, Woodfall, Orion, Yellowbill, 1984 148
7. *The Accused*, Paramount pictures Corporation, 1988 151
8. *Little Man Tate*, Orion Pictures, 1991 155

Reproduced by kind permission of the Kobal Collection

Acknowledgements

In the knowledge that most people read these only in order to see who's dating whom, I'll keep this brief (the gossip's in the text). My thanks then to Matthew Frost, Stephanie Sloan and Gemma Marren at Manchester University Press. Also to the (anonymous) readers at the Press who gave me food for thought and sound advice. Thanks also to my colleagues in the Drama Department at Manchester University who facilitated my research time by ridding me of large tracts of administration. Thanks to Paul Heritage for lending me his book collection, and for complimenting me on mine and to Silvia Davini for being so enthusiastic.

Thanks to Sara Ahmed, Jane Howcroft and Rachel Driver who each read chapters of this book in its later stages. Thanks to Angela and Tessa for looking forward to reading it. Special thanks to Lisa Diedrich who commented widely and with good humour and affection.

Thanks also to Fiona Jackman at Kobal, who was both helpful and enthusiastic in allowing me to riffle through files of films relevant and not strictly relevant to this book.

Special thanks to beautiful Pratibha Parmar for her enthusiasm and commitment to the excavation of popular culture!

Thanks to the cat for sitting on the delete button only when necessary, my Uncle Paul because he wanted a mention, Doris for always making me talk to teachers at parties, all my family in fact, but especially my Ma and Pa and brother Carl who encouraged me in this project even while hoping it wouldn't have *lesbian* emblazoned quite so colourfully in the title.

And finally, thanks to Karen, the most charming woman in the world, always.

Introduction: (In)appropriate(d) others or how Vanessa Redgrave turned me lesbian

A few years ago a friend, Rachel Driver, and I, were asked to give a talk on lesbians and film to our local university lesbian, gay and bisexual society. The remit seemed clear – a brief survey of the history of lesbian representation in the movies to date, necessitating an obvious, albeit limited, progression through *Maidens in Uniform* (Leontine Sagan, 1931, Ger), which I had come across on a sexualities film course, and which I guessed most of the group would not have seen, though I suspected they would respond to its famed dormitory kissing scene as positively as I had. Following this we would give a brief mention to another film course favourite, the French school romance *Olivia* (Jacqueline Audry, 1951, Fr), then on to *The Killing of Sister George* (Robert Aldrich, 1968, US), a brief excursion into lesbian-feminism (the films of Jan Oxenburg, most particularly *Home Movie* (Jan Oxenburg, 1975, US), featuring strongly here as usual) and finally into the independent/mainstream crossovers *Personal Best* (Robert Towne, 1983, US), *Lianna* (John Sayles, 1982, US), *Desert Hearts* (Donna Deitch, 1985, US) and the then just released *Salmonberries* (Percy Adlon, 1991, Ger). As we were sitting around and talking about film in relation to our own lives, however, we realised that, though we had come across these films as important lesbian representations on courses at university and in our own post-coming-out viewing,[1] they were not the films that had had the most profound effect upon us as we were growing up. Other films had meant more to us, including film texts with no obvious, or only a slight, lesbian component. For me it was the lesbian frisson, always framed by a compulsory heterosexual recuperation, of *Julia* (Fred Zinnemann, 1977, US) and *The Bostonians* (James Ivory, 1984, GB) that had had a formative impact. At the age of twelve or thirteen I also fell in love with Meryl Streep, starring in *Silkwood* (Mike Nichols, 1983, US) at the time, a passion which, appropriately or inappropriately, informed my reception of each of her films from that date on. For Rachel, with her more nascently perverse (and perhaps more imaginative) tendencies it was *Entre Nous* (Diane Kurys, 1983, Fr), *La Lectrice* (Michel Deville, 1988, Fr), the camp exploits of *Calamity Jane* (David Butler, 1953, US) and the sparky dialogue between Cary Grant and Katherine Hepburn in *Bringing Up Baby* (Howard Hawks, 1938, US).

Looking back, a number of different positions were being negotiated within even these limited identifications and desires. My adoration of Vanessa Redgrave and Meryl Streep informed my reception of all their films, just as Rachel's love of the actress Mio Mio did hers.[2] Her appreciation of a camp aesthetic, before she even knew what this might signify, along with both of our desires for women who stepped out of line, informed our interpretation of film and the pleasures we took in it. Above all, we realised that it was what we as children and teenagers had put into these films that mattered. Our investment in piecing together the lesbian hints and subtexts, the lip-brushing kisses or the look too long held, the *need* in fact, for our nascent lesbian sexualities to bring these moments out in the texts, to make them the focus, was what we took away with us.[3] Cinema viewing was from that moment a transformative process in which we could alter the focus of meaning of a film text, just as when we were adolescents we had read into the narrative what we had most longed to see.

The result was a diverse series of film clips combining both overt and covert representations of our now socially articulated lesbian desires. Vivien and Cay were represented, but so were Doris Day, Vanessa Redgrave, Meryl Streep, James Stewart, Montgomery Clift and Cary Grant. Thelma and Louise and Ripley also featured as testimony to the soon-to-be new vogue in lesbian textual appropriations,[4] but so did Joanna Lumley as the (for me) maternal-erotic sex goddess Sapphire, and David McCallum as Steel. These images reflected our personal and, we surmised, idiosyncratic lesbian desires. Imagine our surprise then when they seemed to resonate with the others, male, female, lesbian, gay and bisexual, in the group. Indeed, our own reflections appeared to set off an entirely new train of inappropriate desires in others. What became clear was that as queer-identified cinema viewers we did not confine our desires to identity appropriate objects.⁵ Our desires rather had relatively free rein within the fantasy space of the cinema. In practice, they seemed limitless.

A few years later I wrote an article, 'Fostering the illusion', which embraced this strategy of queer appropriation to an enthusiastic and celebratory degree. My conclusion there was that 'No film text belongs to any one constituency. It seems as foolish to argue that any text is intrinsically lesbian as to argue that a text is exclusively heterosexual ... [we nevertheless live in] ... a viewing world where we still have the chance to call everything our own' (Whatling, 1994: 195). In many ways I continue to believe this, at the very least because I continue to have a pleasurable investment in cinema as a medium of fantasy appropriation. On reflection, however, I would maintain that my arguments in 'Fostering the illusion' require a more serious examination. This centres for me now on three main issues: how is our reception of films refracted through not only sexual orientation but other signifiers of difference? what is the potential for filmic appropriations as part of a committed queer viewing strategy? and, what underlies appropriation, what are we colonising and/or evading in the things we seek to appropriate for ourselves?

This introduction takes its title from a 1986/7 special issue of *Discourse* edited by Trinh T. Minh-ha and entitled, *She the Inappropriate/d other*. The project of this special issue was to examine the double bind of domination and resistance, the fact that, as Minh-ha puts it, 'one is never installed within marginality, and one never dwells outside it ... there is a Third world in every First world and vice-versa' (Minh-ha, 1986/7: 3). In other words, an other, any other, is both inside – but never quite – the dominant discourse, and outside – but never totally – its regime of interest, subject rather to a series of appropriations, colonisations, representations. In another piece in which the *Discourse* special issue is cited, Teresa de Lauretis appends this thought:

For, as Norma Alarcón put it to me in a seminar discussion, are there really any 'inappropriated others'? I took her question to mean that while there may be – indeed there are – many who are other (than white or socially privileged), insofar as they are named, interpellated, or represented as 'others', they may already have been appropriated. (de Lauretis, 1990: 17–18)

My intention in this book is to bear testimony to Minh-ha's/Alarcón's/de Lauretis's point in arguing that indeed, there are no inappropriated others. Appropriation is a feature of discourse and of the desire which is invested through discourse in acts of representation. In the psychoanalytic terminology which will underwrite at least a part of this book, this describes the way in which the subject constitutes itself through and upon its cathection of another. The heterosexual who repudiates the homosexual who nevertheless continues to operate as the site of repressed fascination; the lesbian who disavows her heterosexual past, whilst incorporating this into the desires she realises as an avid consumer of the cinema; the white cinemagoing public, straight and lesbian-identified, who both exclude and recall the figure of the non-white woman, or indeed man. Appropriation, in these instances, is reflected through a politics of dominance, of colonisation, of absorption (though the structural relation of dominance is reversed in the case of the lesbian who excludes her heterosexual past). How then can I argue for its radical impact as a politics of reversal and recontextualisation?

For Gayatri Chakravorty Spivak, appropriation reflects a process of self-consolidation which is always grounded upon the colonisation and, in one sense or another, the elision, of the other. Spivak locates this process within 'the history of imperialism, in the epistemic violence that constitutes/effaces a subject that was obliged to cathect (occupy in response to a desire) the space of the Imperialists' self-consolidating other' (Spivak, 1988: 209).[6] Within Spivak's process the other is employed as sop to he who holds the power of naming. Still, named and abjected and repudiated, lacking the power of self-naming, banished to the underside of the dominant, we learn from Albert Memmi (1965), Frantz Fanon (1986), Judith Butler (1991) and others that the appropriated is none the less subject to an endless return. For while occupying the space of the other, the dominant is yet dependent upon that other for its own sense of self. The two in fact share a relation of interdependence in which subject and object form an exclusive and inevitable relation by which you can't have one without the other.

In many ways this book will reverse the habitual relation between dominant and other where one of those appropriated others, the lesbian, will be the subject of the book as opposed to its object. And within at least some of the lesbian configurations attested to in the chapters ahead, the dominant (heterosexuality) will form the abject other to the previously colonised lesbian subject. At the same time we need to be clear as to what gets appropriated and colonised within this lesbian reversal which is *ipso facto* no more innocent than any other.

A word or two about definition. This book inevitably employs terms – lesbian, queer, community, identification, desire, appropriation, abjection, audiences, texts, amongst others – that have been subject to much necessary debate within contemporary cultural and sexuality theory. Some of those debates will be referred to or revisited in the chapters that follow, chapter three in particular dealing with the intersection between desire and identification, chapter four with the meaning of abjection, the function and scope of appropriation as a visual politics and the relation between audiences and texts, and chapter five with a circumscribed notion of community. I do not want to pre-empt those discussions here. Still, some immediate attempt at definition will be made around the area of the lesbian.

The subtitle of this book should perhaps be *Desire and the Movies*. Its subject is in fact lesbian desire. What, however, do I mean by this? For our immediate purposes the term *lesbian* describes the subject who enters a cinema or video store with a self-named (motivated by sex, politics, sociality or any combination of the above) identity as lesbian. Such a lesbian self-naming as it remains strategic, situated and multiple is meant to elide any essentialism implied in the term. This lesbian is crucial to the concept of this book, whose subtitle, *Fantasising Lesbians in Film*, implies a certain commonality of vision. Inferences of lesbian commonality are fraught with dangers, however, and thus for safety's sake, the lesbian subject most clearly implied in this book is the one I know best, that is, myself. If other people recognise something of their own identifications and desires in the categories discussed below, all well and good. However, the intention of this book is to expand the possibilities for lesbian identification and desire, not to proscribe new ones; and thus disagreement, disaffection and disavowal are welcomed as much as any avowal of my arguments herein.

At the same time as I hold to a notion of myself as a lesbian subject who reads films through a self-consciously lesbian desire, however, I will argue that the images so read need not themselves self-consciously articulate lesbianism. My argument is that there is no such thing as a lesbian film. Films are rather lesbianised by the individual (or in some cases collective) viewer. The good thing about this is that, in practice, there are as many lesbian readings of films (and hence lesbian films) as there are lesbians in the audience.

In the contest between audience and text in this book, the audience definitely comes off the better. This is not, however, to argue that the text has no effect on the choices made by audiences.[7] One appropriates what is there, straining to read into it those elements which are not there. In this sense the text sets up the terms of representation and of resistance, colonisation and refusal which structure any appropriation of the dominant by the margins.

Nor is it to argue that textual representations somehow reflect 'the truth' about lesbians. Throughout this book the term *lesbian* will be employed in order to describe characters on the screen. This use of the term should be understood as a shorthand description for the cultural connotations of lesbianism, however, and not necessarily conflated with the lesbian subject who watches. Where appropriate, the distinction between screen representation and lesbian subject will be highlighted through the use of the term *'lesbian'* (in quotation marks) for the former.

Nor, in reading self-consciously as a lesbian, do I believe that all lesbians do this all of the time. It is as likely that lesbians will employ the cinema to temporarily 'pop out' of their lesbian identity as Tamsin Wilton puts it (Wilton, 1995: 157), as they will to seek its reflection in diverse cinematic images. That my focus in this book will be to look self-consciously as a lesbian should not preclude other possibilities. In addition, I believe, and at points will argue, that the cinema offers women who do not self-name as lesbian, who may actively repudiate such an identification, a space for the realisation of private same-sex fantasies. It is not the scope of this book to describe these. However, I want to make it clear that, despite its broadening of identificatory categories, this book only ever describes half the story. In this sense the term *lesbian* is both a necessary and an insufficient category of description, but then again, what's new there?

The scope of this book is idiosyncratic. The majority of my filmic examples are taken from the mainstream Hollywood cinema. Others can be more comfortably placed within the independent, largely but not exclusively US, sector. None of the readings appended is intended to be either definitive or particularly thorough. I include them where they facilitate an argument, rather than as readings in themselves. They are united only by their function as examples which have sprung to mind as a result of my thoughts on lesbians and cinema over the years. Reviewing the book I worry that this leaves them seeming rather decontextualised; of context of production, of different points, or histories, of reception. Each of these issues will be taken up in chapters five and four. A guiding word to the reader would be to remember that this is a study not of the lesbian film,[8] but of a way of looking lesbian. This is its scope and its limitation.

The argument of this book is that interpretation lies largely (though not exclusively) with the desire of the spectator. She has enormous power to shape the meaning of a given film text, and, if she recognises herself as a lesbian (that is, as someone who is generally excluded from the remit of dominant film production), enormous investment in appropriating the films she loves to her own desires. To 'look lesbian' (Graham, 1994) is to situate one's sexual orientation at the heart of one's viewing practices. The scope of this book will be to situate those viewing practices within a multiply potential interpretative framework.

Chapter one will attempt an examination of the current status of appropriation as a strategy of reading in relation to a number of contemporary feminist and lesbian feminist texts and contexts. This chapter will ask, amongst other things, how far can a politically informed lesbian feminism go with this strategy? This question is picked up and explored in greater detail in chapter three where I will ask not only how lesbian desire alters the focus of film interpretation but also how it might be constituted by the cinematic forms in play.

Chapter two examines the relation between psychoanalysis and feminist film theory. Through a critical reading of a number of feminist film and/or psychoanalytic theorists I will draw attention to the limitations of psychoanalysis as a means of exploring lesbian cinematic desire. I will then demonstrate its uses when informed by a self-consciously appropriative lesbian politics. This chapter really serves as a means of mapping the terrain for chapter three, which will utilise a modified psychoanalytic model in exploring the relation between cinematic identification and desire. Chapter three will also explore some of the variety of lesbian spectatorial positions, utilising psychoanalytic concepts of identification and desire to explode the traditional demarcation between being and having through the figure of the femme lesbian whose potential desire for another femme destabilises the conventions by which lesbian cinematic desire is usually understood.

Chapter four engages with some of the pros and cons of appropriation as a strategy of both subversion and containment. It also argues that, despite being shortchanged by Hollywood, maligned or otherwise misrepresented when 'we' appear at all, lesbian spectators have long been intent on appropriating the Hollywood scene to our own agenda. Indeed, rather than bemoaning the fate of filmic lesbians who are variously represented as sick, sinful, narcissistic, psychotic or dead, lesbian spectators are able to turn the cinema of abjection into a perverse pleasure in looking.

Chapter five considers the importance of gossip as a medium of cultural knowledge and the exchange of sexual information. It will argue that, though the alleged sexual profile of a particular star is interesting and a part of the aura that accumulates around a cult of personality, the ability to lesbianise a given star lies ultimately with her (or perhaps even his) viewership. The notion of the extra-filmic, not only in the form of gossip, star interviews, profile and biography but as a feature of the fantasy desires and daydreams of the subject who watches has been given little consideration within cinema studies to date. In part this is due to the deeply personal nature of the area, often a bar to formal academic research. Still, I will argue in this chapter that the investment of the viewer in shaping the meaning and significance conferred upon a text becomes a fundamental part of its reception. Chapter six will put the argument of chapter five into practice with an examination of the star profile and some of the films of Hollywood icon and alleged lesbian Jodie Foster.

The concluding section of the book asks why looking has come to be so important within the frame of reference of contemporary cinematic studies, and of lesbian cinematic desire. It will suggest some of the limitations of looking lesbian but also the necessity of appropriating an already predominating scopic economy to a lesbian frame of reference.

Finally to a question about style. Academic film texts have generally taken two forms: either an in-depth, psychoanalytically informed, often structuralist account of a few specific films, genres or auteurs, or a methodological study of particular, limited, film audiences and/or practices. It will be clear in reading this book that the latter was never an option for me. How would one ever collect, never mind quantify, the various and contradictory pleasures of an audience that I believe crosses so many divides? The first option is closer to my intentions but still hopelessly limiting. My scope is not a few films confined to a specific genre, auteur or psychoanalytic paradigm but just about every film that has affected me since the age of ten. To be sure, psychoanalysis provides a framework of sorts but, as chapter two will describe, it is a framework that, when employed within a lesbian context, needs be accompanied by a self-conscious deconstruction. In short, this book attempts to develop a personal vision of the cinema in which the findings, the experiences and the pleasures are mine. The hope is, however, that they will resonate with the reader in a way which, if it does not always confirm my thesis, will at least open up new areas within the debate.

One final word – or is it demurral? – on the subject of appropriation. As any theorist writing at the end of the twentieth century knows, it has become a feat of impossibility to testify to all one's influences, or even to render a sufficient account of their ontology. Whilst theoretical and academic integrity has led me to never wittingly misrepresent another writer in this book which embraces feminist, psychoanalytic and post-colonialist writing as only its most obvious influences, it should be clear that what I offer is only partial glimpses. I have not read all that there is to read in feminist, post-structuralist, psychoanalytic and post-colonialist theory, rather I have taken what I felt I needed from each of them. The result is, I am sure, an argument built upon blind spots, but, and as well, a politics of appropriation that thrives on its eclecticism. The mistakes I make (and I am sure there are many) are mine. I hope they won't spoil the reader's enjoyment of the larger (or is it the smaller, more intimate?) view.

Notes

1 In making the claim that these films are important examples of lesbianism in film, I am aware that each has a very different status within the history of lesbian representation.

2 The way in which the characters Redgrave plays in *Julia* and *The Bostonians* skirt the line between covert homoeroticism and the tantalising possibility of a more overt desire, registered with my own nascent desires to the extent that I would send my entire family out of the house so as to view the films in private, so intense (and also of course so shameful) were the images to me at the time.

3 I suspect in fact, that, contrary to the various political bids to have lesbianism named on the screen as an overt and visible identity, at this point it was the very covertness of the representation that appealed to me. I have wondered, in the course of writing this book, whether this desire for the covert is a feature of my own perverse desires alone, or whether it is shared by others. Certainly, as I argue in chapter four, it is a trope which for me has continued beyond adolescence and into my adult viewing preferences.

4 *Appropriation* is a term which will be more properly investigated in chapters one and four. Some provisional definition seems necessary, however. The *OED* definition, to appropriate, is to 'take possession of; take to oneself, devote to special purposes' and this seems to me fitting as a description of what I was doing with Vanessa Redgrave all those years ago. On the whole, however, I prefer the more colloquial term 'stealing', since this retains the notion of appropriation as a form of cultural misreading, a self-conscious appropriation of the dominant meaning to a lesbian point of view.

5 My deployment of the term *queer* in this instance is a self-conscious attempt to expand the definitional category *lesbian*. Queer appropriations are not limited to gender-'appropriate' same-sex identifications but might embrace the 'inappropriate' desire for, say, the heterosexual male, or the heterosexual couple, or even the heroine's pet dog.

6 For Paul Willemen, too, appropriation is a strategy marked by a process of self-consolidation. In a recent reading of nationhood, for example, he utilises the term 'appropriative projection' (Willemen, 1995: 28) in order to describe the way in which readers of one cultural sphere project their belief world on to another cultural sphere. Whilst our deployment of the term is quite different, it needs to be recalled that as a use of the other for the shoring up of the self, appropriation, even as a subcultural strategy, is never innocent.

7 I am aware also of the dangers of regarding myself, in the words of John Fiske, as 'typical of the people in general' (Fiske, 1989: 178). As Jostein Gripsrud argues, in Fiske's assumption 'a critical consciousness in audiences parallel to that of the researcher is simply taken for granted ... Fiske seems to believe that he can leave behind his academic training and the political socialization that went with it when he enters Disneyworld or other spheres of popular culture, as if he could switch at will between the disparate elements of his "postmodern" subjectivity' (Gripsrud, 1995: 121–2). Now it is probable that I have read more film studies and looked at more films from an academic/critical perspective than the average reader, and that this has no doubt influenced my arguments around cinema and spectatorship. I am aware then of falling into overbearing generalisations about audience response, and would be as wary of claiming a general lesbian-eye-view of the cinema as of arguing that, say, reading films through a camp sensibility is limited to those of us who identify as queer. Nor is there anything innately radical about looking as a lesbian. The cinema can confirm one's worst or most unconscious prejudices, as well as offering one a new perspective on an old world. Nevertheless, I do believe that audiences, acting in multiple and contradictory and searingly ambivalent ways, do work on films against their dominant grain of reception. Through the course of this book I will be looking to various writers working in film studies today – Carol Clover, Yvonne Tasker, Judith Mayne spring immediately to mind – who seem to be arguing along with me that perhaps the most interesting thing about films is the audience which watches them.

8 Other texts have attempted this far more successfully and thoroughly. See for example Weiss (1992).

The appropriateness of appropriation

i Audiences and texts

The power that has been accorded to the audience or individual viewer within film studies to date is far from established. A now apocryphal tale tells of the first screening of the Lumière brothers' *The Arrival of a Train at La Ciotat Station* (Louis and Auguste Lumière, 1895, Fr). In this instance audiences are reputed to have screamed in fear as they watched the locomotive speeding towards them. Whether a true story or merely an early example of good marketing, this tale inaugurates the notion of the essentially passive audience, of an audience more acted upon than acting, duped to respond en masse to the cynical machinations of the dominant cinema.[1] This is an argument that is pursued with more refinement through the Frankfurt school, Walter Benjamin's ([1936] 1970) and Theodor Adorno's ([1963] 1991) responses to mass culture reflecting both the perceptions and limitations of their time and place of writing.[2] Its logical mode of development ends in the consensus arguments of Noam Chomsky (1988 and 1989), for whom capital, and the vested interests it supports, remain the bottom line and *raison d'être* of popular culture.

It will be clear from the arguments I pursue in this book that I am not a close adherent of Chomsky. Still, it would be blind of me not to recognise the influence of production and marketing decisions since these operate as the backbone of the Hollywood financial system. Indeed, the operation of finance, and the artistic compromises that necessarily accompany it, often determine a film's very mode of articulation on the screen.[3]

In the contemporary debate over the relative dominance accorded to texts and audiences, on the other hand, it is the audience which has largely triumphed with the emergence of notions of the individual reader or 'interpretive communities' (Gripsrud, 1995: 9). Such theories develop the critical debate beyond the modernist notion of the sanctity or purity of the text and understand reception as a series of readings, or even of misreadings.[4] This move has recently been criticised by a number of theorists for what they see as its cultural relativism, with both Jostein Gripsrud and Teresa de Lauretis describing the conclusions reached, at their extreme, as 'silly' (Gripsrud, 1995: 9 and de Lauretis, 1994: 140). It is true that where the notion of the audience tends to promote an interpretive free-for-all, where readers are assumed to jump from one reading to another without reference to the specific context of reception, cultural relativism is often the result. Accordingly, where readership is set within a situated account of, for example, a reader's race, class, gender, sexual orientation (and all the other differences – age, educational background, (dis)ability, nationality – that are often less consciously a part of the theoretical matrix of difference), it is less liable to generalisation. Not that these factors need be determinate. They do, however, have an impact. Of course, within the fantasy investments of the desiring audience whose operation is the concern of this book, the tendency is to override difference in the pursuit of sameness. That is, that whilst race, sex, gender, class and all the other distinctions between subjects obviously do influence the mode of appropriative desire of spectator to screen (where indeed difference can be a positive spur to spectatorial fascination), the tendency of fantasy desire is to elide the differences between, say, desired character and spectator, proliferating instead points of fantasised connection. Suffice it to say then that I am aware of the dangers of appeals to the audience even as I am intent on promoting the jubilance of my own readings of the text against its ostensible meaning.

At the same time, any account of filmic reception that refused to take issues of production as well as of reception on board would seem fatally solipsistic. Chapter five, in focusing upon the construction of the Hollywood star as heterosexual, will accordingly give some examination to this area. For now one question insists: why give time, energy and hence validation to Hollywood films by looking lesbian at them, when as an industry Hollywood remains sexist, racist and heterosexist (amongst its other sins) in the images it purveys? I have no adequate reply to this other than the populist response that mirrors Hollywood's own, that is, that Hollywood matters because it is what the people want. Even to those who accompany their viewing with a concerted anti-sexist, anti-racist, multisexual, deconstructivist irony (and, if recent studies are anything to go by, there is more of this, albeit in contradictory and confusing manifestations, in your average cinemagoing audience than one would think),[5] Hollywood cinema continues to afford a seductive viewing pleasure and power which on their own merits seem worth investigating. Indeed, we should be as aware of condemning popular forms of culture out of hand as of theorising an intrinsic subversion in their impact. Still, one of my anxieties in this book is that, through my proffered strategies of appropriation, I not only give testimony to the varieties and the ingenuity of lesbian viewing strategies but provide a neat apologia for Hollywood indifference to lesbian representation itself. After all, why improve one's record in minority representation if viewers are just going to go on ahead and find pleasure in the images anyway? How radically lesbian appropriations (inappropriate or unlicensed) of Hollywood stars and films shake or undermine the compulsory heterosexuality of the Hollywood system will be the subject of chapters four and five. My earliest hunch is, not a lot. However, are we merely to discard appropriation as a strategy of visual pleasure because Uncle Walt didn't change his mind and let the Queen go ahead and marry Snow White?

At the same time as appropriation remains a strategy whose potential for subversion is always under contention, more recent feminist film criticism has testified to the role that audiences or individual viewers have in altering the focus and interpretation of a given film. As I will describe in section ii, this has become particularly significant as a strategy around same-sex, or more particularly lesbian, cinematic spectatorship, but is also a feature of feminist and race appropriations wherein audiences or individual viewers seek to read a film against its dominant grain of reception.[6] The fact that many different kinds of viewers enjoy films in which they are either not directly represented or deliberately excluded does not mean that such viewers are merely wallowing in their own oppression. As an example, the history of lesbian representation within both the mainstream and independent sectors has been characterised largely by absence, occasionally by misrepresentation and contemporaneously, in perhaps the most ironic configuration to date, by liberal colonisation.[7] Still, the cinema remains a source of fascination and pleasure for many lesbians who, as recent work demonstrates,[8] are more than capable of translating films and appropriating texts to a receptive context of their own. That such textual appropriations are not effected without a certain amount of irony and struggle is also the subject matter of this book.⁹

Appropriation is in many ways the key word of this book, and as such its meaning, scope and implications need to be investigated. The project of this chapter is to begin to ask, what are the possibilities, but also the limitations, of appropriation as a strategy of reception? How are even potentially radically appropriative gestures, for instance a strategy of looking lesbian against the cultural mass of heterosexuality, yet complicit with dominant forms of filmic imagery? Should there be limits to the possibilities of appropriation within a politically motivated lesbian and feminist viewing theory? Are there appropriations that, informed by reactionary or merely naive assumptions, should be deemed inappropriate? Are there indeed some appropriations that are merely beyond the pale? These are all questions that will be considered in this chapter and reviewed in the light of my arguments in further chapters.

ii Appropriate and be damned: feminist readings of the dominant

One possible definition of appropriation is the tendency to read a genre against its received or established interpretation. In the late 1980s a number of important feminist film texts set out to attempt just that. A number of books have been published within the feminist film theory of the last five or so years, all of which depend upon an argument for some kind of generic appropriation of the traditional filmic space to non-conventional cross-gender, cross-racial or cross-sexual identifications. The reception of film texts or genres which had previously been condemned by feminists as misogynistic or racially exclusive or heterosexist by definition, is in some cases being revised, subverted, reinterpreted and recuperated to a feminist or racially invested reading. The mode and degree of appropriation, revision and subversion varies from text to text, and none of these writers argues for a total or unambivalent acceptance of the terms of the genre they investigate. Still, analyses such as Linda Williams's study of filmic pornography, Carol Clover's re-reading of the slasher/horror film, Yvonne Tasker's investigation of the action movie, and Jacqueline Bobo's reception study of *The Color Purple* (Steven Spielberg, 1985, US) each testify to the revisionist potential of this mode of film criticism.

Such revisions can be characterised as a positive move away from the earlier feminist concentration upon the ubiquity of the male gaze and its framing of the figure of the woman in terms of a sadistically motivated scopophilia/voyeurism. The new appropriative criticism opens up a fantasy space between film text and interpretation, reasserting the potential for variety of audience response, ensuring that the multiplicity and scope of women's viewing pleasures can be registered and explored. Hence, Linda Williams's *Hard Core* (1990) discounts what she sees as the hitherto dominant feminist view that 'if you've seen one porn film, you've seen them all', on the grounds that 'these apparently self-evident texts were fraught with contradiction' (Williams, 1990: x). She continues: 'in the genre where I expected to see the most unrelieved and unchallenged dominance of the phallus ... I saw instead a remarkable uncertainty and instability' (Williams, 1990: x). And concludes:

I began to see that an understanding of how power and pleasure function in discourses in which women's bodies are the object of knowledge could be crucial to any efforts to alter the dominance of male power and pleasure in the culture at large, even in this most masculine of film genres. (Williams, 1990: x)

One appropriates, in this case by infiltration, in order to understand and then to change. In her book Williams situates her subject matter (contextualising it within a history of pornographic representation), critiques it and notes inconsistencies in its modes of both production and reception (film porn is not a monolithic category), and testifies to generic appropriations (through the work of ex-porn-star turned producer Candida Royalle). In the course of the book she also looks at the way in which audiences rewrite the pornographic scene in both predictable and unpredictable ways. One of the most striking instances of this is the way in which the then contemporary pornographic industry was attempting to 'democratize' (Williams, 1990: 230) its mechanisms of representation in order to appeal to an increasingly female or couple-orientated market. Notes Williams: 'The pornographic marketplace is now almost as eager to address women as desiring consumers as it once was to package them as objects of consumption' (Williams, 1990: 230). The role that audiences play in destabilising as well as reasserting conventional sex/gender distributions would perhaps have been even more obvious had Williams turned her attention to the then just perceptible phenomenon of publicly lesbian-produced pornography.[10]

An equally as invested appropriation of a genre formerly deemed irrecuperable is Barbara Creed's *The Monstrous-Feminine* (1993). Creed argues that there is a generic type within horror film which, rather than relying upon the traditional Freudian assumption that women are fearful (as in objects of fear and subjects to be frightened) because, in Freudian terms, they are castrated, reveals women to be objects of fear for men because they carry with them the threat of castration: 'Although a great deal has been written about the horror film, very little of that work has discussed the representation of woman-as-monster. Instead, emphasis has been on woman as victim of the (mainly male) monster' (Creed, 1993: 1). Tracing through the book a number of examples of woman-as-monster from the archaic mother of *Alien* (Ridley Scott, 1979, GB) and the poltergeist witch of *Carrie* (Brian de Palma, 1976, US), the monstrous womb of *The Brood* (David Cronenberg, 1979, Can) and the voracious sexuality of the vampire, to the castrating gaze of Medusa, Creed does not argue anything as simple as reversal of type. Nor does she argue that these images are *ipso facto* feminist:

I am not arguing that simply because the monstrous-feminine is constructed as an active rather than a passive figure that this image is 'feminist' or 'liberated'. The presence of the monstrous-feminine in the popular horror film speaks to us more about male fears than about female desire or subjectivity. (Creed, 1993: 7)

She does, however, hint that some women might enjoy the (albeit temporary) reversal of fortunes experienced within the genre: 'this presence does challenge the view that the male spectator is almost always situated in an active, sadistic position and the female spectator in a passive, masochistic one' (Creed, 1993: 7). Again, an examination of the particulars reveals a complication of the terrain of reception, of the ways in which audiences interpret given texts within a given context.

Carol Clover's *Men, Women and Chain Saws* (1992) reads the modern horror film and what has conventionally been understood as its even more misogynistic underside, the modern slasher. In the course of her book Clover argues that, contrary to initial appearances, horror film audiences are not constructed entirely of sadistically motivated men, braying for sex, guts and violence, voyeuring and pleasuring in the torture and murder of women – though this is certainly a part of it. Nor are the few women in the audience masochistically pleasuring in their own oppression – although they may be. For alongside these conventional binarisms go a series of complicated and sometimes extremely sophisticated mechanisms of identification by which, in Clover's words, gender is rendered: 'less a wall than a permeable membrane' (Clover, 1992: 46). I do not intend to restage Clover's arguments here: her initial chapter, 'Her body, himself', develops as many twists and turns as the 'Terrible Place' she argues serves as the *mise-en-scène* of the horror genre as to render such a summarisation possible. Suffice it to say that through the course of the book Clover manages to stage and restage looking relations within an endless theatre of play and counter-play, engendering multiple and contradictory looking positions for the horror-enjoying audience. Again, however, Clover does not simply conclude that the modern horror film is more feminist than we had thought. She is in fact tempted to argue it is not feminist at all. After all, the figure of the final girl who works so powerfully through her arguments in her first chapter can as easily be a cipher for male identifications as a signal to women that they might triumph over the genre (even and despite its endless return: see her account of the *Texas Chainsaw Massacre* (Tobe Hooper, 1974, US)).[11] The genre remains, however, one marked by an ambivalence of reception as by an audience which revels in its inappropriate alliances, alliances that both deconstruct and reaffirm traditional and non-traditional demarcations of sex and gender.

A near contemporary to Clover's book is Yvonne Tasker's *Spectacular Bodies: Gender, Genre and the Action Cinema* (1993). Amongst other things Tasker wants to redeem the action genre from its reputation as 'dumb movies for dumb people' (Tasker, 1993: 5), a perception she argues to be rooted in false notions of both high (versus popular) culture and class. The action movie is, like any other, a genre 'thriving on ambiguity' (Tasker, 1993: 91). For Tasker, the seat of ambiguity is often the audience itself (an audience which is never composite in its responses) and her book is strong testimony to the appropriative possibilities of film viewing. In part this lies with the text which is by definition open to multiple interpretation. Hence, for Tasker, 'To suggest that meanings are *obvious*, necessarily excludes something of the complexity of popular films. As good products, *efficient commodities*, films are polysemic, speaking or not speaking to different audiences in different ways' (Tasker, 1993: 61). I think Tasker is right to argue that texts, even Hollywood texts that have come to the screen as a compromise of artistic design with marketing and finance, thrive on ambiguity. The way in which this works for and against the individual viewer or group of viewers will be described in my account of the popular lesbian (and straight, and Christian, and lesbian Christian) classic *Fried Green Tomatoes at the Whistle Stop Café* (Jon Avnet, 1991, US) in chapter four.

Central to Tasker's argument for film viewing as a series of partial glimpses is the notion of fantasy, and the individual fantasy investments that audiences bring to a film. This is sometimes about context. Thus, as Tasker notes, to bill *Thelma and Louise* (Ridley Scott, 1991, US) as a lesbian film at a screening for lesbians is 'to assert that there is a space for such identifications within action films like this, even if they don't specifically acknowledge their gay audience' (Tasker, 1993: 29). Even without the presence of a strong receptive context, an individual viewer can fantasise a meaning in the film that need only have the most tenuous suggestion in the text, an argument I shall pursue in chapters five and six.

Many of these readings rely upon a revisionist understanding of sadism and, in particular, of masochism, descended from Deleuze (1971) and developed through the arguments of Gaylyn Studlar (1984 and 1992). For my purposes the most useful feature of both these accounts is their ability to deconstruct the habitual binary relation between the active/sadistic/masculine/male position within film theory and the passive/masochistic/feminine/female. These relations are still in process but they are no longer tied to sex. Men are capable, find pleasure even, in taking up a masochistic position in relation to the filmic diegesis, while women may take pleasure from a sadistic alignment with the focus of the filmic gaze. Such theories, while they need, as always, to be situated, have done much to open up the cinema beyond the limited account of the sadistically voyeuring male and the masochistically positioned female.[12]

In addition to appropriations of genre previously neglected by feminist theory, the last few years have seen a number of lesbian-identified publications whose premise has been to interpret popular culture in the light of audience sexual orientation. As Yvonne Tasker asks, 'What is a lesbian film?' (Tasker, 1994: 172). The answer would seem on one level to be whatever you want it to be, as lesbian-identified readings of *Basic Instinct* (Paul Verhoeven, 1991, US), *Thelma and Louise*, the *Alien* trilogy (Ridley Scott, 1979, GB; James Cameron, 1986, US; David Fincher, 1992, US) and *The Accused* (Jonathan Kaplan, 1988, US), have attempted to subvert film from its apparent foundation in compulsory heterosexual closure whilst undermining mainstream (i.e. heterosexual) feminism's fixation upon the sexual difference that underwrites dominant film theory. A response to the paucity of images of lesbians in the media and popular culture, these articles are notable for their joyful recuperation of mainstream film to a lesbian erotic. Some, such as Ros Jennings's (1995), or Paula Graham's (1994) work on the *Alien* trilogy, or Yvonne Tasker's (1994) examination of a variety of lesbian-tainted films, focus on intra-diegetic ambiguities, teasing a lesbian reading out from between the lines. Often such readings demonstrate a wilful blindness, refusing to accept, even actively disavowing, the heterotextual resolution of the classic Hollywood or independent narrative. Some, such as Ruby Rich's (1993) examination of lesbian and gay film at the end of the 1980s or Louise Allen's (1995) reading of the k. d. lang vehicle *Salmonberries*, investigate the intertextuality between race and sex. Others, such as my reading of Jodie Foster (1994), re-examined in chapter six, focus on the extra-filmic diegesis of stars and their sexualities. All rely upon the input of the spectator to make the connections, forge the alliances, read appropriatively, however inappropriate the context. Once again the intention seems to be to open up the theoretical space in terms of what audiences are doing to film texts or individual scenes, allowing the lesbian viewer (depending upon her in fact), in my own words of some years ago, to cultivate a viewing environment where we 'still have the chance to call everything our own' (Whatling, 1994: 195). The potential, and some of the limitations, of much of this work will be discussed in the chapters that follow.

At least some of the ideology behind this species of lesbian appropriation was itself appropriated from the analyses, strategies and survival mechanisms of black American feminists writing out of and against a culture of misrepresentation or invisibility.[13] Through earlier work, such as bell hooks's account of the oppositional gaze to the reader-response analyses of Jacqueline Bobo, cinema viewing becomes for these writers a series of partial glimpses. For hooks, cinemagoing is a compromise between the pleasure in looking[14] and anger at being excluded from the scene of representation:

With the possible exception of early race movies, Black female spectators have had to develop looking relations within a cinematic context that constructs our presence as absence, that must deny the 'body' of the Black female so as to perpetuate White supremacy, and with it a phallocentric spectatorship where the woman to be looked at, and desired is 'white'. (hooks, 1993: 291)

For hooks, women of colour have a choice (which is never a real choice), either to look the other way, that is to exclude Hollywood images from their frame of vision, or to turn their attention to indigenous imagery in order to represent their desires (a desire which, like the desire for lesbian images, always promises more than it can deliver). The alternative, argues hooks, is to turn a blind eye: 'to close down critique, analysis ... to forget racism' (hooks, 1993: 293). It is a compromise which, hooks says, she is no longer prepared to make, arguing that resistance comes not from altering existing texts but from developing new and alternative ones at the level of production as much as reception:

> Critical Black female spectatorship emerges as a site of resistance only when individual Black women actively resist the imposition of dominant ways of knowing and looking ... Manthia Diawara's 'resisting spectatorship' does not adequately describe the terrain of Black female spectatorship. We do more than resist. We create alternative texts, ones that are born not solely in reaction against. (hooks, 1993: 300)

While this is an important strategy, because of her focus on production over reception hooks can give no account of the way in which audiences invest in existing or mainstream texts except to discount the audience as either racist or oppressed, utterly colonised by the domineering visions of the white supremacist cinema.

For Jacqueline Bobo, on the other hand, popular cinema remains a site of pleasure despite its terms of racial exclusion or colonisation, where the black women she interviewed (later extended into a larger study of the reception of a number of black American literary and visual texts) opted to 'read through the text' (Bobo, 1993: 273) in order to construct their own interpretations of the film *The Color Purple*. Bobo also terms the reading strategies she investigates 'oppositional' but in contradistinction to hooks argues that

> The reactions are oppositional in two respects. First the reactions [of the women interviewed] contradict cohesive reactions by black people to past negative films such as *Birth of a Nation* ([D. W. Griffith, US] 1915), *The Green Pastures* ([William Keighley/Mare Connelly, US] 1936), *Gone With the Wind* [Victor Fleming, 1939, US] ... In the case of *The Color Purple* the outrage against the film is not unanimous ...
> The second way in which black women's reception of *The Color Purple* is oppositional is that it is a challenge to the mandate, given dominant media coverage, that black people should not have positive responses to the film. (Bobo, 1995: 92)

So violent were exchanges about the film that, as Bobo notes, those who opted to defend the film, on whatever level, were 'at risk of having their allegiance to black people challenged' (Bobo, 1995: 93). Nevertheless, women both within the media and outside of its immediate frame of reference continued to invest in the film. Argues Bobo: 'In paying good attention to a film in which aspects of their histories were depicted, Black women were able to extract images of power and relate them to their own lives'

(Bobo, 1993: 285). A relation of looking which was also a negotiation of the racist strategies of the film's director Steven Spielberg (who, as Bobo argues in a close textual reading of the film in chapter two of her book, patently misses the point in so many areas), it is one which nevertheless engenders its own intrinsic pleasures for women in the audience. Most particular was the pleasure in seeing Alice Walker's story writ large on the screen. As Bobo writes:

Aspects of their lives and histories, missing from other well-known works, were depicted for the first time in a medium accessible to a large number of black females. Although they were very vocal in their praise of the film, fuller examination of these women's responses revealed that their seeming conflation of the film with the novel was due to a complex process of negotiation. Black women sifted through the incongruent parts of the film and reacted favourably to elements with which they could identify and that resonated with their experiences. (Bobo, 1995: 3)

As a result: 'Using their own resources, they responded favourably in spite of Spielberg's direction' (Bobo, 1995: 5). What results is certainly a cinema of compromise for these viewers. It is one that nevertheless affords its own visual and narrative pleasures.

Extending this notion of racial appropriation, in an investigation of psychoanalysis through race, Michele Wallace argues that 'Even as the "Law of the Father" may impose its premature closure on the filmic "gaze" in the coordination of suture and classic narrative, disparate factions in the audience, not all equally well indoctrinated in the dominant discourse, may have their way, now and then, with interpretation' (Wallace, 1993: 264). Audiences are not then always delimited to, or defined by, the images they absorb. Wallace extends Bobo's notion of reading beyond the desire for visual representation (the pleasure of seeing black women on screen) towards a strategy of visual appropriation. Hence, she argues, for black female audiences like the one she participated in in the 1950s, some white stars were considered virtually black:

It was always said among Black women that Joan Crawford was part black, and as I watch these films again today, looking at Rita Hayworth in *Gilda* [Charles Vidor, 1946, US] or Lana Turner in *The Postman Always Rings Twice* [Tay Garnett, 1946, US], I keep thinking 'she's so beautiful, she looks black.' Such a statement makes no sense in current feminist film criticism. What I am trying to suggest is that there was a way in which these films were possessed by Black female viewers. The process may have been about problematizing and expanding one's racial identity instead of abandoning it. (Wallace, 1993: 264)

The overt visual presentation of whiteness is overridden by the investment of the audience to secure the screen for its own visual pleasures. Wallace's argument formulates a fascinating countertext to the habitual colonisation of the black or otherwise racially signified star by the dominant white audience and expands the potential categories of identification and desire. Indeed, asks Wallace, if spectatorship can be argued to be bisexual, why not theorise it as 'multiracial and multiethnic' (Wallace, 1993: 264) too?

Between them, these writers articulate some of the terms and dilemmas that inform my own appropriative readings. On the one hand, appropriative reading seems a valid strategy of wilful misreading. On the other hand, there is a danger that appropriative reading merely sustains, as it were by default, the reproduction of the status quo. As I asked earlier, does pleasuring in images, despite their foundation in sexism, heterosexism, racism, even in readings that attempt to counter these elements, merely give credence to the oppressor? Who really triumphs here, the text or the audience? And what if, so intent on working against one's own oppression, in the act of, for example, looking lesbian, one ignores or overrides or colonises as a self-consolidating gesture, the specificities of the oppression of others? What are the politics of pleasure and whose rights might they compromise? Perhaps, as bell hooks insists, appropriative viewing is marked by a cinema of blind spots, a wilful looking away from the racist or heterosexist or classist implications of the narrative, and thus is, in a sense, intrinsically solipsistic.

iii Fantasy appropriations

To return to the question I posed towards the beginning of this chapter, is there no end to the transformative and translatative potential of filmic textual appropriation? Can we, and should we, appropriate just anything and everything? This is in part of course a question about the politics of fantasy. Appropriative readings rely upon cross-gender, cross-sexual, in psychoanalytic terms sadomasochistic, fantasy identifications and desires.[15] In essence they testify to the power of fantasy to forge inappropriate alliances, to read against the semantic probability of the text and through or even around the overt (social, political, personal) identity investments of the audience. In Yvonne Tasker's words: 'the best way to express this might be in terms of what "we" know and what "we" enjoy, since the kind of fantasy investments at work in the pleasures taken from the cinema cannot be controlled by conscious political positions in the way that some criticisms might imply' (Tasker, 1993: 136).

A feminist position would of course want to insert the question of politics at some point. Still, and as Tasker implies, the history of feminist approaches to fantasy testify to an ongoing and problematic relation. Indeed, feminist politics have in the past often sought to inhibit the play of fantasy especially when fantasies have been deemed to take inappropriate courses. Certainly, public fantasies of the sort that have accumulated around lesbian-produced pornography and lesbian sadomasochistic material have been subject to virulent condemnation from some feminist quarters.[16]

Some of these debates have also focused on film, for example with the storming and boycott of *She Must Be Seeing Things* (Sheila McLaughlin, 1987, US) in the late 1980s.[17] Of course the last few years have also seen an outpouring of material in defence, or theorisation, or revelation of fantasy.[18] Such are the politics of defence, however: my sense is that some of the more difficult issues thrown up by fantasy remain unexplored. The difficulty with the terrain is, as Elizabeth Cowie noted some ten years ago, that our fantasies cannot be removed by 'fiat' (Cowie, 1984: 72), and are in fact notoriously resistant to political cleanup. At the same time, I feel that public fantasies of the order that I will be describing in this book, or rather private fantasies that become public once rendered in book form, demand some kind of political investigation. How then situate filmic fantasy within a political framework that neither falls into a politics of proscription nor betrays its intention in a blind belief in the celebration of fantasy's free play? For of course, just as fantasies cannot be removed by fiat, they never work outside of what Linda Williams terms 'the larger relations of power' (Williams, 1989: 49).

My intention is to try to situate notions of fantasy within the social and political space of filmgoing as well as to testify to the operation of fantasy within politically inappropriate contexts. This is not to imply that fantasy can be ultimately contained or legislated within a political framework. It is certainly not to repudiate the notion of politically incorrect fantasies *per se*. It is, however, to acknowledge and attempt to theorise the ways in which our filmic fantasies may be informed by certain social and ideological inscriptions.

The influence of the social upon the psychic, and of the psychic upon the social, has long been subject to debate, however. On the one hand it makes sense to argue that public fantasies of the order of, say, Hollywood film-making tend to be informed by dominant (and frequently sexist, racist, classist and heterosexist) social and political fantasies.[19] On the other hand, if we do not wish to argue that the audiences for these films are then merely duped into making these fantasies their own, we are presumably arguing for some variation in interpretation of collective or social fantasy scenarios. At the same time it seems naive to argue that audiences are somehow untouched by collective fantasies of social domination and desire since, if they bear no influence at all, why utilise them in classic narrative forms? Certainly as fantasy is mediated through language in its public manifestations, it becomes, by definition, social. Simultaneously, when seeking to determine the influence of social factors on fantasy, we are always brought back to the notion of the unconscious. What is the status to be accorded to the unconscious and how far can it be said to reflect or subvert conscious or social processes of interpretation? Given the tendency for the intrusion of inappropriate fantasies into our conscious lives, I would hazard, quite a bit. This is not, however, to say that the unconscious is not covertly influenced by social forms.[20] My sense is that there will be different mixes of the two in any individual fantasy investment, the operation of fantasy being structured by society, but desire often trespassing outside of the socially appropriate to forge inappropriate alliances. Often of course this will be accompanied by a certain amount of public disavowal.[21]

Up to now I have been rather allusive as to the possible nature of these fantasies. Here, however, are some examples of what might under certain terms and conditions be described as inappropriate desires. Interracial, or indeed any, fantasies which utilise a sub(ordination)–dom(ination) framework are always already suspect, as the last decade of debate around consensual S/M has demonstrated. Narcissistic identification with the blonde, white heroines of Hollywood, which perpetuates the racial conflation of whiteness with beauty, is also an area of difficulty, as I will describe in chapter three. A preference for a fantasised world of costume dramas and nice middle-class mores which retreats into a nostalgia for empire while ignoring the classism, racism and moralism which structures that world might be regarded as problematic within all but the most politically naive of contexts. Fantasies about gun-toting criminals are also problematic for those of us who take anti-militaristic ideals to heart, despite the evident fetishistic pleasures to be found in *Blue Steel* (Kathryn Bigelow, 1990, US), *Die Hard* (John McTiernan, 1988, US) and just about every other mainstream Hollywood (and independent) film. Fantasies about Keanu Reeves in the testosterone-fuelled but oh so homoerotic *Point Break* (Kathryn Bigelow, 1991, US) might cause a few problems for lesbians (and straight-identified men) intent on limiting their spectatorial pleasures to the sex and gender appropriate. And, what I deleted in an earlier analysis, but append as a none the less trenchant thought, sexual fantasies about Sarah Tobias dancing for the crowd in *The Accused*, a film which prompts the question, when does voyeurism become as criminal as rape?

Whether we disavow, repudiate, keep quiet about or acknowledge such fantasies, there is an evident problem with employing images of others as fantasy figures especially if those others are configured through dominant sexist, racist or other regimes. Certainly, I would presume that the intertextuality of these two elements engenders a certain amount of disavowal within the politically invested subject. As Paula Graham observes: 'If you ask a lesbian why she enjoyed a film with pleasurable lesbian-erotic undertones but anti-feminist content, she will almost always reply with the classic form of fetishistic disavowal: "Well I know, but ..."' (Graham, 1994: 214). As Graham argues, Freudian fetishism gets around this dilemma since it works, for the male subject, through the displacement of one or more contradictory elements from the site of displeasure into the realm of pleasure. Displeasure continues to underlie pleasure, however, since:

Male fetishistic pleasure in disavowing castration anxiety [an anxiety which the cinema seeks to compensate him for, see chapter two] involves the simultaneous fear of castration. If this fear were entirely overcome (or forgotten) the basis of the fetishistic pleasure would disappear ... In order for [an] image to work for the male spectator, he must 'believe' several contradictory things at once. (Graham, 1994: 214)[22]

Hence, Graham suggests, spectatorial pleasure thrives upon its relation to unpleasure. As a result, cinema spectatorship, be one lesbian or straight (though this is not to imply an intrinsic commonality between the two), seems marked by ambivalence, contradiction and surprise. At the same time, it can seem profoundly predictable.

iv Fantasising the dominant

I thus have to conclude that the project of making my own erotic unconscious participate in the reading process, far from guaranteeing some sort of radical or liberating breakthrough, brings me face to face with the political incorrectness of my own fantasy life. (Johnson, 1993: 165)

As I have hinted above, despite the appropriative potential of individually invested audiences, the cinema may help to structure fantasy in some predictable ways. Sexism, classism, heterosexism, racism all inform the cinematic scene in multiple and often covert ways. It is the latter that I want to focus on in this section. Racism operates in Hollywood of course first at the level of production – who tends to get employed and who does not. The history of black American representation in Hollywood has been one marked by absence.[23] The visual representation of other ethnic groups even more so. Even today, where black American, a few Latin American, Native American and Asian Pacific stars and directors are gaining recognition, the general impression of Hollywood is of a place where whiteness continues to reign ideal.[24] Such an ideology works all the more seductively at the level of representation, where discreet forms of exoticisation,[25] and erasure through colonisation,[26] take effect.

All of these issues inevitably have an influence upon reception. In general lesbian appropriative studies, unless the remit has specifically focused upon race, have tended to reflect the ethnocentrism of the Hollywood star system and the mainstream studies that have been done on it. In part this is due to the whiteness of the images of women perpetuated within the Hollywood system. It is difficult to appropriate to lesbian she who is not even visible as woman. This difficulty is reflected in a text such as Andrea Weiss's *Vampires and Violets* (1992) which finds itself attending to racial differences through an acknowledgement of their relative absence from the stage of mainstream (and indeed much independent and avant-garde) lesbian representation.

This is not to say that interesting work is not being conducted in this area. A recent article by Louise Allen stresses the binary reconfiguration of same-sex desire through the visual signification of racial difference in the film *Salmonberries*. Charting the relationship between a mixed race (Inuit–white) woman, Kotzebue, and Roswitha, a white woman from the former East Germany, the film is insidious in its deployment of race as a signifier of sexual difference:

> what is at stake in a reading of *Salmonberries*, is how discourses presenting lesbian butch and femme as 'subversive' or normative gender roles can be seen to employ racial signifiers ... in order to articulate a 'subversion'. Therefore in attempting to 'subvert' one set of normative and hierarchical practices (heterosexuality) it is possible to reaffirm further hierarchical relations (racial) difference. (Allen, 1995: 75-6)

The lesbian identity that emerges triumphant out of this binary is, Allen argues, always white:

[Richard] Dyer has exemplified how, in popular culture, the ideal woman is white and blonde, and we can see how Roswitha is desired because she is just this. It also appears that Kotzebue's desire for Roswitha is bound up with a desire for white identity, and more specifically white *lesbian* identity. Kotzebue's revelation of how she had been in the 'dark' before she found 'bright' Roswitha may refer at one level to how Roswitha helped her discover her 'true' identity: however, the light/dark connotations in this statement suggests that a Native American identity (indeed any black lesbian identity) is undesired and that whiteness and brightness (a white lesbian identity) is more desirable. (Allen, 1995: 79)

Whilst, as I have noted above, racial difference is often represented within the mainstream cinema as desirable through exoticisation, I think that Allen's argument, as it reflects upon the configuration of sexual and racial difference within both mainstream and independent cinema, is by and large right. Certainly it is an argument I shall return to in chapter three in discussing the configuration of lesbian butch and femme in terms of their various, and predictable, racial inflections. The subtlety of argument in Allen's work points to the need to be aware of what is being configured, what erased, in lesbian representations on screen and in theory. Generally, and I include my own work in this condemnation, exclusion on the screen has been compounded by ignorance in the text. This text will try not to repeat and thus consolidate these elisions whilst bearing testimony to their influence.

One theorist who has recently foregrounded Hollywood's inflection of dominant racial fantasies is Lynda Hart (1994). Unfortunately, for me at least, she aligns this with a textual politics that is decidedly anti-appropriative. For Hart, mainstream cinema is informed by a white supremacist, heterosexist agenda which marks the white feminine woman as 'The woman, overdetermined as both heterosexual and white ... a representational absence that is necessarily constituted by a displaced "presence"' (Hart, 1994: 107).[27] This leaves lesbians, whom Hart describes as 'women who act alone', and non-white women who fall out of the bounds of the white supremacist ideal (since they are redundant within the white supremacist *procreative* ideal) outside the bounds of the feminine:

What is already out of bounds, and therefore already criminalized, are nonwhite women and women who act alone i.e., without men. Women of color and white lesbians have committed 'unladylike' behavior by virtue of their race and sexual preferences alone. That much should by now be evident. (Hart, 1994: 107)

This system does not, however, secure a parity between lesbians (who as Hart notes are usually coded white even within the paradigms of feminist theorists) and non-white women. For as Hart notes in a chapter concerned with an analysis of the film *Single White Female* (Barbet Schroeder, 1992, US):

> What is curious, then, and cannot go unremarked because it attains its power precisely because of its invisibility, is that these *representations* are so overwhelmingly of *white* women in the particular formula I have been interrogating ... These lesbian 'ghosts', it would seem, have a certain privilege. As the specters in the machine of white, heterosexual patriarchy, their invisibility affords them a certain power that makes them particularly threatening ... If they are, in a sense, wish-fulfilling ghosts, or, in some cases, the white heterosexual male's worst nightmares realized, they are nonetheless produced by a desire that wants them to be almost, but not quite 'like' their dreamers. Gender preserves the distance within sameness. Racial difference, however, perhaps does not appear because it would constitute an alterity that could eliminate the pleasure which undoubtedly attends the terror. (Hart, 1994: 107–8)

In the case of non-white women, doubly excluded from the regime of representation, Hart's response is not to seek out instances of their imaging within the mainstream, but rather to reflect their exclusion from the white heterosexual and lesbian symbolic.[28] Thus she argues:

> Rather than falling into the trap of 'positivity' or 'presence', a pitfall that too often occurs when white feminists turn their lens to focus on women of color, I want to persist in my negative critique, pursuing the absences that ground the figures which do appear. (Hart, 1994: 110)[29]

Following Hart, race will be figured as an issue in this book not so much in terms of suggesting a recuperative or appropriative politics for non-white audiences – for a white academic this would be profoundly inappropriate – but in terms of acknowledging both the general absence, and the always potential colonisation, when 'present', of images of colour, within even a racially conscious lesbian appropriative cinematic politics.[30] The dangers of this are as evident as its investigation is imperative. It is some years since Cripps (1977), Bogle (1988), and Dyer (1988) began to chart the configuration of whiteness as both ubiquitous and unmarked within the popular cinematic culture, and still the conflations continue. As Marylin Frye notes, any debate remains skewed by the continued domination of the white perspective, even within a revisionist context: 'for I think it is an aspect of race privilege to have a choice – a choice between the options of hearing and not hearing. That is part of what being white gets you'

(Frye, 1983: 111). As a result: 'Every choice or decision I make is made in a matrix of options. Racism distorts and limits that matrix in various ways' (Frye, 1983: 112).

At the same time, if appropriation is available to white lesbians as a tenable cinematic strategy (and the argument of this book, in contradistinction to Hart's own, will be that it is), then appropriation as a strategic possibility, albeit differently situated, imbricated through the double representational lack of sex and race, must be available to lesbians of colour also. One way through the miasma of domination and resistance is suggested by Kobena Mercer in his retrospective of photographer Robert Mapplethorpe. Mercer traces his own reception of Mapplethorpe from an early fascination with the 'illicit object of desire' (Mercer, 1991: 169) formulated by Mercer and a friend over Mapplethorpe's text *Black Males*, a fascination combined with distaste at the 'racial discourse of the imagery' (Mercer, 1991: 169) and the objectification of the subjects on display, to a framing of Mapplethorpe's estate within the context of homosexuality and the censorship his work was subject to following his death from AIDS in 1989. Context, argues Mercer, changes the focus of interpretation and of the relation between 'authors, texts and readers, relations that are always contingent, context-bound and historically specific' (Mercer, 1991: 169–70). The incorporation of a racially conscious viewing subject, though it will not necessarily determine the spectatorial experience, will certainly impact upon it. That this impact might have positive as well as negative consequences does not mean that it is any less racially inflected. As Peggy Phelan notes, the relation between subject and its various others is always one of fascination as well as of violence, a species of self-consolidation that needs the other as violently as it repudiates it:

The relationship between self and other is a marked one, which is to say it is unequal. It is alluring and violent because it touches the paradoxical nature of psychic desire; the always already unequal encounter nonetheless summons the hope of reciprocity and equality; the failure of this hope then produces violence, aggressivity, dissent. The combination of psychic hope and political-historical inequality makes the contemporary encounter between self and other a meeting of profound romance and deep violence. (Phelan, 1993: 3–4)

As this book will demonstrate, this relation is configured not only through the matrix of race but also through sexuality, namely the intertext of the homosexual with the heterosexual. It is also configured through the relation between the old and the new, of what I term in chapter four the nostalgia for abjection in contemporary lesbian cinematic spectatorship. It is also a feature of the relations I describe between the desiring audience and the star detailed in chapters five and six. Each example of cinematic appropriation discussed in this book is accordingly marked by a tension between, and a negotiation of, the line between romance and violence. For, as I argued in the introduction, no appropriation, however much it sees itself as invested in a discourse of radical reversal (for example, looking lesbian), is *ipso facto*, more innocent than any other.

I began this section with a quotation from Barbara Johnson's reading of *The Accused* in which she begins to theorise her investment in reading as a lesbian. In her piece Johnson notes the sometimes embarrassing hiatus between conscious political aim and unconscious desire where she reads her desire for Kathryn Murphy, one of the film's protagonists, as structured around the prohibitive/productive order of the patriarchal symbolic:

> If I do nevertheless feel that *The Accused* presents me with a plot that corresponds to my own fantasies, I have to acknowledge the role of the patriarchal institution not in impeding those fantasies but in enabling them. Murphy is attractive to me because she is a powerful woman turning her full attention to another woman precisely *within* the patriarchal institution. (Johnson, 1993: 165)

Part of the pleasure Johnson garners from the character has to do with the power Kathryn Murphy manifests as a player in the patriarchal world of the courtroom and the negotiating table. As a result: 'Any attempt to go from this reading to theorise (my) lesbian desire would therefore have to confront the possibility of a real disjunction between my political ideals [which, for an avowed feminist, are anti-patriarchal] and my libidinal investments' (Johnson, 1993: 166). As Johnson notes, however, the tension continues to proliferate in the relation between political conviction and fantasy desire which form an uncomfortable symbiosis. The tendency is to see the former as motivated by good intentions and the latter as guilty by definition. Still, as Johnson reminds us: 'if the unconscious is structured by repetition and the political by desire for change, there is nothing surprising about this. The question, still, would remain one of knowing what the unconscious changes and what the political repeats' (Johnson, 1993: 166). For me, fantasies of the order I detail here are always a little bit guilty. That this does not necessarily detract from their pleasure is one of the ironies of reception at work in this text.

v **The limits of appropriation**

Fantasy and its various psycho-social investments certainly introduce some new problems into the notion of appropriation. At the same time, and as I will develop over the next chapter and chapter three, fantasy, both appropriate and inappropriate, remains integral to the structuring of identification and desire within cinematic relations and to the visual pleasures they afford. In general, recent feminist textual appropriations of individual films and film genre have been both interesting and enabling. I would also argue that they are imperative to subjects, those of us especially who are affected by sexism, racism, heterosexism and all the other ablisms temporarily set on the sideline, who are by and large underrepresented on the silver screen. However, and at the risk of curtailing the fantasmatic possibilities of the filmic space, I have to ask, where textual appropriation rests upon a colonisation of filmic imagery which itself appropriates dominant cultural fantasies around race, sex, class, or homosexuality, is it in turn rendered invalid by association? The terrain of fantasy is remarkable as a space where as subjects we exercise scant concern for the appropriateness of our desires to the world we inhabit or to the consensual rights of those who inhabit them, but does this mean that we should just go ahead and have them anyway? My preliminary answer is yes, but it is an avowal fraught with theoretical, if not (in my fantasies at least) ethical, anxiety.

Notes

1 More recent examples of this tendency can be seen in the 'video nasty' debates in Britain in the 1980s, which played into a moral panic which predicted that the minds of the nation's children would be corrupted by a daily dose of sex and violence. Characterised by a simplistic causality (for example in the media association of the killing of James Bulger with the video horror *Child's Play* (Tom Holland, 1988, US)) and a censoriousness that crosses the political spectrum, such debates look set to play on the fears of concerned parents for years to come. For an account of a situated history of film censorship see Kuhn (1988) and Robertson (1989).

2 Criticised for years as elitist, both Benjamin's and Adorno's arguments have recently been subject to something of a critical renaissance. Jostein Gripsrud, for example, argues for a progression in Adorno's writings from the cultural pessimism of his early work to the development of a sense of audience agency in the later (see Gripsrud, 1995: 7–8).

3 For accounts of the financial ordering of the old Hollywood studio system, see Bordwell, Staiger and Thompson (1985). For an account of the New Hollywood, see Schatz (1993) and Tasker (1996).

4 See Fiske (1989), Feuer (1989) and the lesbian readings introduced in section ii.

5 See section ii of this chapter. Though I must confess upfront my agreement with Gripsrud (1995: 8–14, 136–7, 160–1, 185–6) that, when talking about audiences reading ironically or camply or sub-

versively, one has to be careful to testify to not only the variability of reception but also to the dangers of reading too much politically into audience reaction. Since this is not an audience study in the conventional sense, these dangers seem limited. Still I must emphasise that in my occasional invocations of audience I am more than aware of the potential for contradictions and ambivalence in such an appeal.

6 For an account of reading through race, see my account of the work of Jacqueline Bobo in section ii of this chapter. Though situated within the new queer politics of the 1990s, the origins of lesbian textual appropriation perhaps lie in the work of Elizabeth Ellsworth (1986), whose account of published feminist responses to *Personal Best* demonstrates the influence of the interpretive community over the received text. Ellsworth demonstrates that lesbian readers of *Personal Best* skew their interpretation to a lesbian reading even to the point of ignoring the film's heterosexist denouement. In the words of Jackie Byars: 'the text does not exert the primary limits on interpretation ... it simply provides the opportunity for discursive struggle' (Byars, 1991: 262).

7 The sheer number of 'lesbians' represented in the wake of the new vogue in lesbian chic makes it clear that it was largely fiscal concerns (to which I would add notions of public morality in the sense that the public can pay only for what Hollywood deems at the time they will want to see) that had prevented Hollywood from exploiting this subject in the years before.

8 See in particular Budge and Hamer (1994) and Wilton (1995), both of which collections promote the jubilance of reading lesbian over the dominant heterotext.

9 For an informative and engaging account of the ups and downs of appropriation as a strategy for subversion, see Erica Rand's *Barbie's Queer Accessories*. Though the question, 'how queer can we make Barbie?' is debated throughout the book, the passage quoted below summarises many of the issues involved, and should be recalled at many points in my own text: 'I suggested earlier that what people tell and remember may be distorted to privilege queer moments for many reasons. These reasons include their sense about what makes a good narrative or what is called for in terms of Barbie memories ... and the likelihood that unusual or troubling memories about Barbie are simply more memorable ... there is a danger, then, of overestimating the number of queer moments ... I argued above that hegemony/counterhegemony and conformity/resistance are of limited use partly because so many acts and interpretations cannot be determined to be one or the other or be fixed at some particular point between. A bigger problem lies in the question of what we would glean from labeling acts of consumption in this way if we could do so. Incidents of anti-Mattel [Barbie's manufacturer] Barbie consumption do not even necessarily signify a consistently or thoroughly resistant stance on the part of those consumers who describe them either toward Barbie or toward what (according to the consumer's perception) she stands for' (Rand, 1995: 147).

10 See Smyth (1990) and Dunne (1990).

11 Indeed, Clover seems to prefer the first reading, arguing at one point that 'the final girl is, on reflection, a congenial double for the adolescent male' (Clover, 1992: 51).

12 For an account of this position see Mulvey (1975), Doane (1987) and Kaplan (1984).

13 See for example Wallace (1990) and Bobo (1991).

14 Which she notes, is only legitimately offered to an (in this case black American) audience through the medium of the cinema or television screen, a pleasure in looking which was also about 'contestation and confrontation' (hooks, 1993: 290). This being the oppositional gaze referred to in the title of her article, a look which both takes pleasure in looking and resists, in the words of Manthia Diawara, 'complete identifications with the film's discourse' (quoted in hooks, 1993: 290).

15 The definition of fantasy in use at this point is taken from the account developed in Laplanche and Pontalis (1983: 314–19). For these writers the scope of fantasy (or phantasy) encompasses 'conscious phantasies or daydreams, unconscious phantasies like those uncovered by analysis as the structures underlying a manifest content, and primal phantasies' (Laplanche and Pontalis, 1983: 314). It is the first order of conscious fantasies or daydreams which I am interested in. This is not to argue that these are not related to the order of unconscious or even primal fantasies investigated by Freudian psychoanalysis. As I argue, the unconscious certainly has its part to play in the conscious articulation of desire. Its investigation is not, however, my specific aim here.

16 Witness accounts of what have come to be known as the feminist sex wars of the 1980s, debates which precipitated conflicts amongst feminists around the issues of lesbian- and feminist-produced pornography, consensual sadomasochism and lesbian butch–femme. See in particular the work of Sheila Jeffreys (1986). See also Linden, Pagano, Russel and Leigh Star (1982).

17 For the background to this event see Ardill and O'Sullivan (1989).

18 Snitow (1984) and Vance (1992) remain the foremost accounts of the area and include rhetorically impressive, albeit preliminary, investigations of the pleasures and contradictions of fantasy. The work of Pat Califia (especially 1988 and 1994) remains passionately committed to a radical exploration of the possibilities of inappropriate fantasy. On the theoretical front, Cowie (1984), Stern (1982) and most recently de Lauretis (1994) are excellent accounts of the terrain.

19 See Bordwell and Thompson (1993) and Hart (1994).

20 For a complex account of some feminist negotiations of the relation between the psychic and the social, see Brennan (1990).

21 Fantasies, though having a public face, are in essence private. Most of us would metaphorically die if we saw our fantasies paraded within the public sphere.

22 In Freudian readings, fetishism has been understood as a male trope. More recently Elizabeth Grosz (1991) has attempted to read it through a lesbian appropriative politics, a reading which I assume Graham is herself appropriating here.

23 See Cripps (1977) and Bogle (1980 and 1988).

24 Certainly, the increasing sway of the black dollar remains, as Bobo notes (1995: 169–70), a consideration, though, as with faith put in the gay and lesbian pink pound, I think its influence can be overestimated. Hollywood seems more than capable of appropriating the two to its own brand of (bland) liberal pluralism.

25 For an account of the colonisation of images of blackness through cultural exoticisation, see hooks (1992).

26 For examples of this, see Judith Mayne's (1993: 142-56) reading of

the literal erasure of Whoopi Goldberg from the scene of *Ghost* (Jerry Zucker, 1990, US). Also, Tasker's reading of the buddy genre (1993: 35–53).

27 Her reasoning behind this is twofold. In the first place ~~woman~~ is constituted as an absence within the patriarchal symbolic. This no-woman is nevertheless a white no-woman: 'For it seems impossible not to conclude that the Woman produced in the discourse of psychoanalysis and the lesbian who ghosts her entrance into representation – both of them things that are "(no)-things" – are "white (no)things"' (Hart, 1994: 106–7). Within the binary relation that defines black as less than white, however, whiteness must come to connote something. Hence: 'within the terms of racial difference as it has been constructed as a binary opposition ... the nonwhite things are (some)things – indeed perhaps the thing itself. That is, what is "nonwhite" becomes inscribed with a certain immobilizing positivity, a "presence" that stabilizes and hence creates the illusion that there is no possibility for historical change' (Hart, 1994: 107).

28 Hart does not believe that lesbianism can be represented in film except as a function of white heterosexual patriarchal desire. Her arguments are thus, as I have noted, severely non-appropriative.

29 Jane Gaines, quoting Marylin Frye, makes a similar point in arguing that white, middle-class feminists should not do what we have historically done, which is to 'assume responsibility for everyone' (Gaines, 1988: 13), since it is in turn an exercise of racial privilege to assume that one can encompass (as a kind of smoothing out) differences between women.

30 Indeed, I would suggest that it is easier to construct a (white) lesbian out of mainstream Hollywood images than a non-white woman of whatever orientation. I would argue that this is in part because lesbian appropriative readings rely upon the invisible or semi-visible signifier of sexual deviance, whilst racial appropriations depend largely upon the visible signifier of race (the presence of non-white people) within the text.

Psychoanalysis and the lesbian supplement

2

i Identity

That the sustenance of a subject's identity depends upon the fantasy appropriation of an other (as its object) should come as no surprise once we acknowledge the Lacanian paradigm that underlies much feminist and other film criticism. This chapter will then attempt a preliminary account of Lacanian psychoanalysis through readings of his work proffered by film theorists and other critical sympathisers.

For Lacan, a sense of self first comes about when a child (always gendered male in his 'neutral' writing) is held by its mother before a mirror:

> This event can take place ... from the age of six months, and its repetition has often made me reflect upon the startling spectacle of the infant in front of the mirror. Unable as yet to walk, or even to stand up, and held tightly as he is by some support, human or artificial ... he nevertheless overcomes, in a flutter of jubilant activity, the obstructions of his support and, fixing his attitude in a slightly leaning-forward position, in order to hold it in his gaze, brings back an instantaneous aspect of the image. (Lacan, 1977: 1–2)

The self that is reflected in the mirror represents a totality, a pleasing and affirming image of uniformity and coherence. Indeed, Lacan refers to it as the 'Ideal-I' (Lacan, 1977: 2). He notes, however, that this sense of self is immediately a divided one. For Jacqueline Rose, the reflection in the mirror operates primarily as a fiction, with consequences both negative and positive: 'This image is a fiction because it conceals, or freezes, the infant's lack of motor coordination and the fragmentation of the drives' (Lacan, 1982: 30). At the same time, however, this fiction is 'salutary for the child, since it gives it the first sense of coherent identity in which it can recognise itself' (Lacan, 1982: 30). The fiction works to confer upon the child the 'anticipation of self-mastery and unified identity' (Silverman, 1988: 7).

Such confirmation is necessary to the constitution of a sense of self. In being fictional, on the other hand, this pursuit is founded in a permanent sense of disappointment as the ego ideal proves impossible to realise. Thus, as a sense of self-coherence is continually striven for and undermined, so its ideal mirror image will be endlessly pursued, inaugurating an ongoing symbiosis of desire and disappointment, or, as Lacan terms it, lack. This relation is figured by Lacan as one of alienation:

> the important point is that this form situates the agency of the ego, before its social determination, in a fictional direction, which will always remain irreducible for the individual alone, or rather, which will only rejoin the coming-into-being of the subject asymptomatically, whatever the success of the dialectical synthesis by which he must resolve as I his discordance with his own reality (Lacan, 1977: 2).

As David Rodowick argues, the mirror reflects an image that both is, and is not the child, internalised as its only coherent image of self and yet marked as other to it: 'As a result, the distance between subject and object is simultaneously formed and cancelled' (Rodowick, 1982: 7). This is a necessary process in the sense that self-recognition rests upon a sense of difference from all that is other to itself. This moment is articulated in the mirror when, for the first time, the child becomes aware of the distinction between it and its mother. Up to this point she (or her substitute) has enjoyed a more or less unbroken union with the infant. In the mirror, on the other hand, the mother is rendered separate and visibly distinct for the child, as the object to its subject. As Kaja Silverman argues:

> the child makes its self-discovery through a process of subtraction – through the understanding that it is what is left when a familiar object (e.g. the mother) has been removed. Subjectivity is thus from the very outset dependent upon the recognition of a distance separating self from other – on an object whose loss is simultaneous with its apprehension. (Silverman, 1988: 7)

Hence, two figures are set up within this relation; the child's sense of itself as a separate entity and the child's sense of its mother as other to itself. At this point, as Merl Storr notes, the child 'has no need of a definite decision or choice in favour of one or the other' (Storr, 1993: 60). However, with the advent of the symbolic order, figured in the child's negotiation of the castration complex,[1] a decision must necessarily be made:

> as soon as the subject passes through the castration complex ... and thereby becomes 'sexed', he or she must choose according to the familiar Freudian pattern. Masculine desire chooses anaclitically, that is chooses the image of the mother to fill the place of the 'other', and strives for the desire of the (m)other through 'having' what she lacks – namely the phallus; feminine desire chooses narcissistically, that is chooses its own image as 'other', and positions itself in the heterosexual relation as 'being' the phallus, the object (signifier) to be exchanged. (Storr, 1993: 60)

As Storr makes clear, this inequality between the sexes, that is the male's symbolic possession of the phallus and the female's relative dispossession,[2] is compensated for within the heterosexual relation by the woman's inhabiting of the position of object of exchange, and the man's situating of himself as subject within that exchange. He objectifies her as being the phallus in compensation for his fear of not having it.

This separation along sex lines is obtained once the subject enters into the symbolic order of language. Language sets up a distance between the subject's sense of self (its identification with the pronoun 'I') and the subject's sense of itself in relation to the external world, since both of these concepts are dependent upon a series of significations that bear meaning not in themselves but only in relation to each other. To clarify, the simplest relation between a concept (or signified) and the image used to describe it (its signifier) is that of a one-to-one correspondence in which the image relates to the thing described. The example Lacan gives is of a tree, a concept which is designated by the signifier 'tree'. In this account the signified (a tree) and its signifier ('tree') appear to share an unproblematic, self-evident, unmediated relation of meaning.

As Lacan goes on to demonstrate, however, this assumed correspondence between concept and image is in fact profoundly inadequate. To illustrate this inadequacy he gives another example, that of two doors, identical except for the fact that one is marked 'ladies' and the other 'gentlemen'. Within this relation of signifier and signified the distinction between the two doors (how they signify differently) can be understood only, first, in relation to each other – how they are different, that is, as Jane Gallop asks, how are they 'not the other?' (Gallop, 1982: 10), and, secondly, how they are understood in relation to what Lacan terms a signifying chain, by which he means 'the contexts in which signifiers have been learned' (Gallop, 1982: 10). We will return to this notion of context of learning in time. For the moment let us stay with language and its impact upon the securing of the subject in a relation of alienation. As Silverman makes clear, it is the non-coincidence, the non-essentiality of the relation between the signifier and the signified that sets up the distance between the subject and its object(s):

> When we say that language takes the place of the real, we mean that it takes the place of the real for the subject – that the child identifies with a signifier through which it is inserted into a closed field of signification. Within that field of signification, all elements – including the first person pronoun which seems transparently to identify the subject – are defined exclusively through the play of codified differences. Not one of these elements is capable of reaching beyond itself to establish contact with the real. The door closes as finally upon the subject's being as upon the object. (Silverman, 1988: 8)

The result is a secondary alienation through the mediacy not of sight this time but of speech.[3]

Subjectivity, as I have noted, requires the distancing of the subject from that which it has formerly considered indistinct but now recognises as an object apart from itself. The mother's breast, its own faeces, a loved blanket, a toy, all count in this relation. Separation of the self from these desired objects is necessary to the development of subjectivity. However, the past aura of such objects continues to exercise a power over the subject, which, as a result, are described by Lacan as 'objets petits autres', or, as Silverman puts it, as 'objects with only a little "otherness"' (Silverman, 1988: 7). The longing for such objects both testifies to the violence with which the subject must separate itself, and to the sense of lack which this separation engenders. For Lacan 'the objet (à) is always bound to the orifices of the body' (Lacan, 1982: 164) as 'something from which the subject, in order to constitute itself, has separated itself off as an organ, [and which consequently] serves as a symbol of lack' (Lacan, 1978: 103). As Silverman concludes: 'The object thus acquires from the very beginning the value of that without which the subject can never be whole or complete, and for which it consequently yearns' (Silverman, 1988: 7).

As Jane Gallop notes: 'The objet A is a domestication of the Other' (Gallop, 1982: 40). Note how she employs the capital A as an indication of this domestication, the capital reflecting upon and recalling the site of the radical Other which though sought after can never be obtained. For Lacan, the radical Other (designated by the capital A for Autre) is inappropriable and thus unobjectifiable. As a subject one cannot cathect upon the radical Other as it has no correspondence in the real. What one has as a subject is a mediated relation with a variety of *objets à*, where: 'The object A sets itself in place of the Other which cannot be glimpsed' (Gallop, 1982: 40). As an analogy, Gallop cites the condition of 'Woman', a signifier which operates as the radical Other in that 'She' can never be defined. The domestication of the objet A as in images of women, can, however, operate as a cover, disguising the impossibility of Woman.

As I noted earlier, within the Lacanian construction of the heterosexual relation, the female partner sets herself up as object to the male's subject, where she narcissistically constructs herself as the object of desire and cathects on to him as signifier of her desire. As Lacan makes clear, however, this relation only ever operates as a partial compensation since the substitution of the radical other with a succession of *objets à* can only ever be approximate and thus unsatisfactory. He is never adequate as the representative of the symbolic transcendence of the phallus and thus she must resign herself to disappointment. She can never be all-sufficient as object of desire and therefore he is consigned to the pursuit of his desire in other women. As a result, the heterosexual relation can only ever function as a compensation:

Because this object is always already lost, the other person is encountered as lacking; man and woman are 'one for the other the Other'. Sexual relation exists therefore only in the imaginary and only in so far as each pretends to be what will make good the lack in the Other. Any semblance of sexual rapport thus hinges on the phallus, the pretence that the objet A exists in a form capable of making good the lack: the man must appear to have it, the woman must engage in the masquerade that she is it ... Consequently, for both the man and the woman, Lacan can say, loving is giving what they do not have; and the manifestations 'are entirely propelled into comedy'. (Lapsley and Westlake, 1992: 32)

In other words, the heterosexual relation is postulated upon an endless fiction of being and having, an appearance, a seeming, endlessly desired and endlessly disappointed, to be endlessly and fruitlessly pursued. Hence, as Lacan observes: 'a "to seem" ... replaces the "to have", in order to protect it on the one side, and to mask its lack in the other' (Lacan, 1977: 289).[4] As Peggy Phelan notes, however, the impossibility of desire is also its success: 'The desire for the real is impossible to realize ... but that impossibility maintains rather than cancels the desire for it' (Phelan, 1993: 14).

For me, the relation between the subject and the *objet à* is primarily one of colonisation, an appropriative fantasy which frames the relation between the subject and the *objet à* in terms of a self-consolidating otherness. But what is the relation of all this to the cinema? Cinema is the scene in which the relation between subject and object is visually played out. Indeed, as Silverman argues, 'It is this irrecoverability of object to subject, this irreducible distance separating the representation from the real, that cinema has often seemed destined to overcome' (Silverman, 1988: 8).

Traditionally, Lacan's argument is interpreted in relation to the way in which the filmic space constructs the image as a fetish (the *objet à* in other words), which compensates for lack, where 'the viewing subject protects him or herself from the perception of lack by putting a surrogate in the place of the absent real' (Silverman, 1988: 4–5). Within film this lack is compensated for in two ways, both directed through male desire and operating upon the body of the woman. In the first instance compensation is anticipated through an investigation of the original trauma of castration, played out through the dissection of the figure of the woman on the screen. For David Rodowick, this involves 'investigating the woman, demystifying her mystery', and is 'counterbalanced by the devaluation, punishment or saving of the guilty object' (Rodowick, 1982: 5). The recent spate of female psycho-killer movies illustrates this point well, where a beautiful woman – Glenn Close in *Fatal Attraction* (Adrian Lyne, 1987, US), Rebecca De Mornay in *The Hand That Rocks the Cradle* (Curtis Hanson, 1992, US) – is first set up as the perfect recipient of male desire, being feminine and sexy and good in bed, or with the children, and then, following her exposure as a fake, is subjected to furious assault and, ultimately, death. The placing of the right of execution in the hands of the good wife (formerly devalued, by the end of the film elevated to the status of madonna mater), is merely the latest twist in this perverse cinematic playing out of sexual and family relations.[5]

In the second instance, compensation is sought through the construction of the figure of the woman into a fetish so that her body operates as a focus of pleasure, becomes reassuring, rather than a threat. The overvaluation of the female star is one example of such a fetish where: 'the physical beauty of the object [is hypostatised] transforming it into something satisfying in itself' (Rodowick, 1982: 5). Both of these approaches function as disavowals of lack through the projection of either pleasure or unpleasure. The first represents the projection on to the woman of the male's lack, for example his fear of castration. Projection is here a form of defence and is linked to disavowal or the projecting on to others of that which one does not want to acknowledge in oneself: 'This set of emotions attests to nothing so much as a successfully engineered projection, to the externalising displacement onto the female subject of what the male subject cannot tolerate in himself: castration or lack' (Silverman, 1988: 16) The second strategy operates as the securing of pleasure through the projection of an over-abundance or fetish. Both are examples of self-consolidation through the colonisation of some image of the other, in this case the body of a woman. In 1975 of course Laura Mulvey exposed the sexual politics of this substitution, arguing that classic narrative cinema is grounded in a sadistically inclined voyeurism wherein the female character is appropriable first to the gaze of the (presumed to be male-controlled) camera, then to the gaze of the male protagonist on the screen and finally, completing the circle, to the gaze of the male viewer. For Mulvey, cinematic pleasure is thus grounded in a classic scopophilic relation:

> In a world ordered by sexual imbalance, pleasure in looking has been split between active/male and passive/female. The determining male gaze projects its phantasy on to the female figure which is styled accordingly. In their traditional exhibitionist role women are simultaneously looked at and displayed, with their appearance coded for strong visual and erotic impact so that they can be said to connote to-be-looked-at-ness. (Mulvey, 1975: 11)

By such terms, the cinema exists solely for the viewing pleasure of men.

ii Psychoanalysis's heterosexual imperative

Evident in these approaches is the heterosexual imperative of the psychoanalytic formulation, that is that such relations depend upon the institution of sexual difference as the polarisation of male/female, masculine/feminine, subject/object, active/passive, sadistic/masochistic. When I argue that the foundations of psychoanalysis lie in the assumption of sexual difference I do not seek to imply that the foundation of psychoanalysis is simply biologistic, a trust in the absolute distinction between male and female, in the anatomical distinction between the sexes.[6] Nevertheless, as these binary structures continue to operate as the discursive currency of the psychoanalytic terrain, they engender not a problem or two for a same-sex understanding of desire.

The psychoanalytic foundation in sexual difference is made clear in Lacan's work where he argues that the subject is constituted (as male or female) by its position within the pre-existing signifying chain of culture which sexes subjects male or female.

As I noted above, Lacan gives the example of two children who are riding along on a train. When it stops at the station the little boy cries out that they have arrived at the entrance to the ladies' toilet. The little girl retorts that, on the contrary, they have arrived at gentlemen. The moral of the story is that 'Interestingly it is the girl who sees "Gentlemen" and the boy who sees "Ladies"; as if one could only see the sex one is not, as if the sex one is outside of could be perceived as a whole, unified locus' (Gallop, 1982: 10). In Gallop's reading of Lacan, culture informs our understanding of sexual difference which it structures in terms of a binary focus, ladies for men, gentlemen for women. What frequently goes unnoted about this ordering of psychic reality, however, is its foundation not only in sexual difference but in compulsory heterosexuality.

As an example, Merl Storr (1993) argues that in certain configurations of Freudian and Lacanian thought, the lesbian is understood to be a homosexual man. The rationale behind this lies in Freudian accounts of male homosexuality which figure this as an anaclitic object choice in the sense that the homosexual man is unable to detach himself from an over-emphatic attachment to his mother.[7] This over-emphatic attachment is reputedly spawned through sibling rivalry where a younger son attempts to usurp his brothers in pursuit of his mother. This desire then becomes orientated through repression towards those same male rivals, where they are now taken up as the loved objects. In the female homosexual this rivalry is transposed to the plane of the social, where the lesbian competes with men as: 'holders of desire and the claimants of sex ... [who] work against each other as rivals' (Lacan, 1982: 96). She must then look for a woman who will allow her to restage the anaclitic–narcissistic relation in pretending to be the phallus which the masculine-identified lesbian seeks to possess.[8] Within this paradigm, the female homosexual is allowed access to an active anaclitic object choice which none the less locates her very firmly within the masculine. As Storr argues, within this Freudian–Lacanian model 'desire [is always conceived of] in heterosexual terms: if not narcissistic then anaclitic, if not heterosexually feminine then heterosexual masculine, all desire must be one or the other and there must always be a difference – precisely a sexual difference between the two' (Storr, 1993: 65).

At other times and in other essays, notes Storr, rather than situating lesbianism in terms of a masculine pursuit of an anaclitic choice, Lacan, in re-reading Freud, situates lesbianism on the side of the narcissistic, a conventional position for the female. Re-reading this construction, however, Storr argues:

The distinction between the anaclitic and the narcissistic type of object-choice is maintained on the condition that one's primary object-choice is based on the sexual(ised) difference between the image of oneself as ideal or model (the narcissistic choice) and the image of one's mother as model (the anaclitic choice). What both Freud and Lacan conveniently forget of course is that, for a woman, the sexual object which resembles herself, will also resemble her mother ... [Hence] the female sexual object who is the image of both myself and my mother confounds the Freudian structure of 'female homosexuality' – heterosexuality by any other name – and reveals lesbian desire as simultaneously a narcissistic relation and an anaclitic object-choice; as in fact a desire which renders the distinction between these terms – and hence the very definition of either – meaningless. (Storr, 1993: 61)

As Storr points out, the lesbian 'thus succeeds twice over in her narcissistic quest of loving herself. Female homosexuality is, in this sense, not a failure of Freudian femininity, but, on the contrary, an excess of it' (Storr, 1993: 56). She concludes: 'The female homosexual is just too much of a woman' (Storr, 1993: 57). Those familiar with recent trends in lesbian appropriative politics will recognise the subversive mischief in Storr's account. The result is that within Storr's formulation, lesbian desire, rather than being ancillary to the masculine, a mere tawdry imitation, or inferior to the feminine, an interminable wannabe, in fact exceeds the terms of relation implied by both.

So lesbianism, in Storr's formulation, is excessive to psychoanalytic thought while at the same time exposing its insufficiency. Some of the implications of Storr's argument can be seen in relation to what is a key text in the feminist reinvestigation of Freudian–Lacanian psychoanalysis, Jane Gallop's *Feminism and Psychoanalysis: The Daughter's Seduction*. In the final chapter of the book Gallop discusses reinterpretations of the *Dora* case, Freud's 'Fragment of an analysis'.[9] Discussing the symbolism that cathects upon the figure of Frau K, Gallop argues that both Freud and Dora retain an imaginary identification with Frau K as uncastrated: 'phallic, omnipotent, omniscient' (Gallop, 1982: 147). Whilst arguing that this identification is plainly fantastic – no such power accrues to Frau K as a woman bound to the symbolic order of patriarchal exchange – Gallop none the less pursues this imaginary (and in Dora's case, loving) attachment with a strange persistence. What follows her point about the imaginary is a supplementary point, an odd inclusion, which itself seems excessive to the text:

What has been said of that love in the present text is that Dora sees Frau K as the phallic mother, infallible, non-substitutable. My argument has subordinated this homosexual love to the important psychoanalytic and feminist question of the relation between transference and radical contestation. Dora's love for Frau K has been cited here as an instance of the imaginary, which is to be taken as a criticism. But the 'more' I have to say is about the beauty, the eroticism, the affirmative quality of that love ... And somehow beauty and affirmation, sexuality as pleasure and joy rather than murderous assimilation, seem to find their place only as a supplement to the political, theoretical argument. (Gallop, 1982: 148)

This theoretical and political argument is amongst other things that there is a tenable, albeit contested, relation between feminism and psychoanalysis. Lesbianism is in Gallop's account, as she notes, somehow in excess to this relation, subordinated to the theoretical exchange between feminism and psychoanalysis whilst remaining excessive in promising something intangibly 'more'.[10] Yet, as Storr's argument demonstrates, the relationship between feminism and psychoanalysis cannot be understood while lesbianism remains supplementary or, worse, subordinated, to the text, but only when it is recognised, incorporated as something which upsets the paradigmatically heterosexual foundation of the text. This, I believe, Gallop does recognise, though she covers over her recognition in another substitution. In her penultimate chapter Gallop questions Kristeva's celebration of a radical heterosexuality grounded in the meeting between two discourses, the semiotic maternal of Sollers and the rational theoretical of Kristeva which form 'an intermingling of two opposites which keep their opposite identities, a contamination of the opposition, a risking of difference and identity' (Gallop, 1982: 126). Gallop questions this celebration on two grounds, which she situates in opposing texts on the right- and left-hand sides of the page. On the right-hand side of the page she questions Kristeva's celebration of the maternal position in *L'Hérèthique* which Gallop fears folds in upon itself, less a radical doubling and redoubling of the subject–subject(s), mother–child, maternal–paternal engagement than a retreat into 'homogeneous fantasy' (Gallop, 1982: 129). On the left (an unwittingly ironic play on the western cultural association between left-handedness and homosexuality?) she questions the cultural and political inscription of heterosexuality as radical: 'A militant feminist question nags me. How can you privilege a relation called "heterosexuality"? Does this not support the heterosexism of our culture, the oppression of homosexuals, the oppression of homosexuality?' (Gallop, 1982: 127). Gallop then tries to justify Kristeva's deployment of the term in arguing that radical heterosexuality, rather than operating in terms of an Irigarayan desire for the same (a veiled hommosexuality),[11] emphasises heterogeneity and thus is open as a model of appropriation to homosexuals too where 'any relation between members of the same sex which allowed their difference, did not assimilate both to one fantasy, would be heterosexual' (Gallop, 1982: 127). In so doing, however, I would argue that Gallop, in substituting heterosexuality (albeit radical) for homosexuality, consolidates rather than subverts the cultural subordination of the latter to the former (since when is heterosexuality not also implemented on the assimilation of both partners to the one fantasy?) Meanwhile Gallop concludes her reading of Kristeva on the right-hand side with a palpable sense of relief at the trace of the heterosexual in Kristeva's otherwise claustrophobic account of the maternal. Of course, if we are to believe Gallop, the dilemma between her reception of the right- and left-handed texts remains unresolved (the two texts remain situated, never one without the other). Still her left-hand doubts remain subordinate to the right-hand text which finally and literally underwrites it. The dilemma remains unresolved but underwritten, testimony to the way in which the possibility of the lesbian is figured by Gallop as an ongoing seduction, albeit one that is subject to sublimation as the underwritten, inexpressible supplement to the heterosexual politics of the text.

Yet if we appropriate Gallop's reading of Lacan in an earlier part of the book we realise how the excessive nature of the lesbian supplement might be incorporated into a psychoanalytic politics of excess. In chapter four of the book Gallop argues that Lacan's 'annoying and embarrassing insistence [upon the terms] "phallus" and "castration"' (Gallop, 1982: 55) works as a kind of excess, an over-playing in order to play out the terms to their logical (in)conclusion: 'Maybe he's using them up, running the risk of essence, running dangerously close to patriarchal positions, so as to wear "phallus" and "castration" out, until they're thoroughly hackneyed' (Gallop, 1982: 55). She also demurs: 'maybe not' (Gallop, 1982: 55). Still the possibility has been introduced and can be taken up, appropriated for a different use, in relation perhaps to the over-playing of narcissism and anaclisis in Storr's formulation, appropriated by what is otherwise viewed as excessive to the text, the partially admitted, always subordinated and supplementary lesbian excess.

iii 'Her adorable white body':[12] lesbian psychoanalytic appropriations

Despite a formerly widespread mistrust amongst lesbians of a system that has long sought to exclude them, lesbian theoretical appropriations of psychoanalysis now proliferate. Two examples, Judith Roof's theorisation of lesbian excess in *A Lure of Knowledge* and Judith Butler's 'The lesbian phallus and the morphological imaginary', will serve to give some understanding of the various terrains at stake.

As opposed to Gallop, who as I have argued reads lesbianism as supplementary to the text of psychoanalysis, for Roof it is psychoanalysis that needs be put under question, less to argue its redundancy than to expose its more productive insufficiencies. In her chapter 'Freud reads lesbians' therefore, Roof testifies to the evasive strategies employed by Freud in first ignoring and then justifying his ignorance of Dora's unconscious attachment to Frau K. Roof notes, for example, how Freud begins the case study with a reflection upon the 'very considerable current of homosexuality' (Roof, 1991: 60) that he finds in all subjects, but then ignores the implications of this finding in his determined pursuit of a heterosexual identification for Dora. Knowledge, notes Roof, is a production, which is always already shaped by the desire of the knower. Accordingly, desire sets the terms by which knowledge can be obtained and understood. Hence: 'as Freud's enactment of the interrelation of knowledge and desire illustrates, the reading may be more important than the source; the imbrication of desire in reading tends to find what desire is looking for' (Roof, 1991: 215). To Roof, Freud's (mis)engagement with lesbianism in the *Dora* case presents a veritable map of misreading in which the analyst's inability to see is compounded by his desire not to look. In a complicated argument Roof traces the elisions and mistiming throughout the *Dora* case study, interpreting Freud's reluctance to engage with his patient's unconscious desires through the replacement of knowledge with a series of disavowals from his 'rhetorical gentility' (Roof, 1991: 183) to his own 'vaguely homoerotic friendship' (Roof, 1991: 181) with Wilhelm Fliess. As with all narratives of self and other, Freud's metaphors can be revealing. With respect to *Dora* Freud characterises lesbianism in terms of a pre-oedipal current that 'in favourable circumstances often runs completely dry' (Roof, 1991: 185). The retention of a lesbian commitment into adulthood is hence characterised in terms of a regression. Freud however then notes that this pre-oedipal lesbian current may be reactivated by the experience of unhappiness in heterosexual love, an unhappiness which precipitates a return to prior channels. As Roof put it: 'if the straight stream [of heterosexual oedipal desire] is blocked, the water runs to "older" channels' (Roof, 1991: 185). This metaphor can, however, be read against the stream of interpretation. Freud first employs his metaphor of the river current in an earlier passage on the perversions (in which homosexuality is included) which he characterises by the following metaphor:

> A stream of water which meets with an obstacle in the river-bed is dammed up and flows back into old channels which had formerly seemed fated to run dry. The motive forces leading to hysterical symptoms draw their strength not only from repressed normal sexuality but also from unconscious perverse activities. (Freud, 1905: 51)

As Roof argues, what Freud's account makes clear is that the perversions are 'always present ... are really diverted circles that return to a previous place and time' (Roof, 1991: 185). Hence:

> Like his own text that acknowledges that he already knows what he subsequently forgets, perversions – lesbian sexuality – refer back to a place one has already been; they are always already there, but abandoned until excess forces the libidinous or textual current, back in their direction. (Roof, 1991: 185)[13]

On the one hand then, lesbianism operates as a blockage, a regressive clinging to old forms which inhibits proper development. On the other hand it represent a 'breaking open' (Roof, 1991: 212), an unresolved ambivalence which disturbs the gendered dualities of Freud's account of female sexual development. In other words, lesbianism in Roof's account figures as the spanner in the works, the supplement which is both central to the configuration of oedipal sexuality and at the same time excessive to and disruptive of it:

> This strange inside/outside position of the passages on lesbian sexuality is characteristic of the ambivalent location of lesbian sexuality in Freud's work. Always in two places at once in the center and on the outside, known and forgotten, it is outside by virtue of its centrality; it is central because of its eccentricity. (Roof, 1991: 179)

This excess of lesbian sexuality, rather than acting as a supplement to the text as in Gallop's work, in Roof's underwrites the narrative of heterosexual development which tries, and fails, to overwrite it.

Beginning with an account of Freud's 'On narcissism', Butler (1992) argues the relation between pain, erotogeneity and bodily materiality, observing:

> The essay 'On narcissism: An introduction' (1914) is an effort to explain the theory of the libido in terms of those experiences which seem at first to be most improbably conducive to its terms. Freud begins by a consideration of bodily pain and asks whether we might understand the obsessive self-preoccupation on the part of those who suffer physical illness or injury to be a kind of libidinal investment in pain. And he asks further whether this negative investment in one's

own bodily discomfort can be understood as a kind of narcissism. (Butler, 1992: 133–4)

Whilst noting the pathological implications of this negative narcissism, Butler argues that for Freud such bodily pain is a 'precondition of bodily self-discovery' (Butler, 1992: 133), since 'that libidinal self-attention is precisely what delineates a body part as a part' (Butler, 1992: 135). What is more, and as Freud continues, 'the familiar prototype of an organ sensitive to pain, in some way changed and yet not diseased in the ordinary sense, is that of the genital organ in a state of excitation' (Freud, 1914: 84). As Butler observes, it is to be inferred that the genital organ Freud is referring to is the penis. However, as Freud continues to extrapolate the relation between pain and libido, Butler argues that it becomes clear that Freud does not wish to confine erotogeneity to this body part alone, assuming indeed as accepted knowledge 'that certain other areas of the body – the erotogenic zones – may act as substitutes for the genitals and behave analogous to them' (Freud, 1914: 84).[14] As Butler notes, two rather interesting things can be deduced from this. On the one hand those other body parts the erotogenic zones, are 'synthesized and summarized by the prototypical male genitals' (Butler, 1992: 136). On the other hand, the erotogenic zones are said to act as substitutes for the male genital organ. In other words, the primary signification of the phallus is 'reversed and erased' (Butler, 1992: 136). As noted above, the phallus operates in Freudian (and Lacanian) thought as the primary signifier: 'that which originates or generates significations, but is not itself the signifying effect of a prior signifying chain' (Butler, 1992: 136). In this case, however, as Butler notes, the phallus is that which is 'generated by a string of examples of erotogenic parts' (Butler, 1992: 136). Though Freud subsequently tries to restore the phallus as 'prototype and then as originary site of erotogenization' (Butler, 1992: 137), none the less the phallus continues to operate in terms of a 'fundamental transferability' (Butler, 1992: 137). As Butler argues:

it is clear from the metonymic trajectory of Freud's own text, the ambivalence at the center of any construction of the Phallus belongs to no body part, but is fundamentally transferable and is, at least within his text, the very principle of erotogenic transferability. Moreover, it is through this transfer, understood as a substitution of the psychical for the physical – the metaphorizing logic of hypochondria – that body parts become phenomenologically accessible at all. (Butler, 1992: 138)

Of course, and as Butler acknowledges, to argue for the fundamental transferability of the phallus is not to discount the fact that 'the phallus operates in a privileged way in contemporary sexual cultures' (Butler, 1992: 162). She does, however, argue that 'To insist ... on the transferability of the Phallus, the Phallus as transferable or plastic property, is to destabilize the distinction between being and having the Phallus' (Butler, 1992: 138). Since men do not really possess the phallus and women cannot ever really be it, 'precisely because it is an idealization, one which no body part can approximate adequately, it is a transferable phantasm' (Butler, 1992: 160).

One of the ways in which phallic properties might be transferred is through a lesbian appropriation of the phallus, the morphological imaginary referred to in Butler's title. In Freudian–Lacanian terms such a lesbian appropriation would be understood within a representational economy wherein the lesbian effects a copy, an imitation, of the phallic heterosexual original. As Butler argues, however, if the sovereignty of the phallus is dependent upon its status as non-transferable, 'if this attribution of property is improperly attributed, if it rests on a denial of that property's transferability ... then the repression of that denial will constitute that system internally and, therefore, pose as the promising spectre of its destabilization' (Butler, 1992: 138–9). This non-transferability of the phallus, rather than being foundational, is, however, merely an effect of its articulation as original. Similarly to Butler's analogy of the judge who institutes the compulsory nature of heterosexuality through a series of discursive affirmations,[15] the ontology of the phallus is also grounded 'in no other legitimating authority than the echo-chain of [its] own reinvocation' (Butler, 1993: 107). Hence: 'in so far as any reference to a lesbian Phallus appears to be a spectral representation of a masculine original, we might well question the spectral production of that "origin" one which, as we have seen, is constituted in Freud's text through a reversal and erasure of a set of substitutions' (Butler, 1992: 139).

The lesbian phallus which Butler imagines is, as she observes, 'a fiction, but perhaps a theoretically useful one, for there does seem to be [engrained in its possibilities] a question of imitation, subversion and the recirculation of privilege that a psychoanalytically informed reading might attend' (Butler, 1992: 159). As a result, Butler calls for an: 'aggressive reterritorialization' (Butler, 1992: 160) of the phallus in order that it may come to signify beyond its naturalisation in a male heterosexual morphology. Lesbian appropriations of the phallus are particularly appropriate within this context since the signifier operates only as one among many within the lesbian relation. Thus, though it partakes of a certain masculinisation, it remains tied to the economy of the lesbian. Hence: 'When the Phallus is lesbian, then it is and is not a masculinist figure of power; the signifier is significantly split, for it both recalls and displaces the masculinism by which it is impelled' (Butler, 1992: 162). Indeed 'the offering of the lesbian phallus suggests that the signifier can come to signify in excess of its structurally mandated position; indeed the signifier can be repeated in contexts and relations that come to displace the privileged status of that signifier' (Butler, 1992: 163).

This section has of course represented only a few of the recent theoretically informed lesbian incursions into the psychoanalytic. In so doing, however, it has attempted to show how psychoanalysis is both a fundamental structuring relation in many accounts of lesbian desire (and thus to the arguments in the chapters that follow), and in need of a fundamental overhaul if it is to work productively with the accounts of lesbian identification and desire articulated in this book.

In fact, I should say that my use of psychoanalysis at all stages of this book has been accompanied by a marked ambivalence. On the one hand, and as Elizabeth Grosz notes in criticism of its dominance, it remains 'the preferred ... discourse of sexual pleasure and sexual desire within lesbian theory' (Grosz, 1995: 158). Certainly it has become the structuring concept in feminist film theory. An account which utilised contemporary feminist film theory but failed to acknowledge its debt to Freudian–Lacanian thought would read as rather odd. On the other hand, psychoanalysis structures the subject into a theoretical paradigm which seems hopelessly constricting to an account of lesbian desire. As Grosz asks: 'Why do we need psychoanalysis to think lesbian desire? What are the limits of its explanatory power regarding subjectivity and desire, the points beyond which it risks incoherence and contradiction? Who are the subjects unable to fit into its explanatory schemas?' (Grosz, 1995: 158). Indeed, having completed a number of accounts of Lacanian psychoanalysis, Grosz has spent the last few years attempting to theorise lesbian, and other, desire beyond and outside of a psychoanalytic framework.[16]

Much as Grosz's work reads as highly interesting, and is certainly a refreshing change from the dominance of the psychoanalytic scene, and much as I have my doubts as to the appropriateness of psychoanalysis for explaining the trajectory of my own desires, I nevertheless have to admit that as a *fictional fantasy* of desire in lack (the endless pursuit of a desire fuelled by a disappointment which translates itself into more desire), the Freudian–Lacanian account reads for me as a profoundly seductive one. This is not to invest it with any essential truth. It is to argue for its continued deployment within this book as a fantasy scenario for the exploration of my lesbian desire in relation to the cinema.

Notes

1 Where, according to Freud, the girl child must come to terms with her self-evidently castrated state, that is, her non-possession of the phallus, whilst the boy child, witness to the girl's castrated state, must come to terms with the threat of castration which, thenceforward, hangs over him. As we shall see, this hypothetical relation between the sexes is foundational both to Freudian psychoanalysis (including its Lacanian revisions) and to the looking relations that inform psychoanalytic accounts of the cinema. As I shall describe in this chapter and the next, however, its structuring of relations between the sexes in terms of a masculine/active/anaclitic and a feminine/passive/narcissistic binary need not be definitive.

2 I recognise of course that there is some debate as to the male's metaphorical, or literal, possession of the phallus. On the one hand Lacan (1977: 289) argues that possession is of a symbolic order only, less a fact than a relation of seeming. On the other hand, and as Gallop (1982) argues, it seems impossible to separate symbolic possession from the overwhelming distribution of power in favour of men in real terms. What does seem evident is that, as Butler puts it, the masculine subject's 'seeming self-grounded autonomy attempts to conceal the repression which is both its ground and the perceptual possibility of its ungrounding ... the demand that women reflect the autonomous power of masculine subject/signifier becomes essential to the construction of that autonomy and, thus, becomes the basis of a radical dependency that effectively undercuts the function that it serves' (Butler, 1990: 45). As will be clear throughout this book, any claim to subjectivity rests upon the absorption, objectification, repudiation or abjection of another subject at some point or another. As will also be clear, these others effect an endless point of return upon the subject.

3 What is not clear from this discussion is that the alienation of the subject through language is multiplied for women through the structure of sexual difference. Women are doubly alienated, first, through the non-coincidence of language to meaning (an alienation that affects all subjects) and, secondly, where language is appropriated through a sovereign gesture to the order of the phallus (for readings of how this appropriation is effected see Irigaray (1985a) and Wittig (1992: 76–89). I would like at this point to introduce a third order of alienation, that which affects lesbians who are thrice alienated through the addition of the compulsory heterosexual ordering of language; see Wittig (1992).

4 Hence: '"having" and "being" are, in Lacan's terms, finally to be understood as comedic failures that are nevertheless compelled to articulate and enact these repeated impossibilities' (Butler, 1990: 46).

5 Not that I deem this genre to be entirely without its merits. In the first place it can amuse for its blatant playing out of heterosexual male anxieties, and in the second, and as I argue in chapter four, since its 'pathological' women remain the focus of the film's narrative and of its generic pleasures.

6 Even Freud's essay of that name substitutes the cultural for the bio-

logical, at least if one reads between the lines of its own footnotes (see Mitchell 1974: 46–7).

7 With the onset of oedipus of course, the boy is supposed to turn his anaclitic desire away from his mother and on to her substitute, which he finds in other women. In other accounts, as Storr goes on to describe, both Freud and Lacan figure male homosexuality as a narcissistic attachment to the self, which ego ideal one then seeks to realise in the pursuit of others.

8 What does go unnoticed in this configuration is the motivation of the feminine-identified woman who agrees to take up the narcissistic position. Is she merely lying to herself as to the identity of her beloved?

9 This is of course one of Freud's most famous cases, the tale of a young woman, 'Dora', who was brought to Freud suffering from a number of 'hysterical' symptoms, most notably an irritating cough. During the analysis Freud uncovers a veritable web of family romances, including Dora's father's relationship with a family friend, Frau K. Fixating upon the attempted seduction of Dora by this woman's husband, Freud ignores, or rather fails to register the significance of, the bond between Dora and Frau K. It is only some time after Dora terminates the analysis that Freud, reviewing the situation in his postscript, begins to recognise the significance of the relation that has grown up between the two women. This has become one of the most analysed of Freud's case studies. Some notable readings include Gallop (1982) and Bernheimer (1985).

10 It should be noted that the ambiguity is compounded where Gallop supplements her 'more' with Cixous's (Cixous and Clément, 1986) reading of Dora's lesbian desire. In so doing Gallop supplements her own political analysis of Dora's refusal to accept the exchange of women by men (which Gallop characterises as her refusal of the 'massacre' involved in the 'barter' of women) with the thought that 'one should add to that what there is in Dora of a very beautiful, staggering, feminine homosexuality, what there is of the love of women' (Gallop, 1982: 148). In both texts then, the one built upon the other, lesbianism is both supplementary and excessive to the political scene.

11 See Irigaray (1985b).

12 This phrase signifies Dora's love for Frau K in Freud's text. The whiteness of Frau K's body should serve as an ironic reminder, not merely of western culture's hypostatisation of the fair woman but also of the ethnocentrism that underwrites the psychoanalytic scene. Ironically, in a chapter devoted to an account of the lesbian supplement, what has remained supplementary to my own text, at least up to this point, is the acknowledgment of a racial context. In part this is because, as Jane Gaines observes, 'the psychoanalytic model works to block out considerations which assume a different configuration, so that, for instance, the Freudian–Lacanian scenario can eclipse the scenario of race–gender relations' (Gaines, 1988: 12). This is an elision which, though the absence of multiply racial images and gazes from the dominant scene will continue to be testified to, will not be repeated in the chapters that follow.

13 In a further complication of her argument Roof then links this metaphor of perversion as current with the progression of the narrative which is also described by Freud in terms of an unnavigable river (see Roof, 1991: 185).

14 An example would be a sexually induced rash.

15 See Butler (1993: 107).

16 See Grosz (1995, 173–85) and Probyn (1995: 1–18).

Fantastic desires 3

i Identification

'There are experiences that I have had through watching films that have reminded me of who I am and erm ... like a, almost like a ... oh there's a word for it ... damn ...'

'Recognition?'

'... yeah, recognition of a sort of consciousness, and there's nothing like that, I think. Once again it allows you to be brave in your life in ways that you might not have been had you not had the opportunity to experience something very dramatic and impactful in a safe environment.' (Jodie Foster, talking to Melvyn Bragg)[1]

In chapter one I referred, albeit briefly, to the ways in which contemporary lesbian film studies appropriate the popular culture to a lesbian point of view. In that chapter I testified to the power of this kind of appropriation, its celebration of lesbian desire and its ability to read between the lines of mainstream heterosexual culture. One of the problems with characterising this type of appropriative strategy, however, is that one tends to imply a notion of lesbian desire as somehow a given, as always already there, prior to the text upon which it operates. In one sense this makes perfect sense – god forbid that the multiple and contradictory subjects that name themselves lesbian should be the sum reflections of a medium such as Hollywood cinema! Still, as I noted when discussing the social and psychic significations of fantasy in chapter one, I do believe that cinematic representations and the fantasy desires they precipitate have an impact of sorts upon the desiring subject. Hence, one of the questions I intend to ask in this chapter, and proffer some answers to in the next, is, how might lesbian desire be constituted within, and by exposure to, a filmic culture? To what extent do the films I watch have a part to play in the constitution of my lesbian identity and the desire it predicates itself upon?

In chapter two I began to explore the psychoanalytic foundation to desire and to describe some key lesbian interventions into what is by and large a heterocentric, and ethnocentric, psychoanalysis. In this chapter my hope is to combine the two elements (desire as radically appropriative and desire as constructed) in order to examine a possible relation of lesbian subjectivity to the cinema.

Since our focus is the cinema, however, we need not only to separate the notion of desire as constructed and constructing, but also to examine the somewhat contentious psychoanalytic and cinematic relation between desire and identification. This is all the more important where I will be arguing in section iii that the two work might in conjunction.

Jackie Stacey, writing on the subject in her book *Star Gazing*, isolates three understandings of identification within the filmic context. Two are of a commonsense order. The first 'refer[s] to a set of cultural processes which describe different kinds of connections between spectators/readers and fictional others' (Stacey, 1994: 130). Hence, on the most popular level identification has 'meant sympathising or engaging with a character' (Stacey, 1994: 130). This is often complicated through the notion of point of view: 'This involves not only visual point of view, constructed by type of shot, editing sequences and so on, but also narrative point of view, produced through the sharing of knowledge, sympathy or moral values with the protagonist' (Stacey, 1994: 130). As Stacey goes on to observe, however, there is another level upon which identification has been understood within film theory (as opposed to the popular reception of films) and this is the psychoanalytic. Thus, she notes: 'Within psychoanalytic theory, "identification" has been seen as the key mechanism for the production of identities' (Stacey, 1994: 130). If we recall the account of the Lacanian mirror stage in chapter two we can better understand what is meant by identification on these terms. If we remember, self-identity is grounded in the perception of one's ideal self in the mirror. What is reflected through the medium of the mirror is ones self as one would like to believe it appears to others. We love this image of ourselves. It operates then as a narcissistic device which, as Stacey points out, 'is a necessary part of the development of all subjectivities' (Stacey, 1994: 131). To follow the argument through, again from chapter two, quite simply the cinema operates as another, larger and grander mirror. We aspire to be that which we identify with on the screen since it offers to us our ideal ego image.

So far in this chapter we have been considering identification without reference to the spectre of sexual difference. This is, however, a blind spot, since, as I argued in the last chapter, sexual difference structures both the psychoanalytic and the cinematic scenes. We find, for example, that identification and desire, or in Freudian terms narcissism and anaclisis, are understood as largely gender specific concepts. For as Stacey notes, though narcissistic desire may be part of the psychic formation of all subjects, 'the cultural construction of femininity in terms of physical appearance ... shapes the meanings of such narcissistic object relations for female spectators' (Stacey, 1994: 132). Women, if we recall the Mulveyan paradigm described in chapter two, connote 'to-be-looked-at-ness' (Mulvey, 1975: 11). Their function within the cinematic narrative is to attract and retain the male gaze. Hence, in identificatory terms women are confined to the position of object of the male gaze, allowed no active investigative look, aspiring only to emulate the passive beauty of the female star. Only (white) heterosexually identified men, or so the argument goes, have access to an active, anaclitic desire which they realise through their objectification of the female star. For women, then, identification operates as a monolithic and oppressive system, one complicit with the dominant workings of patriarchy. As Ann Friedberg puts it:

Identification can only be made through recognition, and all recognition is itself an implicit confirmation of an existing form. The institutional sanction of stars as ego ideals also operates to establish normative figures. Identification enforces a collapse of the subject onto the normative demand for sameness, which, under patriarchy, is always male. (Friedberg, 1982: 53)

As Mary Ann Doane argues, identification, at least within dominant cinema, depends upon the framing of a body. This is how recognition of an image by the spectator is obtained:

The mechanism of identification with a character in the cinema pivots on the representation of the body. Narrative is a mise-en-scène of bodies and while images without bodies are perfectly acceptable within its limits, it is the character's body which acts as the perceptual lure for the anchor of identification ... The affective value of [the cinematic] moment, strengthened by both lighting and the movement into the frame, is tied to the spectacle of the recognizable face – the very ability of the cinema to manufacture the pleasure of recognition. (Doane, 1980: 26)[2]

Though the male body can be structured within this relation of the look, owing to the patriarchal emphasis of the cinema, it is more usually the woman's body that is foregrounded in this way. Hence, if women are to take pleasure from the cinema they need to identify narcissistically (and hence masochistically) with the woman on screen who operates as vessel for the scopophilic investments of the male gaze. Not having access to the mechanism of the look, women operate as objects of the look.

This relation has been figured as a fundamentally oppressive one for women, or rather I should say, for white heterosexual women, since it is their over-presence as image within the cinema which renders them all too predictably visible. This is a problem, and I am not arguing for a minute that such images ever come close to reflecting the multiple possibilities of what it means to be a white heterosexual woman in the world. Nevertheless, even as burdened by the image Hollywood imposes upon them, such women at least have a body to identify with. The situation for other kinds of racially identified heterosexual women and Caucasian and non-Caucasian lesbians, however, is palpably one of lack. What then of lesbians, of all races, who choose not to be party to the conventional structure of the look between men and women, but who still seek to see themselves, and their desires, represented on the screen?

In chapter two I described the advent of the child into subjectivity through the Lacanian model of the mirror. It was noted in that chapter that the self reflected in the mirror is not a representation of the self in reality but of an ideal self. Though this ideal self functions through a relation of alienation or lack (that is, that it is never obtainable in reality), still I would argue that the ideal-I also functions at the level of the social, that is between the *Innenwelt*, one's sense of ideal self, and the *Umwelt*, or the way in which the outside world confirms and validates that sense of self. What, however, if one's *Innenwelt* does not correspond with one's sense of the *Umwelt*. What, indeed, if it has no visual object of identification or desire in the *Umwelt*, for example, in a world where lesbians are not perceived to exist? For a long time this was the world of Hollywood cinema, a cinema in which lesbians were either invisible or, when visible, coded in predictable, stereotypical ways.[3] How then project a lesbian desire beyond or, as I will suggest in chapter four, through these cinematic caricatures?

According to Mary Ann Doane, women spectators' relation to the cinema is often couched in terms of excess. Women, according to the dominant view, do not possess the ability to distinguish between image and reality, their cinematic identifications are thus marked by over-identification. Doane isolates the example of

Mia Farrow, whose uplifted face in *The Purple Rose of Cairo* (Woody Allen, 1985, US) illustrates the power of the cinematic image to shape reality for the female spectator:

> Toward the end of Woody Allen's *The Purple Rose of Cairo*, there is a close-up of some duration of Mia Farrow in spectatorial ecstasy, enraptured by the image, her face glowing (both figuratively and literally through its reflection of light from the movie screen) ... What the shot signifies, in part, is the peculiar susceptibility to the image – to the cinematic spectacle in general – attributed to women in our culture. Her pleasure in viewing is somehow more *intense*. The woman's spectatorship is yet another clearly delineated mark of her excess. (Doane, 1987: 1)

Of course, within the filmic fantasy Farrow's character succeeds in realising her fantasy identifications to the point where the force of her desire brings the hero down from the screen and into the 'real world', where, as Doane notes, 'he rapidly falls in love with her, fulfilling her spectatorial dreams' (Doane, 1987: 1). Farrow's over-identification with the scene set out in the film within a film allows her to realise her desire within the extra-filmic text of the film. What I will argue in the following pages is that the lesbian viewer, through the force of her lesbian-identified desire, attempts something similar, bringing the possibility of lesbian cinematic pleasure, if not quite into the realms of the real, then at least into view.

ii Gauging the limits between identification and desire

> It is also testimony to the vitality and fluidity of desire that it so easily appropriates whatever channels are available to it. (Bright, 1991: 152)

As lesbians we are often expert at the art of inserting ourselves into the filmic text which, as it is inscribed into a heterosexual economy, affects to exclude us but which on an individual viewing level offers us various points of access. This insertion of oneself into the text may be overt, as in the appropriative strategies of lesbian photographer Deborah Bright who literally inserts herself into film stills, cheekily placing herself between Spencer Tracy and Katherine Hepburn, popping up alongside a recumbent Vanessa Redgrave, or stealing the limelight from George Segal as she captures the roving eye of an obviously bored Glenda Jackson. Evidently there is nothing intrinsically lesbian about the films that Bright employs, the characters they present or the actresses who play them.[4] It is rather what Bright projects of her own desire on to these images that transforms them. For, as she argues, 'the lesbian subject roams from still to still, movie to movie, disrupting the narrative and altering it to suit her purposes, just as I did when I first watched those films' (Bright, 1991: 154). I would argue that Bright's work performs a witty re-enactment of what, from the privacy of the darkened cinema or the domestic sofa, many of us do, that is insert ourselves as desiring subjects into the film text. This is not a simple strategy. As I shall make clear in chapter four, for me it is structured, at least partly, through a relation of alienation. And to be sure, in reading lesbian desire into films which offer little narrative opening for the lesbian viewer, one is guilty of committing a certain amount of semantic violence on the text. These are often texts which have to be appropriated to a lesbian erotic by force, taken and adored. Within the economies of individual lesbian viewing pleasure, however, and as resistance to the hegemony of heterosexual desire in the cinema, this can be only to the good, and in any case reinforces resistance to the notion that a text must possess a single narrative function. For, as Bright's work shows, the individually desiring viewer is free to make virtually what she wants of a film text, knowingly subverting its narrative hegemony. What this engenders is a textual munificence as we make a text with no obviously lesbian credentials into something we can call our own by the insertion of ourselves as desiring subjects into the filmic scenario.

Of course there will be resistances in any text where one's identification with and/or desire for a character might be limited, even curtailed, certainly frustrated by the narrative closure of the text. I am not then arguing for the text as some kind of utopian free-for-all. As I noted in chapter one and will take up further in chapter four, the pleasure afforded from these appropriations is never *ipso facto* either subversive or transgressive. Still, I do want to maintain a celebration of the kind of lesbian viewership that operates perversely upon the text, reading it against its obvious or established meaning, my argument being that at a given moment there are always multiple possibilities for access to fantasy desire and identification. To an ever increasing degree, this is being recognised in the lesbian film criticism that circulates within contemporary discourse where a new understanding of the complexity and variety, the contradictoriness and occasional paradoxes of lesbian viewing are all being testified to. Nevertheless, certain blind spots continue to operate around the poles of identification and desire, something which will, in part, be the focus of this chapter.

As I noted in chapter one, the forging of a lesbian body by appropriating and hypostatising the covert or even disavowed significations of lesbianism (or at least of non-heterosexuality) in a figure such as Sigourney Weaver's Ripley or Jodie Foster's Clarice

Starling is just one strategy available to the lesbian-invested viewer. Readings of the latter film will be discussed in chapter six. The former, since she is so often the focus of both heterosexual feminist and lesbian critical cinematic writings, deserves some discussion here, particularly as readings of the various lesbian investments made in the character more than illustrate the complexity of the terrain between identification and desire.

As Paula Graham in her interesting and complex reading of the lesbian look in cinematic science fiction argues, 'Lesbian identification in the *Alien* trilogy lies firmly with the "Amazon"' (Graham, 1994: 197). Ripley is strong, independent, focused, muscled: according to Graham classic identificatory material for the lesbian viewer therefore. In a reading of the last scene in *Alien*, however, where Ripley faces her final battle with the alien in vest and pants, Graham, testifying to the 'double-edged' (Graham, 1994: 197) nature of the Amazon, both independent sister and 'daddy's brain-child' (Graham, 1994: 197), argues that the 'sexualization of Ripley's body functions as a disavowal of the lesbian implications of her "phallic subjectivity"' (Graham, 1994: 200–1). The strategies of identification, desire and disavowal, which, Graham argues, succeed Ripley's sexualisation, deserve extensive quotation:

Without her masculine clothing, Ripley appears feminized as a vulnerable sexual object. *The lesbian spectator generally resists identification with the feminine object and may slide into the phallic position in the classical scopic relay* ... This evokes a familiar lesbian strategy for resisting objectification and then coping with the 'impossibility' of reciprocal female subjectivity: 'phallicised' female sexual subject desires self-as-other female reciprocally ... The lesbian resists passive objectification by adopting a 'phallic' agency, yet desires a woman as sexual object. This paradox structures conflicts around lesbian sexual identity. (Graham, 1994: 201, my emphasis)

What I find interesting in this model is that we are to identify with Ripley only when masculinised, and desire her only when she is feminised. Of course on one level this makes perfect sense where Graham is merely utilising the classic psychoanalytic binary where femininity = passive and masculinity = active. As we learnt from Carol Clover in chapter one, such a distribution, albeit reflective of socially inscribed gender positions, is not binding: men and women do cross the divide between passivity and activity, masculinity and femininity. Nevertheless, I believe that in employing this model Graham manages to conflate the binary positions of masculinity and femininity with gender performance with the unfortunate consequence that lesbian identification is, albeit covertly, structured around the figure of the butch. I find this tendency amongst some lesbian critics to situate Ripley as a butch narcissistic ideal over and above her position as an object of lesbian anaclitic desire (which operates only when she is feminised) rather interesting.[5] As lesbians we are supposed to want to be Ripley, to admire and seek to emulate her bemuscled body and focused intensity. We are supposed only to be able to desire her, however, when she is feminised by the text (a feminisation which, as a consequence of the scopic pleasure invoked, as Graham notes, engenders certain feminist anxieties about the passive situation of the objectified body). For me, however, admiring Ripley for her muscles and independence and cinematic 'spunkiness' means not that I want to *be* her (though in the course of writing this book I have often wished to emulate her mental focus), but to *have* her, to possess her, *at the site of her masculinity and her femininity*, as the object of my *femme lesbian anaclitic desire*. The fact that this requires an understanding of objectification as extending beyond the merely passive and feminising is only one of the difficulties (the binary focus of psychoanalysis being another) that inhibit me from making such identifications, consolidating such desires in theory if not in practice.

The difficulty, it seems to me, accumulates around the figure of the lesbian femme. For Andrea Weiss the narcissistic position is not readily available to lesbians: 'Since lesbian images have been chronically absent from the screen ... [hence] it is questionable whether lesbians would enter into the spectatorial position of "over-presence" of narcissistic or masochistic over-identification' (Weiss, 1992: 40). Weiss therefore situates lesbian spectatorship with the masculine-identified or butch lesbian, a manoeuvre we also witness in the work of Bright, who in her photographs visualises the possession of the heterosexually identified femme (albeit butchy-femme) star by the visibly identified butch lesbian subject. While I believe this over-simplifies the construction of butch lesbian identification and desire, it quite clearly, and most worryingly, erases femme lesbian identification and desire from the specular equation. Weiss admits that she cannot account for femme lesbian desire, which remains 'largely a matter of speculation' (Weiss, 1992: 42). In Bright's work too the lesbian femme is rendered invisible as the heterosexually identified woman intercedes as the object of (butch) lesbian desire. The lesbian femme is doubly negated therefore, first as lesbian, then as feminine object of desire. What place then for the lesbian femme within a psychoanalytic account of cinematic identification and desire?

The socially inscribed looking position for women is of course the narcissistic, and presumably the lesbian femme, even where her gaze is addressed towards another woman, is deemed to find her cinematic pleasure in this. Narcissistic desire is of course, if we recall the Freud of chapter two, aspirational and non-object-focused. Can it, however, be eroticised? According to Jackie Stacey, it can. Indeed, in *Star Gazing*, her account of the identificatory strategies employed by a group of British women through the 1930s, 1940s and 1950s, she argues for an eroticisation of the (in this case heterosexually identified) female spectator's identification with the woman on the screen, even perhaps where this is not consciously articulated. This does not mean that all of the feminine fascinations she refers to in the book are covertly homoerotic. Nor that there is no specificity in consciously articulated lesbian desire (I do not for a moment believe that Stacey is attempting to reintroduce a Richian concept of the lesbian continuum, with its unfortunate, but seemingly inevitable, consequent desexualisation of lesbian desire).[6] Rather, in Stacey's own words: 'I suggest that identification between femininities contains forms of homoerotic pleasure which have yet to be explored' (Stacey, 1994: 29). She continues:

My concern with the possibility of homoeroticism in the forms of fascination between women available to all women in the cinema audience assumes that pleasures of spectatorship work on unconscious as well as conscious, levels ... This is not to argue that identification is the same as desire, or only contains desire, but rather to try to open up the meanings of both categories to enable a fuller understanding of the pleasures of the cinema for female spectators. (Stacey, 1994: 29)

Though the identifications described by Stacey can be read in terms of a conventional interpellation into femininity – one learns appropriate femininity by watching other women – Stacey argues that the intensity of feeling experienced pushes identification into desire. Observes Stacey: 'The passion for female stars experienced by spectators is striking in its intensity: it is difficult to see *Calamity Jane* forty-five times in a fortnight!' (Stacey, 1994: 138) as one respondent recalls doing. She also notes that such passion is often relegated in recollection to the status of adolescent crush. Indeed, Stacey's respondents often seem embarrassed by the intensity of their feelings forty years on. Still, as Stacey acknowledges, the impact of such crushes can continue into adult life, lasting through a lifetime's adoration. Thus she quotes a woman whose passion for Deanna Durbin began at nine and continues to this day. The language is, as Stacey notes, laden with romantic conventions:

> In the late 1930s, when I was about nine or ten, I began to be aware of a young girl's face appearing in magazines and newspapers. I was fascinated. The large eyes, the full mouth, sometimes the wonderful smile, showing the slightly prominent but perfect teeth. I feel rather irritated that I do not recall the moment when I realised that the face belonged to a very lovely singing voice beginning to be heard on the radio record programmes. The face and voice belonged to Deanna Durbin. (Stacey, 1994: 139)

That the woman testifies to her adoration while invoking her marriage, children and grandchildren as proof of her heterosexuality illustrates the tension at work between identification and desire. As Stacey concludes: '[often] the contrast to heterosexual devotion is made by the spectator herself, but the homoerotic connotations of such attachments are left implicit' (Stacey, 1994: 138).

The form and implications of such identifications remain by and large unexplored within cinematic studies and, unfortunately, it is not within the scope of this book to attempt to rectify this. What intrigues me is the way in which one might apply Stacey's hunch about heterosexual identifications to the lesbian femme whose object is not the lesbian butch, but another femme – how might her narcissistic cinematic identifications be infused with an anaclitic desire which if not exactly deemed to be impossible, has certainly been ignored within accounts of lesbian visual pleasure? This is the project of section iii of this chapter. First, however, a necessary detour. Stacey's position has of course been notoriously attacked by Teresa de Lauretis (1994), who criticises a number of lesbian theorists for what she sees as their conflation of identification and desire at the expense of what she terms a mature lesbian sexuality. Hence in *The Practice of Love* de Lauretis criticises Stacey's textual appropriation of mainstream films such as *All About Eve* (Joseph L. Mankiewicz, 1950, US) and *Desperately Seeking Susan* (Susan Seidelman, 1985, US) in Stacey's oft-cited piece 'Desperately seeking difference' for recuperating lesbian desire to a '"childlike" wish ... a kind of identification that is at once ego-directed, narcissistic, and desexualized, devoid of sexual aim' (de Lauretis, 1994: 117). For de Lauretis, Stacey's (and others') concentration on films that have no overt lesbian content means that:

> the 'feminine desire' Stacey pursues ... is still a form of identification with the image of woman, if a powerful and attractive womanhood a feminine role-model or ego-ideal, and a quintessentially heterosexual one; it is not desire between women, but indeed intrafeminine, self-directed, narcissistic 'fascinations'. (de Lauretis, 1994: 120)

De Lauretis juxtaposes such identifications with her own reading of Sheila McLaughlin's *She Must Be Seeing Things* which she theorises as an example or a film resonant with a textually visible lesbian desire:

> McLaughlin's film locates itself historically and politically in the contemporary North American lesbian community with its conflicting discourses and (why not say it) instinctual vicissitudes, posing the question of desire within the context of actual practices of both lesbianism and the cinema. (de Lauretis, 1994: 122)

Though I would agree with much of de Lauretis's reading of McLaughlin's film, I nevertheless demur at her criticism that appropriations of non-lesbian identified-films necessarily operate as 'heterosexist' (de Lauretis, 1994: 120). For me, Stacey's response to de Lauretis's attack, that she is 'not de-eroticising desire, but rather eroticising identification' (Stacey, 1994: 29) certainly requires more substantiation. What forms might this desire take? What if its homoeroticism were overtly recognised by the heterosexually identified woman? What are the possibilities for a lesbian-identified viewer? These are issues which are frustratingly – though, given the composition of her survey and the restrictions of methodological work in general (where one is not granted the right to probe with such questions), inevitably unanswered, within her work. Still, I believe that her notion of the feminine as object of erotic fascination for women as well as for men deserves more consideration than de Lauretis is prepared to bestow upon it.

iii Femme to femme: a love story

> Femmes have been seen as a problem through the decades both by those who never pretended to be our friends and now by those who say they are our comrades. (Nestle, 1992: 144)

> 'How,' he asked, 'could the feminine one be the real lesbian?' (Martin Gottfried, quoted in Russo, 1981: 164)

One of the things that struck me upon first reading de Lauretis's impressive *The Practice of Love* is the difficulty she appears to have with theorising a visible position for the femme. Of course, where it takes 'two women, not one, to make a lesbian' (de Lauretis, 1994: 92), the femme remains integral to the lesbian dyad and indeed de Lauretis hints at her role within this as a comparable one to the butch, where she too inhabits 'the place of a woman who desires another woman, the place from where each one looks at the other one with desire' (de Lauretis, 1994: 88). Certainly, de Lauretis's project is to open up a theoretical space for the negotiation of multiple points and configurations of lesbian practice, identification and desire. Still, where the butch tends to figure as a category on her own, indeed has a whole chapter devoted to her self-individuation,[7] the femme is rendered, relatively speaking, invisible. This may have something to do with de Lauretis's own narcissistic identifications; it is certainly reflective of a more general failure to visualise the lesbian femme within contemporary theory.[8] As Joan Nestle's words, first written in 1984 and appended as introduction to this section, make clear, the lesbian femme, the lesbian whose personal style and social identity manifests itself, to varying degrees, through the cultural trappings of femininity, has been ignored by the dominant heterosexual culture, and treated with suspicion within her own lesbian culture.

As Nestle describes, the femme has always been a problem for heterosexuality, since she appears to exhibit all the prerequisites of heterosexual femininity – and thus of heterosexual desirability – whilst exercising a 'deviant' object choice in that her passion is directed towards other women. As a system, heterosexuality of course operates on the basis of a binary structural differentiation, male/female, masculine/feminine, heterosexual/homosexual. Within this system lesbians are lesbians and women are heterosexual where lesbianism is figured as the opposite to heterosexual femininity and hence, in the most restrictive of readings, aligned with a masculine identification and object choice. As I will describe later, this limits the potential scope of identification and desire for the butch lesbian as it ignores the participation of the femme. By implication, lesbians who are visually indistinguishable from heterosexually identified women, pose a particular threat to the system of differential heterosexuality. In the early part of the twentieth century the sexologist Havelock Ellis responded to this threat by attributing some other (any other) mode of physical deficiency to the femme lesbian, implying, for example, that such women are unattractive to men since they exhibit a physical or emotional immaturity. Thus he tells his readers: 'On the whole, they are women who are not very robust and well developed, physically or nervously, and who are not well adapted for child-bearing' (Ellis, 1925: 222). He concludes: 'One may, perhaps, say that they are the pick of the women whom the average man would pass by' (Ellis, 1925: 222). Hence, though nominally designated a woman by Ellis, the femme lesbian remains inadequate on all counts of 'proper' femininity. By the 1950s her press has not improved. Here the lesbian femme is described by psychologist Frank Caprio as that apotheosis of all things regressive, weak and indulgent, the primary narcissist:

The feminine type of lesbian is one who seeks mother love, who enjoys being a recipient of much attention and affection. She is often preoccupied with personal beauty ... the clinging vine type who is often thought and spoken of by elders as a little fool without any realisation of the warped sexuality which is promoting her actions. (Caprio, 1953: 19)

As Nestle points out, in articulating femme lesbian identity in this way, that is, as marked by absence of choice, as reactive rather than proactive, 'the femme lesbian is stripped of all power, made into a foolish woman' (Nestle, 1992: 143). She concludes: 'Historically, we have been left disinherited, seen neither as true inverts nor as grown women' (Nestle, 1992: 144)

In the theories of the sexologists the femme is characterised as the (inadequate) woman 'to whom the actively inverted woman [in other words the butch] is most attracted' (Ellis, 1925: 222). She is therefore designated as passive to the 'proper' invert's active. Surprisingly, some of the vestiges of this logic are found in subsequent feminist responses to the femme. Thus, in the context of some 1970s feminism, femmes are viewed, as Sue-Ellen Case puts it, testifying to a bizarre twist of feminist logic in the work of *Lesbian/Woman* authors Del Martin and Phyllis Lyon, as 'lost heterosexuals who damage birthright lesbians by forcing them to play the butch roles' (Case, 1988/9: 58). As Nestle writes:

If we dress to please ourselves and the other women to whom we want to announce our desire, we are called traitors by many of our own community, because we seem to be wearing the clothes of the enemy ... The message to femmes throughout the 1970s was that we were the Uncle Toms of the movement. (Nestle, 1992: 141)

The logic of the femme's style is lost to a later age eager to impose its own interpretation without heed to receptive context. And the map of misreading proliferates:

In the 1970's and 1980's, the femme is also charged with the crime of passing, of trying to disassociate herself from the androgynous lesbian ... A femme is often seen as a lesbian acting like a straight woman who is not a feminist – a terrible misreading of self-presentation that turns a language of liberated desire into the silence of collaboration. (Nestle, 1992: 142)

Such a formulation echoes the suspicions of the sexologists who see the femme primarily as an imposter, committed neither to heterosexuality nor to homosexuality.

In the 1970s and 1980s, of course, both lesbian butch and femme identities were condemned by the then dominant form of lesbian-feminism which characterised the style as a reactionary and outmoded form.[8] Butch–femme, it was claimed, reinstitutes lesbianism within patriarchal constructions of heterosexual exchange, one woman making her investment in the sartorial, bodily and gestural significations of masculinity, the other being constrained to expressing a conventional heterosexual femininity. The butch–femme investment in gendered dress, thus, according to such readings, imitates heterosexuality and plays out, within a lesbian context, its patriarchal investment in gender inequality. Thankfully, the complex nature and investment of lesbian butch–femme relations have since been explored, detailed and discussed in the work of not only Nestle but Amber Hollibaugh (Hollibaugh, Davis and Nestle, 1992), Madeline Davis (Davis and Kennedy, 1993) and Leslie Feinberg (1992) amongst others. For Nestle, one of the first lesbian feminists to defend the butch–femme relation against the charges that it refigures the oppressive structures and gender inequalities of the compulsory heterosexual marriage relation, the debate is still, nevertheless, charged with irony. Because it is still the butch who visualises lesbianism through her visual investment in masculine dress (the femme is rendered visible as a lesbian when seen publicly alongside her butch lover), the femme remains lesbian, as it were, only by association. Remarks Nestle: 'Butches were known by their appearance, femmes by their choices' (Nestle, 1992: 139).

This emphasis has continued to skew the way in which visibly masculine- and feminine-identified lesbians have continued to be represented and understood. Lisa Walker in 'How to recognize a lesbian: the politics of looking like what you are' argues that there is a tendency in lesbian critics to theorise largely from the position of the butch, conferring upon her the position of active, instigative desirer, whilst confining the femme to the role of passive recipient of her desire. Isolating Sue-Ellen Case's 'Towards a butch–femme aesthetic' in particular, Walker argues:

In each of these passages [discussed by Case] the butch is represented as the desiring subject whilst the femme is represented as the object of desire. Thus, while Case's essay suggests that 'the butch–femme couple inhabit the subject position together – "you can't have one without the other" ..., it could be argued that another meaning behind the phrase is something like 'a femme is not queer without her butch.' While the butch can stand alone as the 'marked taboo against lesbianism,' the femme is invisible as a lesbian unless she is playing the butch'. (Walker, 1993: 881)

Lesbian visibility has tended to depend upon the woman who physically (and by this I include stance, gesture, hair and dress, in other words all the socially inscribed signifiers of what has come to be known as gender performance) identifies herself as butch. As a result, the visual connotation of active lesbian desire in cinema theory remains predicated upon the cultural equation butch = lesbian. As Cheshire Calhoun argued recently: 'Butches figure the lesbian in ways that their feminine counterparts cannot. In their power to generate the question "To which sex does s/he belong?" they invite a reading of them as lesbians' (Calhoun, 1995: 22). Calhoun is swift to point out that she is not proposing a hierarchy whereby the butch lesbian comes to represent the real to the femme's undecided. Her argument is merely that ambiguous gender status operates as the signifier of difference and that the masculine lesbian visualises this in a way that the femme does not. Walker, however, points to some ironies in the predominance of a politics of the visual in the social and theoretical articulation of identity:

> While privileging visibility can be politically and rhetorically effective, it is not without its problems. Within the constructs of a given identity that invests certain signifiers with political value, figures that do not present these signifiers are often neglected. Because subjects who can 'pass' exceed the categories of visibility that establish identity, they tend to be regarded as peripheral to the understanding of marginalization. (Walker, 1993: 868)

Extending this across race as well as sexuality, Walker demonstrates how the right of the woman of colour who can pass as white, or the lesbian femme who appears heterosexual, or the lesbian femme woman of colour who is recognised as neither, to be represented within her chosen community, is put under question, or at least, suspicion.

As has been noted by Weiss (1992) and Allen (1995), amongst others, the (mainstream and art) cinema's response to the problem of sexual sameness has often been to render one of the lovers butch and the other femme.[9] As Michèle Aina Barale points out, this gesture is a colonising one where 'In order [for the dominant, here, heterosexuality] to appropriate the Other, it is represented as similar. Heterosexuality thus seeks to create lesbians whose desires are similar to its own' (Barale, 1991: 237). As Barale also notes, the visual display of sex/gender positioning is often complemented by a difference in hair colour, dark for the butch and blonde for the femme. For Louise Allen amongst others, this distinction is predicated upon the racial construction, dark = bad and blonde = all that is desirable, where as Richard Dyer puts it: 'the blonde woman comes to represent not only the most desired of women but also the most womanly of women' (Dyer, 1988: 48).[10] This is a distinction which, as I noted in chapter one, Allen explores in her reading of Percy Adlon's *Salmonberries*. Though I think Allen is absolutely right in her reading of the interpellation of racial difference (which always returns to the assertion of white privilege) in the film, I find the way in which she positions femm*e*ininity as a result, problematic. For Allen, as for Calhoun, the butch cannot pass since she remains always visibly visible. This visibility is conveyed, she argues, and quite rightly, through more than just dress:

> cultural identification is conferred through dress codes and skin colour ... but it is also conferred through language (use of patois, Asian languages, gay and lesbian language such as palare and 'code names' in lesbian and gay culture), accent, sentence construction, badges, signs, walk, pose, mannerisms, the 'look' etc. (Allen, 1995: 76)

Allen then admits that 'Black people, "white" enough to "pass" have all these forms of identification to employ in order to identify as black, and so do lesbian femmes in order to identify as lesbians' (Allen, 1995: 76). And yet, she claims, in practice 'What happens *most of the time* is that some black people passing as white and some lesbian femmes also use these other (non-visible?) strategies in order to invest in privileges of whiteness and heterosexuality respectively' (Allen, 1995: 76, my emphasis). Though she limits her accusation to 'some' black people, 'some' lesbian femmes, the implication remains, with the two reduced to collaborators until proved innocent. So an essay which is sensitive to the implications of one type of cultural colonisation reads as profoundly insensitive to the configurations of another.

The fact that the cinematic femme lesbian frequently passes as the heterosexual cinematic ideal (that is, feminine and blond), with all the sexual and racial connotations implied by this, does perhaps, as Allen argues, situate her more firmly than the butch within hegemonic discourse. This does not mean that she is not also 'other' to the (white) lesbian, femme, butch (or any combination of the two), identified spectator. It does suggest that her otherness (her manifestation of a socially inscribed femininity, predicated upon her blondeness/whiteness) might be a positive spur to both aspiration (to be that much of a woman *and* a lesbian) and desire (to desire what is other to oneself in the other) for a spectator who feels these culturally inscribed ideals to be lacking in her own look. Recognising then, that an identification with or desire for the femme, be she coded lesbian or not, may well play into racial constructions of beauty as both feminine and white, I nevertheless want to pursue this notion of femme visibility and femme–femme desire, to what are, for me, some of its logical conclusions.

The difficulty of theorising the lesbian femme spectator, particularly if her object of desire is another femme, should be clear, for, when theorising the femme away from the butch, one runs into some persistent social and theoretical impasses. What I want to argue here, namely the possibility of femme–femme desire as an independent lesbian erotic category, seems to be a contradiction in terms. Yet, and in my own experience, the femme figure on screen has constantly operated as both an aspirational (narcissistic) and a desired (anaclitic) category.

As I noted in the last section, for Andrea Weiss the lesbian femme figures as a visual impossibility. A feminine woman on screen is always already recuperable to the voyeuristic male gaze. Two femmes on screen only compound the effect, as Weiss, talking about lesbian vampire movies, here makes clear:

The typical vampire and her victim are both visually coded as heterosexual and feminine, even though the narrative sets them up to be lovers. *They lack the lesbian verisimilitude that would enable them to 'pass' as lesbians*; they flirt with men and dress (and undress) to appeal to male-desire. (Weiss, 1992: 106, my emphasis)

The erasure of the specificity of my own femme–femme desire, and the assumption that because a woman does not pass as butch she lacks lesbian verisimilitude, is breathtaking. To return to the question I raised in the last section, however: is femininity always and only subjected to a passive eroticising objectification, or can it, in the accession to femme*i*ninity, fight back?

While it is largely true that, as Weiss argues, the lesbian vampire in the Euro-horrors of the 1960s and early 1970s were intended to appeal to a male heterosexual audience, I cannot agree that a pandering to male voyeurism necessarily inhibits the articulation of either lesbian identification or desire. Weiss's focus upon the femininity of the lesbian vampire in fact seems to me to be a more productive category than Weiss gives it credit for. For Weiss, the femme lesbian is primarily a dissimulator:

Unlike the 'masculine' images of lesbians in more mainstream films of the late sixties and early seventies – *The Fox* (Mark Rydell, [1967, US]) and *The Killing of Sister George* (Robert Aldrich, 1968), for example – the lesbian vampire fits the stereotype, not of the mannish lesbian, but of the white, feminine, heterosexual woman. Her vampirism, therefore, is doubly disturbing, as she appears 'normal' by society's standards for women and yet is not. (Weiss, 1992: 91)

She dissimulates right into the heart of hetero-patriarchy therefore. The fact that this dissimulation gets lost in the theoretical bid for visibility is only one of the ironies at work in the representation.

Let me get this clear, when referring to femme desire(s) I am not talking about the 'feminine' lesbian, that species of 'gay lady' who has a political problem with identifying as a lesbian, loathes the term even, and 'doesn't know why those butches have to look so masculine'. This position seems to me to express a level of lesbian-hating (and woman-hating) as trenchant as any. Nor do I want to imply a denigration of the butch identity or style in this analysis. The butch is not absent as an erotic category from this analysis, she is merely not its focus. Reversing a trend in the writing of the femme as inevitably partner to her butch, it is the former who becomes the focus, to ask, as Lois Weaver puts it, can the femme dance alone,[11] and, as I would add, can she signify her lesbian desire to another femme, when so doing?

Once again visibility is the crux we return to. The conundrum is clearly articulated in that most loved of critical theoretical film texts, *She Must Be Seeing Things*, a film which flirts with the possibility of the blonde femme Jo's return to heterosexuality, in order to disinvest it of its power to provoke. De Lauretis has argued that it is because of the film's investment in actual lesbian discourse, by implication, the fact that we may know of Lois Weaver (who plays Jo) as a lesbian performer in her own right, that situates her performance of lesbian femm*e*ininity in a realm of authenticity which other femmes such as Vivian in *Desert Hearts*' cannot possibly attain to.[12] De Lauretis is of course extremely critical of *Desert Hearts*'s reputation as a lesbian film, arguing that heterosexuality as an institution permeates its every pretension to lesbian desire.[13] This is true, but ultimately irrelevant. For where, as I argue in this book, there is no such thing as a lesbian film, where films are lesbianised by the invested desire of the lesbian-identified viewer (that the film world may have played a part in the constitution and limits of such a desire can be figured either as the sum of the banality of that desire, or, as I see it, as testimony to cultural ingenuity of the lesbian-identified viewer), both characters, both Jo and Vivian, can at the very least be lesbianised by my own particular lesbian desire.[14]

Take as an example then *Desert Hearts*, a film I hate and love in equal quantities. Even presuming my lesbian identity to be adult and post-oedipal,[15] I confess I am still (deliberately?) confused in my identifications and desires. On the one hand I want to be the seducer in desiring Vivien, desiring to have her. However, I also desire to be her, being loved by Cay. In fact, what I really want is to be as feminine and gauche, as innocent but guilty by default, as Vivian in being loved by Cay, active in my passive seduction of the more experienced woman, nostalgically recalling the power of sitting back and letting it all happen (a nostalgia all the more poignant for me since I never found myself in that position!). At the same time, I want to disavow any identification with Cay, who, arrogant and presumptuous, I consider unattractive as a character. Certainly, I identify with her as the articulator of a positive 'lesbian' desire which makes things happen. The fact that I project this active desire on to Vivian as both respondent and articulator of my own lesbian desire only illustrates how the various relations shift and are too complicated to divide clearly, one into the other. This all seems quite simple to me when sitting in the cinema. It gets complicated when I attempt to theorise it within the spectatorial paradigms (elevated to the species of scopic norm), within film theory. Let me rehearse the various positions again then in the light of conventional understandings of narcissism and anaclisis. When I desire Vivian I take up the masculine, anaclitic position, a position that disinvests me of my femme*i*ninity. When I want to be Vivian, my narcissistic identification precludes an active looking desire. When I want to be Vivian and want Vivian and want to be Vivian being loved by Vivian I enter the realm of psychic impossibility.[16] Of course, on one level, to argue that the cinema allows for the proliferation of lesbian scopic pleasure beyond the rigours of *either* the narcissistic *or* the anaclitic is a profoundly banal conclusion to come to. Its very banality only makes it all the more revealing that the notion has not been more widely incorporated into a structured account of lesbian cinematic viewing pleasure.

iv All mixed up and nowhere to go

Genderbending is as malleable as Mr. Potato Head ... Some butches [even] look like female sex goddesses. (Lamos, 1994: 96)

For most observers, the assumption of heterosexuality is so strong that the femme is easily seen as just another woman's friend. But for those who know where, when and how to look, the femme's sexual preference is as unmistakable as her gender. (Holmlund, 1991: 148)

And yet it is true that my own femme responses to the film femmes were perhaps responding as much to the little bit of butch in their characters as their femininity. Perhaps this is what I have been terming their femme*i*ninity, or rather what I have been appropriating as such. Certainly the characters I have admired and eroticised since childhood have been feminine in non-traditional terms, articulate of mind, voice and body. Does this then position me as femme to their 'butch', a reversal of the position where I objectify them? Or is there a phallicism to their femininity which resonates with mine and, if so, where does that situate either of us? Can I have my cake and eat it in other words?

Elsewhere, as in the cinema, femme–femme or even butch–butch relations have usually been discussed only on the level of an identificatory narcissism, as the celebration and confirmation of sameness. For Arlene Ishtar, relations with other femmes, both on the screen and outside, were conducted strictly on the identificatory, narcissistic level where 'femme women have a particular attraction for me, because they validate me by being role models who teach me that femininity is not weakness' (Ishtar, 1992: 382). Likewise, Leslie Feinberg tells of the tutoring she received in the art of constructing for herself a butch identity: 'A glimpse of butch Al was a glimpse of power, a memory I was afraid to hang onto, and afraid to let go of' (Feinberg, 1992: 82). Initially suspicious of her young protégée, Al takes the young butch: 'under her wing and taught me all the things she thought were most important for a baby butch like me to know' (Feinberg, 1992: 84). The relation is an imitative, admiring one. Within this relation, butches are buddies, femmes are loved sexual partners. Hence the shock of Feinberg's hero Jess, in her novel *Stonebutch Blues*, whose longtime compadre confesses to loving another butch. Walking away from a scene which puts into question her own sense of the world, Jess returns to take up the conversation more than a decade later, a conversation which suggests the complexities of identification and desire which inform even an identity as apparently overt as the extreme butch. Here Frankie tries to explain her feelings to Jess:

> It was only when I admitted it was butch hands that I wanted on my body that everything changed for me. The more I saw what I loved about other butches, the more I began to accept myself. You know what gets it for me, Jess? ... An old bull with graying hair, a cocky smile, and sad eyes. You know the kind of butch with arms as big as your thigh? Those are the arms I want to hold me. (Feinberg, 1993: 273)

Jess's reply is framed within a conundrum that places femme gender style over and above anatomical sex:

> I ran my fingertips over the dark wood near her thigh. 'I love them so much too. But what gets it for me is high femme. It's funny – it doesn't matter whether it's women or men – it's always high femme that pulls me by the waist and makes me sweat.'
>
> Frankie rested her arm.'You and me have to hammer out a definition of butch that doesn't leave me out.' (Feinberg, 1993: 274)

In her description of just a few of the possible combinations of sex, gender and desire, Feinberg implies the limitation of gender identification if it is taken too literally. The point Feinberg begins to articulate is extended by Ishtar, who implies a continuum of gender readings within butch and femme, a continuum of both history and behaviour:

> I am aware that some lesbians change their identities depending on their lovers or the time of their lives. I know a handful of butches who have gone femme and a few femmes who have gone butch, and I say *mazel tov*. I also know quite a few butches who, in the privacy of their own homes, like frilly teddies and makeup (butches in drag or transvestite femmes?). And many many femmes ... who like butches on their back in bed. (Ishtar, 1992: 382)

Another femme, Mykel Johnson, adds: 'One very butch lover told me she thought of me as butch too, and that she was attracted to butch women' (Johnson, 1992: 397). Intersecting gender complications leave us searching for a definition – what are the gender relations at play in such a relation, are we dealing with two 'faggots' (Brown, 1992: 114), or with two butch women? A femme in drag or a butch in denial? What is the relation between gender, sexual orientation and desire where visible difference is not necessarily connoted, where, as Lisa Walker suggests: 'the relationship between a visible signifier of difference and its signified identity might be complicated' (Walker, 1993: 888)? Like Walker, I would argue the limits of the visible for understanding the complicated arrangements of sex, gender, sexuality and desire that operate in even the most visibly articulated of identities. As Judith Butler notes:

> Sexuality is never fully 'expressed' in a performance or practice; there will be passive and butchy femmes, femmy and aggressive butches, and both of those, and more, will turn out to describe more or less anatomically stable 'males' and 'females'. There are no direct expressive or causal links between sex, gender, gender presentation, sexual practice, fantasy and sexuality. (Butler, 1991: 25)[17]

Indeed, she continues:

> Part of what constitutes sexuality is precisely that which does not appear and that which, to some degree, can never appear. This is perhaps the most fundamental reason why sexuality is to some degree always closeted, especially to the one who would express it through acts of self-disclosure. (Butler, 1991: 25)

What this means is that identity is grounded as much in a relation of abjection (what one disavows) as it is in affirmation, a point I shall take up and develop in the next chapter.[18]

That we seem to have departed radically from a discussion of the cinema and its effects suggests to me the lack of a ground of theoretical debate in this area. To articulate the effect of the non-visible on a medium such as the cinema which postulates its effects upon a hyper-visibility is equally as difficult. Still, it is a beginning at least to note that visibility in the cinema may take forms which are merely unnoted by the dominant readings of its effects. To note, for example, that the butch (be this performed through the body of Cay, George, Eli, Kotzebue or Rhett Butler) is as much the object of the lesbian gaze as the femme, and when wounded through the medium of the screen or the rhapsodies of Teresa de Lauretis, all the more explicitly rendered as an object of vanitas. To note also that the femme, in foregrounding her performance as performance, is perfectly capable of operating as returner, engager in, subject of the gaze, all the more so when she turns objectification on its head and renders it as a species of power.

As Cheshire Calhoun suggests: 'the more vigorously one attempts to read femme lesbian sexuality for sex/gender ambiguity, the more powerfully femme sexuality figures the lesbian' (Calhoun, 1995: 22). She does not specify what forms this might take, but a few spring to mind. The embracing of a hyperfemininity, a kind of high femme drag, seems a possibility, as de Lauretis begins to articulate in her characterisation of Jo's striptease in *She Must Be Seeing Things* as: 'the camp reappropriation of feminine gender signifiers' (de Lauretis, 1994: 102). The exhibiting of a femme style with just a touch of butch seems another (certainly this is one explanation for my adolescent fascination with Vanessa Redgrave!). Argues Mykel Johnson: 'Even if she is "beautiful" by ... male standards, a femme dyke may do something to disrupt the image, intentionally break the rules' (Johnson, 1992: 397). And if not in her 'look', is it in her look? Can the femme lesbian articulate, just by looking, and returning the look, that she is both object and subject of the look? As Johnson argues, the femme 'breaks the cardinal rule: her audience is female not male. She flashes her eyes and smiles in a lesbian direction' (Johnson, 1992: 397–8). Whether the object of her look is butch or another femme, the frame of vision remains tied to the economy of the lesbian.

For Christine Holmlund who, in a study comprising a number of what she terms mainstream femme films, determines to examine the mainscreen femme and the 'promises and problems she raises' (Holmund, 1991: 146), it is context which determines the reception of the femme as lesbian. That context changes over time and audience.[19] There is indeed no certainty that the femme, whether operative in lesbian themed films or otherwise, will be recognised by audiences as lesbian. The probability, as with the homoerotic examples Holmlund reviews (*Personal Best, Lianna, Entre Nous, Desert Hearts*), is that she will not, at least not by heterosexually identified audiences. Lesbians, however, may have a different investment and may accompany their viewing with a different concept of reception. It is this investment in a specific context of viewing, argues Holmlund, that renders the femme visible. Though she does not imply a universality of reception even amongst lesbians, still Holmlund wants to argue for the appropriative possibilities of a lesbian context of viewing. Discussing the reception of Desert Hearts she observes:

> When there were significant numbers of lesbians in the audience ... the ... heterosexual public space of most movie theatres was temporarily redefined as an extension of lesbian community space. Lesbians met other lesbians ... They subverted and supplemented the narratives of all four films, vocally, and as a group ... For once, the presence of lesbian looks and desires – in the audience, if not the text – and the eagerness of lesbian audiences to look at and see themselves in the movies – were hard to ignore. (Holmlund, 1991: 165)[20]

Though, as Holmlund notes, there are limits to the commonality of this temporary lesbian point of view with issues such as race, class, notions of community, all impacting upon the context of seeing, still the need for a flexible approach to understanding films otherwise consigned to the annals of heterocentrism seems necessary. To reiterate, what often seem most interesting to me about the movies are the audiences who watch them.

It seems to me axiomatic that the cinema, far from being about the confirmation of one identification or desire over the other, aids the proliferation of both into multiple configurations of inappropriate identifications and desires. Thus one might identify as a femme with the hyperfemininity *and* the butchiness of the Hollywood femmes but also with the male butch heroes. This could be an aspirational desire – it may be, as in my own, object-focused as well – to wish to be the femme on the screen as confirmation of my own (not always unanxious) investments in femme*i*ninity, and to desire her and want to possess her as deeply as any Hollywood hero. That this leaves me, theoretically speaking, identifying with the butch while appearing to be the femme is only one of the ironies engendered by the visibility/invisibility conundrum. That this might translate to the butch who not only may desire to possess the femme – usurping, as in Deborah Bright's work, the prerogative of the male cinematic hero – but is also fascinated, to the point of fantasising a likeness, by her femme*i*ninity, is a possibility I would at least like to postulate. Her both aspirational and anaclitic attachment to the hero I now virtually take for granted.

Whilst fantasising the proliferating possibilities for identification and desire within the cinematic scene, however, I must emphasise that I do not intend to fall into the trap, which de Lauretis critiques so extensively, of suggesting a fantasy free-for-all which she characterises as the 'optimistically silly notion of an unbounded mobility of identities for the spectator-subject' (de Lauretis, 1994: 140). The limitations of a fantasy desire such as that of the lesbian femme, interpellated as it is within significations of race and class, sexuality and beauty, means that, as de Lauretis writes:

> the question of spectatorial desire and identification in any particular film must rest ... on ... the spectator's subjectivity and what I have called subjecthood; that is to say, not only her or his psychic and fantasmatic configuration, the places and positions that she or he may be able to assume in the structure of desire, but also the ways in which she or he is located in social relations of sexuality, race, class, gender etc., the places she or he may be able to assume as subject in the social. (de Lauretis, 1994: 129)

That, as de Lauretis argues, these cannot be determined from the start, that subjects who appear to hold a clear racial or class or sexed or gendered position may not always articulate their fantasy desires through these positions in any clear or coherent way also needs to be noted.

I asked, at the beginning of this chapter, whether the cinema might be not merely refracted by, but also partially constitutive of lesbian identity and desire. I am aware, drawing to the end of the chapter, that I have not really answered this question. My belief is that the cinema, cinematic fantasies, do have an impact upon the constitution, the scenography, of lesbian desire. As I suggested in chapter one, our cinematic fantasies may be constructed through the most dominant, most predictable, most banal of conditions. The relative influence of the dominant over the appropriative remains, however, under dispute. Perhaps de Lauretis sums it up in arguing that

> when it comes to engaging the spectator's fantasy and identification, a film's effects are neither structural (if structural is equated with universal) nor totally structured by the film (by its fantasy, narration, or form); rather, they are contingent on the spectator's subjectivity and subjecthood (which are themselves, to some extent, already structured but open to restructuration). (de Lauretis, 1991: 130)

Perhaps it will be clearer to the reader from this account of my own cinematic investments.

Notes

1 *The South Bank Show*, ITV, 12 March, 1995.
2 For Richard Dyer (1988) the most recognisable face is also the face framed within a light which reifies that face as white. Some of the ironies underlying Hollywood's hypostatisation of the white female face are explored in Julie Dash's short film *Illusions* (Julie Dash, 1982, US), for an account of which see Mayne (1990: 59–67).
3 For an examination of the ways in which lesbians (and gay men) have been represented by Hollywood before and after the Second World War, see Russo (1981) and Weiss (1992).
4 For Bright celebration stems partly from the fact that 'the cinematic traits these stars shared in their films from the 1940s to the mid-1960s included supple, athletic bodies in tailored suits, strong facial features, dominant rather than subordinate body language, displays of superior intelligence and wit, and (by definition) roles that challenged conventional feminine stereotypes' (Bright, 1991: 152).
5 To be fair to Graham, whose work I admire, she does subsequently conflate identification with desire in the 'homosexualized' (Graham, 1994: 211) body of the masculinised action heroine. Even here, however, desire and identification are still figured around the butch in a way which consolidates this position, or so I would argue, at the expense of what I term femm*e*inine desire.
6 Adrienne Rich (1980) of course theorised a continuum between platonic female bonding and lesbian desire. This position has since been, rightly, much criticised by lesbians intent on forging a specificity for lesbian desire.
7 In which de Lauretis extrapolates on the metaphor of the wounded butch.
8 For accounts of which see Wilson (1983) and Nestle (1987).
9 Of course the butch is often a Hollywood butch (i.e. virtually a femme anywhere else) and thus, outside of the bounds of the strictly visual terms of the cinematic, barely worth the title.
10 The distinction is all the more apparent given the almost total absence of lesbians of colour from the mainstream, and, with notable exceptions, independent screen.
11 A question she puts to the audience in her work, *Faith and Dancing* (joint commission It's Queer Up North and Gay Sweatshop).
12 See de Lauretis (1994: 122). De Lauretis lambasts what she sees as a certain vogue in lesbian imaging which celebrates the moment of coming out at the expense of a more mature and individuated lesbian desire. This is a vogue which encompasses straight male representations such as John Sayle's *Lianna* and feminist and lesbian-produced material such as Donna Deitch's *Desert Hearts* or *I've Heard the Mermaids Singing* (Patricia Rozema, 1987, Can) and *When Night is Falling* (Patricia Rozema, 1995, Can). While I agree with de Lauretis to an extent, I do think that these films negotiate a more complex terrain of identification and desire than she allows. I believe in fact that such films play on a nostalgia for a time when lesbian desire seemed innocent and new, a perfectly valid fantasy to sustain within a cinematic context, and reason, I would surmise, for the popularity of such films with lesbian audiences.
13 See de Lauretis (1990) and (1994: 114).
14 That this desire might predicate itself upon, or elide, the class differ-

ences between the two seems further testimony to the way in which cinematic fantasy erodes unpleasurable conflict between the subject and her desires.

15 A condition which, quite rightly, de Lauretis (1994) argues we should aspire to in our cinematic identifications and desires. Though I also believe that the countenancing of a self-conscious pre-oedipal regression is also a pleasurable part of the fantasy remit afforded by cinema.

16 This last point is of course comprised of a certain amount of rhetorical disingenuousness. Many film critics, among them de Lauretis (1994), Graham (1994), Jennings (1995) and Tasker (1993), do theorise the possibility (in different ways) of both a narcissistic and anaclitic facet to lesbian desire. My point is merely that the first two at least appear to do so from the definitional position of the butch (whether characterising her as wounded or as phallic).

17 Butler situates this reading of incorporation as psychic mimesis alongside an argument for a primary mimetism where 'Mimetism is not motivated by a drama of loss and wishful recovery, but appears to precede and constitute desire (and motivation) itself; in this sense, mimetism would be prior to the possibility of loss and the disappointments of love' (Butler, 1991: 26). Butler then concludes that which comes first, loss or mimetism, is impossible to decide. What is important is that the psychic subject is 'constituted internally by differently gendered others and is, therefore, never, as a gender, self-identical' (Butler, 1991: 27).

18 Indeed, I am beginning to feel that it is a mistake to consider lesbian appropriations solely in terms of their avowal of particular images. For an avowal is often accompanied by a disavowal of sorts, and my suspicion is that what we look away from, or in some other way disavow, is, as Butler notes, just as constitutive of the kind of lesbian identity one espouses. What of the effect of, for instance, an internalised homophobia in even the most adult and post-oedipal of lesbian identities? Certainly, whom one does not find attractive, who operates as an object of fear and even loathing, or of repulsion as well as fascination, of disavowal as well as of desire, seems to me to be as crucial a component of a lesbian cinematics. That I only begin to suggest some of the possibilities for what I have termed abject desire, in the next chapter, is perhaps indicative of the difficulty of the manoeuvres that have to be set up in its defence.

19 As Andrew Britton notes: 'Subversiveness needs to be assessed not in terms of a quality which is supposedly proper to a phenomenon, but as a relationship between a phenomenon and its context – that is, dynamically' (Britton, 1978: 12).

20 Nor are experiences of public commonality of reception confined to expressions of lesbian solidarity. On viewing *Showgirls* (Paul Verhoeven, 1996, US) on the first evening of its screening in Britain, we few coupled women spotted through the audience were temporarily united in our muffled giggles and outright guffaws as the (largely single) men sat between us, their solitary pleasures audibly disrupted.

4

'In the good old days when times were bad':

The nostalgia for abjection in lesbian cinema spectatorship

i Preliminaries

With the advent of the cinema stereotypes of the lesbian, which draw so heavily on the visual, were represented in increasing variety. Here we find the lesbian in a range of guises: mannish imposter (*Walk on the Wild Side* [Edward Dmytryk, 1962, US]), fanged vampire (*The Hunger* [Tony Scott, 1980, US]), virginal victim (*Vampire Lovers*, [Roy Ward Baker, 1970, GB]), predatory school teacher (*Vampire Lovers*), man-eating monster (*Basic Instinct*), child-woman (*The Killing of Sister George*), chic femme beauty (*Les Biches* [Claude Chabrol, 1968, Fr/It]), narcissistic double (*Single White Female*), prim professor (*Desert Hearts*), sophisticated seducer (*Morocco* [Josef von Sternberg, 1930, US]), tomboy (*The Fox*), frustrated nun (*Extramuros* [Miguel Picazo, 1985, Sp]), depressed loner (*Rachel, Rachel*, [Paul Newman, 1968, US]), suicidal depressive (*The Children's Hour* [William Wyler, 1961, US]). (Creed, 1995: 86)

These were the stereotypes I grew up with, and whose transgressive power I grew to love. For what Creed's list does not indicate is that, though the vampire of *The Hunger* was indeed fanged, she was also Catherine Deneuve and then Susan Sarandon in a classy tale of designer evil and ironic bequest.[1] And though *Basic Instinct's* Catherine Trammel is a man-eating monster, she is also, to many of the lesbian spectators who watched her wreak havoc in the world of Nick Curran, wealthy, independent and damned sexy. Heterosexual male fantasy nightmare she may be, but her character is also fraught with lesbian erotic possibilities should the lesbian-identified (or otherwise-) identified-spectator choose to plumb them.

It's not just audience, however time also changes the context of reception. These days the mannish imposter of *Walk on the*

Wild Side might be overtly celebrated as the glamorous butch, Barbara Stanwyck's star persona only adding lustre to her representation of the evil Jo. Certainly, as I will describe towards the end of the chapter, the configuration of the lesbian as mannish imposter operates as cipher, a suitable excuse for the otherwise unlicensed looking of her audience.

To be sure, within the dominant narrative of compulsory heterosexual recuperation each of these images represents a transgression within obvious constraints and is always (or almost always) recuperated by the end of the film (though it is not insignificant that much of the narrative energy of the diegesis is spent in forging the lesbian's recuperation). Hence Martha Dobie has to die at the end of *The Children's Hour*, for it is indeed what the classic Hollywood (which is also the compulsory heterosexual) resolution demands. Nevertheless, as with the death of Ruth in the contemporary *Fried Green Tomatoes at the Whistle Stop Café*, it will be argued that a good cinematic death merely puts into focus the love that dared not speak its name in life, but which in death sings its sorrows to the heavens.

In this chapter I will argue that there are elements in these infamous texts which may yet be isolated and appropriated for the extra-filmic pleasures they afford a knowing and invested audience. The cinematic lesbians of old, and the contemporary representations that hark back to them, may have been evil, but they were evilly seductive. They may have been doomed to die but while they lived they were everything I, at least, desired.

This chapter makes no facile claim that such readings are *ipso facto* subversive, however, and my arguments will accordingly be situated within a more general discussion (developed from chapter one) as to the radical or recuperative implications of appropriative readings. What it does argue is that the bad old images of old, and the contemporary films that hark back to them, operate through what I have elected to call a nostalgia for abjection. The various meanings implied in this phrase will be illustrated throughout the chapter. However, a preliminary attempt at definition seems necessary. My *OED* definition of abjection reads as follows: 'Abject, ... brought low, miserable; craven, degraded, despicable'. As you can see, the association between such terms and a celebratory reading of lesbian desire is not obvious. The terms are in fact more familiar as pejorative descriptions of lesbian life. What am I doing then in reappropriating terms of obloquy to an account of lesbian cinematic desire? In one sense this is simply an attempt to turn the dominant back on itself, to steal the terms that have formerly oppressed us, utilising the abject in the best of Kristevan (1982) senses as a productive and ambiguous category for the cultivation of a productive and ambiguous lesbian desire. On the other hand it is simply the attempt to theorise (and justify and defend) a practice in which I have long indulged but which seems to contravene at least the public face of lesbian cinematic debate (which has tended to focus on the need for positive images). On the simplest level then, this chapter is an attempt to look back on a few of the cinematic images that are argued to have oppressed lesbians for so long and re-read them in the light of the pleasure that they continue to afford me.

Why term this practice nostalgic, however? As Vito Russo observes: 'In Queen Christina, Garbo tells Gilbert that, "it is possible to feel nostalgia for a place one has never seen." Similarly, the film *Queen Christina* [Rouben Mamoulian, 1933, US] created in gay people a nostalgia for something they had never seen on screen' (Russo, 1981: 65). This notion of nostalgia works most evidently, and in the terms of the Dolly Parton song that titles this chapter, as a rewriting of the past. The terrible past, when viewed through the rose-tinted perspective of recollection in repose, offers up a different story (for the terrible past always resonates more strongly than the anodyne happy ending). Once removed from the immediacy of its terrors, its demands become strivings, its resolutions a triumph of will over adversity. It is in this sense, amongst others, that the tribulations of filmic lesbians enter the filmic heritage, serving as a legacy of triumph in defeat. Tragedy, punishment, death frame the narrative, iconicise it even,[2] in a way that the longed-for happy ending cannot. Indeed, it is in the desire for a happy resolution, always foreclosed, that nostalgia establishes its real impact. It is in this sense that nostalgia, the desire for what has never been and never will be, operates as the Lacanian dream of abundance, for ever potential, and inevitably unrealised, which endlessly proliferates desire.

And it is in this sense that a nostalgia for what has never been seen is a motivating factor for a contemporary lesbian desire which seeks its representation in the spectre of abjection. In the second half of this chapter I will isolate the elements which I believe are instrumental to the cultivation of a lesbian nostalgia for abjection, dealing in section iv with the lesbian vampire, a figure which straddles the poles of both abjection and transgression. In section v I consider the contemporary vogue in lesbian 'psycho' killers,[3] reviewing the homophobic link between lesbianism and criminality and reassessing its implications in the light of the genre's popularity with its lesbian fans. Finally, in section vi I argue that at least some lesbian filmic desire is informed by a persistent desire for the heterosexual scene, a desire which functions as both abject and transformative within a lesbian appropriative context.

In her introduction to her foundational work, *Vampires and Violets*, Andrea Weiss defines the relation between lesbians and the cinema in terms of a 'love–hate affair which involves anticipation, seduction, pleasure, disappointment, rage, and betrayal' (Weiss, 1992: 4). For Weiss, the pleasure is always, or almost always, countered by the betrayal. Indeed, she goes on to argue that it is not until the advent of feminism that the cinema begins to address the spectatorial needs and desires of lesbians (through lesbian independent film-making). For me, on the other hand, born in the late 1960s, looking lesbian from the late 1970s, brought up on a diet of miserable, self-hating, perverse or merely covert 'lesbian' images, the pleasure is and always was grounded in the expectation of disappointment, the love born under the cloud of hate, the seduction in the potential for betrayal.

What I will argue in this chapter is that cinematic images of pathological lesbians work for a contemporary lesbian audience through a sheen of nostalgia, which renders them generative rather than inhibitive. The extent to which this nostalgia is a product of our own age remains unclear. On the one hand I understand it as specific to a lesbian erotics which plays on a nostalgia for what I would term the well-of-loneliness effect, a nostalgia that operates as an antithesis to what often seems like the Laura-Ashleyisation of contemporary lesbian culture.[4] That such a desire is specious in terms of the homophobia and violence that continue to shadow the expressions of our right to live as lesbians is to me only further evidence of its effect: nostalgia is always blinkered. At the same time, I am struck by a remark of Andrea Weiss's, where, even in praising the lesbian feminist interventions of the 1970s, she acknowledges somewhat ruefully that 'I have yet to see a contemporary film with a lesbian theme which has the erotic power of Marlene Dietrich's performance in *Morocco*' (Weiss, 1992: 162). Weiss's point is perhaps testimony to what I describe in section v as 'the erotics of the lesbian taboo',[5] an erotics of abjection which depends upon the veiled sign, the covert and inhibited desire, to convey its interests.

My feeling is that even as images of pathological lesbians are read in the context of their immediate production and reception as negative, with the effecting of a degree of distance their status alters in the memory of the viewer. Certainly, trawling the ideas expressed in this chapter around seminars and lecture halls this past year, I have been struck by the correspondence my own desires have found with the thoughts of women who lived through those times. Indeed, the more violent debates have accumulated around the new images of abjection rather than the old. It is on these that I will largely focus then. For it is the contemporary and near-contemporary images of lesbian abjection, too new to be easily reviewed through the sheen of nostalgia, that I believe require the more immediate investigation.

First, however, some necessary paradigms. In chapter three I argued that the cinema offers up a space of identificatory abundance which depends on the active, investigative desire of the individual lesbian viewer to mark its products as lesbian, but which is therefore not limited or determined by the heterosexist paradigms of its production. At the same time I noted that the actual representation of lesbians on the screen is still characterised by a certain lack, a lack of images and in particular a lack of what are deemed to be positive images. Most recently this representational absence has been attacked by lesbian- and gay-identified pressure groups such as Queer Nation, the Gay and Lesbian Alliance Against Defamation (GLAAD) and OutRage!. They respond to the mainstream, big budget success of films like *The Silence of the Lambs* (Jonathan Demme, 1992, US) and *Basic Instinct*, both of which portray queer serial killers,[6] or rather killers who, because of the way in which the narrative diegesis is set up, will be perceived as lesbian or gay by the majority of the audience.

Within debates around positive imaging, films are often gauged on two counts. Firstly they are gauged on their visibility, whether they present images of lesbians that are apparent to everyone in the audience. The question of degree will be taken up in the next section. Secondly they are gauged on their positivity, their ability to reflect (as opposed to distort) the (posited and positive) reality of lesbian life.

Of course the first question that strikes is, positive for whom, whose lesbian life represents the reality? These days this injunction is generally succeeded by the demand that cinematic images represent the variety of lesbian life, that the complexity of lesbian existence can be reflected to the same degree as the complexity of heterosexuality is reflected on screen. The question as to whether heterosexuality and particularly female heterosexuality is adequately reflected on screen remains a trenchant one. It seems, however, fair to argue that on such grounds lesbian images would thus at least compete with others in an open market. The likelihood of this event materialising within mainstream Hollywood cinema is another issue, of course. More significant a problem, however, is the fact that images, even within a subcultural context, always compete within relations of domination where some will be considered positive over others for what are often covertly political reasons. Positive for whom is not merely a question of personal taste but a political question raised within a context where some people's sexuality is still more acceptable than others.

This becomes clear when we review the texts that are most visible in the positive images debates. On the positive front, *The Killing of Sister George*, *Personal Best*, *Lianna*, *Desert Hearts* and *I Heard the Mermaids Singing* are the names that have featured most strongly over the past two decades of feminist debate. To this list we might add the contemporary cross-over sensation *Go Fish* (Rose Troche, 1994, US) and the new Patricia Rozema feature *When Night is Falling*. On the negative we have *The Killing of Sister George*, *Basic Instinct*, the latest splurge of lesbian psycho-killer movies, and just about everything else made before 1967. The fact that *The Killing of Sister George* features in both my lists is indicative of the contentiousness of the positive images debate. None of these films is in fact posited as being unambivalently positive in its representation of lesbian lives. *Sister George* is as hated by as many lesbians as love it; *Lianna*, *Desert Hearts* and *I've Heard the Mermaids Singing*, though they often meet with popular approval, have been subject to virulent critique on the theoretical front.[7] Such films, however, contradictory and ambivalent about their subject as they often are, yet represent for someone their iconic experience of lesbianism.

Now icons, as we know, are of necessity personal, albeit sometimes subject to public validation. Often central to their effect is a validation of the coming-out experience – sometimes indeed such films are felt to have been instrumental to coming out. This is perhaps one of the reasons for the intensity of the debate over an individual film's worth. What seems clear is that, as a result of the personal investment placed in particular films by individual viewers, no one film is ever reducible to the evaluation, positive or negative.

Yet it is exactly these two categories that are invoked when talking to lesbians about film. This seems inevitable in the sense that these are all films whose status as lesbian representations remains under debate. However, what we find in discussions such as 1992's *Out* vox pop *We've Been Framed*[8] is that a covert bias is implicated in the terms of analysis whereby certain images will be lauded at the expense of the others. What concerns me in the light of recent debates about sexual representation is this tendency to the reification of certain images over others. It comes as no surprise for instance to learn that in 1992 it was the romantic, bourgeois, orientated *Desert Hearts* that struck a chord in the majority of the hearts of its lesbian viewers since its aspirations, romantic, middle-class, marital, monogamous, were those values most clearly promoted in the contemporary lesbian community.

What most concerns me about the reification of certain lesbian images over others, however, is its unwitting tendency to fix certain images as definitively lesbian. What's wrong with that, you may ask? Well, imagine if a similar claim could be made for the 'definitively' heterosexual film. The appropriative strategies of the lesbian cinematic pleasures described in this book would fly out of the window. What is more, the fixing of texts as definitively lesbian implies a fixing of a hegemonic viewer, and a corresponding fixing of identification and desire. While I recognise the appeal of collective iconisation to a community intent on promoting political solidarity against homophobia, I sense a grave difficulty around the promotion of even an implicit consensus as to what lesbians want. Must we all like the same films and at the same places? If so, there is a marked failure of intention in our current reception theories. For as inter-community debates have proved beyond doubt, we will never, 'as lesbians' agree on just which images are or are not positive.

One of the difficulties with positive imaging, then, is that as a collective political discourse it remains a myth. For what we witness time and again is an inevitable resistance to attempts to delimit lesbian cinematic identification and desire. This is in part the reason why we love to hate certain representations and defend others to the death. Moreover, what the negative call of a pressure group like GLAAD, that 'You don't see yourself up on the screen',[9] fails to theorise in practice is the subjective nature under which much recognition is obtained. For one thing it refuses to allow for the plethora of queer (contradictory, perverse, trans-gendered, heterosexual) identifications made by viewers who look to see their desires reflected in a multiplicity of situations, however incongruous or at odds with an established political and social identity.

What it also fails to recognise is the pleasure we obtain from so-called negative images of ourselves, what are to some the baddies. This becomes a twofold question as it first asks, just who are the baddies? As Cherry Smyth asks: 'is a positive image a good little monogamous lesbian who isn't into S&M, or is it a bulldagger in a dog collar?' (McClellan, 1992: 91). The answer of course is that it depends who's watching. I would supplement Smyth's point with the question, just what kind of narrative pleasure do we miss out on if we attempt to exclude the baddies from the cinematic diegesis? Do we not recoup some pleasure from the fact that they are the ones we *love* to *hate*? Take the example of the headmistress in Leontine Sagan's film *Maidens in Uniform*, a draconian witch, in many readings a trope for the then contemporary rise of fascism. Without her, much of the film's narrative tension would be lost, the eventual triumph of feisty schoolgirl Manuela and her teacher the fabulous Fräulein Von Bernbourg rendered less moving. In addition, and despite the negativity of her representation and role, as she stands as a stylistic opposite to the two feminine (though in von Bernbourg's case, austerely so) heroines, the headmistress is arguably recuperable to her own lesbian erotic.[10] Like the recent *Swoon* (Tom Kalin, 1992, US) a film which in its portrayal of gay killers plays on the line between identification and resistance,[11] such readings render increasingly unsustainable a simplistic distinction between good and bad.

ii Domination and resistance: the paradoxes and possibilities of a contestatory viewership

'We're so starved, we go see anything because something is better than nothing. It's a compromise. It's a given degree of alienation'. This sense of queer readings of mass culture as involving a measure of 'compromise' and 'alienation' contributes to the complexity of queer articulations of mass culture reception. For the pathos of feeling like a mass culture hanger-on is often related to the processes by which queers ... internalize straight culture's homophobic and heterocentrist attitudes and later reproduce them in their own queer responses to film and other mass culture forms. (Doty, 1993: 8)

To appropriate Hollywood images to ourselves, taking them out of context of the total structure in which they appear, will not get us very far. (Kaplan, 1984: 314)

Some critics have even gone so far as to suggest that queer consumers (and producers) of culture are so accustomed to self-consciously inhabiting contradictory viewing/reading positions as to make us preeminently skilled deconstructivists. (Wilton, 1995: 144)

At this point in his characterisation of queer reception, Doty seems to be arguing, somewhat pessimistically, that, as lesbian and gay readers of contemporary culture, we merely internalise and regurgitate its homophobic foundations. On the other hand, in his book *Making Things Perfectly Queer* Doty describes the transformations he effects as 'queer' and therefore as presumably undergoing some process of translation in their iteration.[12] The contradiction at work perhaps characterises, as Doty notes, the complexity of domination and resistance debates in general; in particular, that, after Foucault, the one can always seem simultaneously to be ushering in the other. In a relation born of domination, resistance is always then a matter of context.[13] While I accept this argument implicitly in my account of the transformations, readings and rereadings of the cinema I will describe in this chapter, I do not want to reduce the ensuing debate to the speciousness of Eve Sedgwick's: 'kinda subversive, kinda hegemonic' (Sedgwick, 1993: 15). At the same time I believe, with Sedgwick, that we need to be aware of the dangers of 'glamorizing the closet', of 'presenting as inevitable or somehow valuable its exactions, its deformations, its disempowerment and sheer pain' (Sedgwick, 1991: 68).

I am sure that in this chapter I step closer to this possibility than perhaps even Sedgwick herself. For one of the arguments of this book is that the closet does indeed impart a glamour not found in the more visible gestures of the contemporary lesbian culture. My fear is that in arguing that pain and death and tragedy can be seductive tropes in the articulation of lesbian desire, I perhaps emblematise my own relative privilege (the pain, death and tragedy that impacts upon my own life is limited, relatively speaking), though, and, as I will argue subsequently, I do suspect that the groundroots of pain which affect anyone who 'comes out' as lesbian or gay are a powerful incentive to abjection. Most clearly operative in such a trope, however, is the notion of fantasy. It is in the fantasy of pain and anguish, because reflected upon in repose, that the seductions of abjection lie, not in its all-too-present reality. These thoughts, then, are less about lived realities than the translation of imperfect reality into fantasised desire. And since when has fantasy been the provenance only of the privileged?

Judith Mayne (1993) states the problem of a politics of ambivalence quite clearly in calling for attention to be paid to the way in which we theorise film texts either as totally dominant or, when read against the grain, as radically contestatory, or liberatory:

One of the largest problems confronting spectatorship studies is the simultaneous affirmation of diversity and the recognition that 'diversity' can easily function as a ploy, a way of perpetuating the illusions of mainstream cinema rather than challenging them. Put another way, there is no simple division between the cinema which functions as an instrument of dominant ideology, and the cinema which facilitates challenges to it. (Mayne, 1993: 78)

Thus there are contradictions and ambivalences, blind spots in all texts which facilitate multiple and contestatory readings. One can read against the grain without upsetting its hegemonic reception. Indeed, as Yvonne Tasker notes, many texts work deliberately to promote the potential for multiple ideological readings: after all, even *Rambo* (*First Blood Part II*, George Pan Cosmatos, 1985, US) relies upon a certain ambivalence of reception.[14] To argue that certain films can be read as transgressive does not preclude their still being read in line with dominant assumptions. As an example, I have argued elsewhere for a reading of *Fried Green Tomatoes at the Whistle Stop Café* as lesbian (Whatling, 1994). My argument grounded itself in the fact that a lesbian-identified viewer or audience is able to piece together the lesbian subtext that informs the film and thus make of it a lesbian narrative. However, the text offers very little encouragement to heterosexually identified audiences to do the same. They can leave the cinema with their heterosexual assumptions unchallenged. An example of mainstream cinema where everybody goes away happy, *Fried Green Tomatoes* perpetuates rather than challenges dominant relations of seeing, despite its lesbian potential.[15]

For Lynne Pearce this is a result of the way in which texts interpellate different audiences at different times, depending upon the ever-shifting balance of power between the two. Audiences search for a 'sign of their own preferment' (Pearce, 1995: 168). This desire is then sometimes appeased, sometimes disappointed (I would argue that it is in the negotiation of the two that desire proliferates), a condition which Pearce describes as 'exciting but nervewracking' (Pearce, 1995: 168). In this sense, the lesbian negotiation of *Fried Green Tomatoes* is both an act of faith and an act of semantic aggression. As a result, in arguing for a lesbian appropriation of the film I would want to maintain as a matter of course the structuring relation of heterosexuality within the text. At the same time I do not believe that the structuring of a text within dominant reading relations is necessarily an impediment to lesbian viewing pleasure or a lesbian appropriative politics. For the very fact that a film like *Fried Green Tomatoes* works upon the level of suggestion offers a certain amount of licence to the lesbian-identified viewer. A text like *Fried Green Tomatoes* requires an effort of translation. The response of the desiring and, importantly, informed (in the sense that she recognises the allusions and picks up on the textual hints) viewer is to forge the links in a text which will transform covert lesbian components into a coherent lesbian narrative. As such, the film serves as a seductive text to the knowing observer, the force of whose lesbian desire is to resexualise its meaning, disabusing it of the myth of platonic same-sex. Hence one of the chief delights of this film is that it allows for, even depends upon, the free scope of the viewer's imagination, teasing her to make the connections and fill in the silences. And let us not underestimate the spectatorial pleasure that results from the piecing together of the lingering looks, the long smiles and the moments of finger-tips barely touching that form the covert lesbian subtext of such films.

As a strategy, this seems particularly important in the case of *Fried Green Tomatoes* as this process relesbianises its co-screenwriter and author of the book on which the film was based, Fanny Flagg, a writer whose lesbianism is diluted by Hollywood but who allows just enough to get through to encourage a lesbian reading.[16] In addition, it is precisely because such films work on the level of the covert, depending upon the individual viewer's subcultural knowledge to piece together the lesbian coding within the text (for example the butch–femme coding of Idgie and Ruth's relationship),[17] that these films vindicate the lesbian viewer of any responsibility for the veracity (or otherwise) of the representation. As distinct from the overt 'lesbian' text whose burden of representation we carry with us (Does it represent us fairly, if not will all lesbians be equated with its assumptions? Am I embarrassed by the images unveiled? Am I at least so anxious at the thought of being misrepresented that I cannot even enjoy the images when attractive to me? All questions which apply to lesbian-produced or lesbian-featured images), the covert representation of lesbianism as, for instance, platonic friendship, at least allows us to make of it what we want. Since we owe the dominant cinema nothing, in one sense its images are up for grabs, there for us to make of them what we will. What the covert text also offers us of course is the thrill of the forbidden, the nostalgic sense of lesbianism as taboo, its images, rendered covertly, for our eyes only.

As Judith Mayne insists: 'The most promising and influential work on spectatorship assumes the necessity for understanding cinema as ideologically influenced, but not necessarily monolithically so' (Mayne, 1993: 78). She continues: 'The challenge, then, is to understand the complicated ways in which meanings are both assigned and created' (Mayne, 1993: 81). Thus, as readers of popular culture, we have to be as aware of declaring texts monolithically oppressive as we do of declaring their various misreadings as intrinsically radical, the first because it reduces readers to the level of dupes, the second because it confers a potency upon the social effects of the reading experience which, at the very least, seems misplaced. In the same way, we have to be aware of arguing that just because an individual or group of spectators have a non-traditional relation to heterosexuality (for example as lesbians) their textual appropriations are inevitably radical. As Mayne warns, 'the sheer fact that a spectator or group of spectators makes unauthorized uses of the cinema is no guarantee that such uses are contestatory' (Mayne, 1993: 80). Spectatorship is habitually both complicit and contestatory.

How then to argue for a strategy of appropriation while recognising the structure of domination that informs the appropriative context? For me, in arguing that the relation of domination proliferates the potential for appropriation, the problem is rendered both less and more crucial. For whilst I shall not argue that such appropriations are intrinsically radical, I do argue that they are an inevitable component of cultural domination, if only for the fact that they are born out of a relation of abjection which continues to inform their reinscription as pleasurable.

iii Deadly pleasures

In a recent article about *Desert Hearts*, Jackie Stacey argues that the lesbian popular romance –

If we take popular to mean both 'use of recognizable Hollywood conventions' and 'appreciated by lesbian audiences', lesbian to denote 'some kind of female samesex desire' and romance to mean the 'sexual and emotional union of two characters having successfully overcome certain obstacles which the audience believed they might not' (Stacey, 1995: 112),

– these days faces something of a double bind. On the one hand, lesbianism as depicted in the cinema is condemned to the old and tragic pathological categories of sin, sickness, frustration and death. Stacey names such films as *Another Way* (Karoly Makk, 1982, Hun), *Personal Best, Entre Nous* and *The Children's Hour. Basic Instinct, Single White Female, Heavenly Creatures* (Peter Jackson, 1994, NZ), *Butterfly Kiss* (Michael Winterbottom, 1994, GB) and *Sister my Sister* (Nancy Meckler, 1994, GB) could be added to render a more contemporary list. The other option, which is no more of an option either, is to render the lesbian film – and Stacey sees the lesbian romance of *Desert Hearts* as being particularly prone to this – as simply just another kind of love in a world where in the end love is universal. Thus Stacey argues: 'if the problems are located elsewhere in the narrative [rather than situating the character's lesbianism itself as the central problem] there is a risk of representing lesbian (or gay) relationships as "just like any others" and denying the specificity of forms of power and oppression' (Stacey, 1995: 111). I agree with Stacey's point that, within the context of intolerance, there is a specificity to lesbian love and its homophobic suppression that needs to be articulated in the movies. However, I do not agree with her argument that *Desert Hearts* makes it all too easy. In fact I was not so sure as Stacey seems about the outcome of the movie. I did not know whether Cay would get on the train with Vivian, and I certainly didn't recall any such unambiguous resolution in the novel to set against the film. However, let's agree with Stacey for now in believing that the first openly marketed lesbian romance film is indeed less a question of will they or won't they than of how they will, and when. In this sense it is possible to read the film as an ironic preamble to that other great contemporary romance, *Sleepless in Seattle* (Nora Ephron, 1993, US), a film whose cynicism and knowing use of romantic conventions operate, as it were, despite themselves. A film which luxuriates in the clichés it manifests to such a hackneyed degree (the starriness of the backdrop to the credits remains a particular favourite), like *Desert Hearts*, *Sleepless in Seattle* operates on the premise that its two lovers will obviously get it together at some point, though how, when and where propels the central narrative movement of the film. By the terms of contemporary rendition of the classic romance then, *Desert Hearts* works, and works well. Both it and *Sleepless in Seattle* represent a utopian fantasy in the midst of harsh unromantic reality. In fact, problems with the former accumulate mainly in relation to its lesbian reception, with the fact that the lesbian romance with a happy ending is, as Stacey admits, such an endangered species that any representative of the genre risks dying the death of a thousand expectations. Why must a film like *Desert Hearts* say something about the difficulty of being lesbian and happy in the world? Why need it articulate issues which are not appropriate or relevant to the utopian premises of its romance? The reason of course is the paucity of representations of lesbians and the consequent burden of representation that any lesbian film must carry. Hence, as a film *Desert Hearts* is made to speak for so many – lesbian and heterosexually identified viewers, feminism and the popular, the mainstream and the independent sectors. Can one film possibly sustain the investment of so many groups? Obviously not.

In contradistinction to the lesbian romance, Stacey argues that there is a tendency in what has been termed New Queer Cinema to pursue the negative at the expense of the facile,[18] in other words to equate difficulty with truth: 'There is a fashionable view in this age of queer cinema that the absence of Hollywood-style, happy-ending romances should not be lamented, since we should not be striving to produce acceptable images of homosexuality' (Stacey, 1995: 93). Adapting Stacey's description beyond the new queer cinema and back into the old queer mainstream, I will argue that, as distinct from the positivist lesbian project of *Desert Hearts* and its cohorts, we expect correspondingly little from these films. As a result, they are released from a burden of representation which otherwise demands the visual elevation of the positive over the negative and the affirmative over the abject. What the new queer films demonstrate – and in so doing they hark back to an older queer which is marked by an equal amount of productive and receptive ambivalence – is that a kiss is just a kiss until it's caught on the winds of doom (and then it becomes an icon). Where such films succeed is where the old clichéd combination of sex and death combine in a deadly tribute to the still-transgressive power of lesbian love. Of course, the fatal linking of sex with death is not confined to lesbianism but operates as a romantic trope within the culture as a whole. None the less, I would argue that as lesbians, particularly attuned to a culture of repression, abjection and denial, we are more than accustomed to pleasuring in this. The lesbian spectator, or at least a certain culture of lesbian spectatorship, is only too happy to pick up and dwell on this to its very last agonising gasp. As a result, films that were formerly read only in terms of a culture of oppression can be reappropriated into a delightful agonistic wherein the tragedy of being the lesbian outside representation is recuperated to the dark glamour of the margins.

iv The eroticism of the lesbian taboo

There has always been a strong tendency towards an eroticisation of the abject or the taboo in lesbian literature and culture. Camille Roy, discussing contemporary lesbian culture, writes:

> I want to draw attention to something that is not there. A peculiar feature of the lesbian community is our invisibility; thus I've heard butch women described as 'the image that can't stand the light of day.' This is a mark of our oppression but it also gives us a kind of buffer zone, or breathing space, outside the demographic. (Roy, 1993: 10)

This habit of standing outside the demographic, the embracing – part prescriptive, part voluntaristic – of the margins, offers the marginalised a freeer (not a free, but a freer) space for the pursuit and production of what I am going to call sexual dreamscapes.

The sexual dreamscape that serves as my focus in this chapter is, however, more often depicted as the stuff of nightmares. It includes amongst its tropes, as I noted in the last section, the fatal link of sex and violence, and, as I will detail in section vi, the conjunction of melancholia with an aspiration which predicates itself upon the impossible desire for the heterosexual scene. Nevertheless, I will argue that the combination of these elements with a certain brand of lesbian romance does not, as decades of feminist criticism have argued, spell a crime against lesbian representation but rather opens up an old and familiar genre to reappropriation as a genre of triumph over death and delight in deviance.[19]

Not that this relation, founded in abjection, is not also a relation of alienation. It can and might be argued that positive or appropriative responses to films that kill lesbians on the screen (whether metaphorically or literally) are a feature of our own subjection to the terms of the homophobic culture in which we subsist, that in finding pleasure in such images we are merely trading in our own oppression. For me, this represents, as I argued in chapter one, a view of cultural appropriation which is simplistic and insulting to those who practise it. I am not blind to the limitations of lesbian filmic representation.[20] It seems clear that much of what one might term our cultural ingenuity as lesbians is born out of a sense of a paucity of representations of lesbianism within the popular culture. The culture that is born out of this is, however, anything but poor.

The image that most clearly denotes this fatal combination of perverse sex and death is of course the vampire. The daughter of the night or lesbian vampire, handsome, mysterious and seductive, who finds sanctuary and sexual prey in the darkness of the night-time city, has been a recurring trope within lesbian culture.[21] This positive appropriation of the genre is in contradistinction to the mainstream opprobrium directed at the lesbian as vampire. As Vito Russo describes, 'The essence of homosexuality as a predatory weakness permeates the depiction of gay characters in horror films' (Russo, 1981: 49). Cultural historian Lillian Faderman describes the links between the two, where the lesbian is represented in the nineteenth century as the carrier of sickness and contagion (the notion of homosexuality as contagion is a familiar homophobic trope). By the late nineteenth century, argues Faderman, the lesbian–vampire association represents a recognisable cultural device in the pathologisation of same-sex friendships.[22] Despite a long history of homophobic representation, however, the vampire continues to straddle a number of discourses, both anti-lesbian and lesbian-appropriative. The heady combination of desire and repulsion, fascination and abjection, illustrates the double-bind between cultural oppression and sexual fantasy. As Andrea Weiss observes:

> Merging two kinds of lesbian outlaws, the lesbian vampire is more than simply a negative stereotype. She is a complex and ambiguous figure, at once an image of death and an object of desire, drawing on profound subconscious fears that the living have toward the dead and that men have toward women, while serving as a focus for repressed fantasies. The generic lesbian vampire both expresses and represses sexuality, but the lesbian vampire especially operates in the sexual rather than the supernatural realm. (Weiss, 1992: 84)

I would argue that the lesbian vampire remains a complex and ambiguous figure, not merely for the living and for men but for lesbians too, her lure being both to seduce and to repulse.

Barbara Creed (1995) describes Hedy's imitation of flatmate Allie in *Single White Female* in terms of classic vampirism. Hedy's adoption of Allie's clothes, hair colour and style is an effect of this vampirism. As the publicity for the film put it: 'Allie's new roommate is about to borrow a few things without asking. Her clothes. Her boyfriend. Her life.' What the publicity does not say of course is that Hedy wants to borrow Allie's boyfriend only so that she can punish him for his betrayal of Allie, the woman she loves as her lost sister.

Single White Female is a film which is pernicious in its treatment of the single woman, demonising Hedy as a boyfriendless, solitary masturbator with no dress sense and thus, within cinematic terms, as inevitably lesbian. Though Hedy at first appears to want merely to be Allie, to have access to all that Allie possesses in terms of self-assurance, physical attractiveness, career, apartment and marriage, we come to realise that she also wants to possess Allie, a 'lesbian' desire she can express only through a regressive and both physically and psychologically violent object fixation upon Allie as her lost sister.[23] Nasty, silly and pernicious in the extreme as the film is, I have to say, however, that, its trite and formulaic ending apart, I thoroughly enjoyed the tensions set up and exploited. The irony at work in the transformation of mouse into monster seemed fitting vengeance in the wake of Allie's complacent notion (in which I would figure her assumption that the whole world is heterosexual and in love with her boyfriend) that the good life belongs to her. Her fascination and horror when she spies upon the masturbating Hedy (who is responding, in a further revolution of the perverse dynamics of voyeurism and desire that inform the film, to Allie and Sam's earlier lovemaking) is both painful to watch (not least in terms of the pathological implications the film encourages us to draw: Hedy plays with herself, hence she must be criminal/regressive/lesbian) and knowingly erotic (in the sense that it rehearses the taboo of looking on at what one should not be witnessing). Finally, the transgressive power of Hedy's desires which will stop at nothing, breaking through the heterosexual dyad to get to the woman she desires, easily plays into certain lesbian revenge fantasies.[24] In this sense Hedy is true heir to the female psycho-killer bitch-from-hell genre, which has a long and austere heritage but was resurrected in the 1980s with *Fatal Attraction*, reproduced in *The Hand that Rocks the Cradle* and parodied in the character of Debbie in the delightful *Addams Family Values* (Barry Sonnenfeld, 1993, US).[25] Vindicated of the absurd marketing strategy that argued 'It could happen to you',[26] these films can now be read very much in the way of the slasher genres detailed by Clover (1992), that is, as moments of gender transference and catharsis, in which the audience first cheers the 'monster' along to ever more terrible deeds, then applauds her demise at the conclusion. And of course the film works hard, as befits the genre, to recuperate these tensions by its end, with the demon slain and the world put to rights. However, in line with generic expectations the fun has already been had and, as distinct from the facile recuperation of a film like *Fatal Attraction* (which ends with the reordering of narrative in the family photograph, possibly ironic in the light of the dead woman in the bathroom, but probably not, considering it's an Adrian Lynne film), *Single White Female* concludes with the heroine Allie left, jobless, apartmentless and boyfriendless, recognising at last that the distance and the proximity between herself and Hedy are but a breath apart. The concluding words of the film – 'I try to do what she [Hedy] couldn't, forgive myself. I know what happens to someone who doesn't' – set up a tension which remains unresolved even by the vicious and bloody death of her nemesis, Hedy.

As Weiss observes, it is important to read the tradition of the lesbian vampire not merely as an instance of cultural homophobia (though this is a part of it) but also in terms of the celebration of a thriving appropriative culture, namely as a means of taking up the homophobic cultural mythology that has defined and delimited us, and making it our own. In this sense, I would argue that it is precisely in her ambiguity, her on-the-edgeness, that the lesbian vampire operates as an interesting, and productive, trope.

The way in which *Single White Female* gauges this line seems particularly productive. What is ironic about Allie's opting for Hedy is that she chooses her as someone in her own likeness.[27]

The film is taken from the novel by John Lutz, *SWF Seeks Same*, and, as Lynda Hart points out, the film is 'terrifyingly unconscious about its segregationism' (Hart, 1994: 113), encouraging the assertion of racial exclusivity, just as it does not consider the potential lesbian connotations of single womanhood. Previous frames have dealt with various stereotypical representations of the flatmate, the working-class butch, the hypersensual black woman, the woman in recovery from she doesn't know what (whom Hart designates radical feminist), and finally the woman who looks like a less attractive, less fashionable (but evidently of the same economic, aspirational and of course racial background), version of Allie. In the first three, lesbianism, racial difference and feminism are all abjected, they are not 'the same' that Allie is seeking. Thus she as heroine, and we as audience, assumed to be white, middle-class and thus also 'the same' are encouraged to distance ourselves from their perverse significations. It is just at the point where Allie, momentarily in tears at the sad plight that Sam's infidelity has brought her to, is about to call the latter, that Hedy walks in. Catching Allie at a moment of vulnerability, Hedy wins her over with tea and sympathy. Hedy, unlike the first three applicants, seems normal, *straight*forward, a rather pale and less flamboyant imitation of Allie herself, same background, same expectations, same colour, same apparent orientation. The tension between Allie and Hedy (and the woman whom Allie was about to call who, as Hart argues, stands as the safe other to Heddy's lodger from hell, but, as I would argue, remains equally under suspicion, silent witness but also ever potential accomplice to Hedy's single woman's excessiveness) lies, as Hart notes, in a dynamic of sameness and difference. Hedy appears to be just like Allie but the more she becomes like Allie, the less she is like Allie.

So where does this leave Allie, who has predicated her approval of Hedy on the assumption of likeness? In a bit of a spin actually. For, as we know, that which both repels and fascinates, disgusts and engenders desire, is, as Julia Kristeva notes, always particularly productive of cultural instability, since the abject is that which 'does not respect borders, positions, rules. The in-between, the ambiguous, the composite' (Kristeva, 1982: 4). Allie is drawn to Hedy as a representation of her like in paler form. The more Hedy becomes like her, crosses the boundary between self and other, the more Allie is confronted by the perverse connotations of her own likeness, which in this case can as easily signify perverse lesbian desire as heterosexual. Hedra, the double-headed monster, is herself.

v Psycho-killer dykes and their lesbian fans

From the outset the film aims to disturb. Kalin's monochrome drama refuses to flinch from the grisly visceral mechanics of the brutal murder. Its unapologetic stance dealing with the callous termination of a child, while simultaneously involving the audience with the couple's tumultuous romance, creates a moral dichotomy, that even the staunchest of liberals may find difficult to take. (Bevan, 1992: 13)

Swoon's director Tom Kalin's response to the accusation that he is perpetuating negative images of homosexuality is touchingly disingenuous:

My main issue about it is that straight people have the luxury of making morally ambiguous movies. There's a long history of such films through the late 40s and early 50s. All these movies like *Double Indemnity*, [Billy Wilder, 1944, US] these kinds of erotic obsessions between straight people. But never, ever are these films used as arguments against heterosexuality. You never have anyone saying 'look, see, there's the evidence, heterosexuality is inherently pathological and leads to murder'. (Bevan, 1992: 13)

I call this off-hand remark in the defence of his brilliant *Swoon* disingenuous since it disavows the way in which heterosexuality operates as the dominant relation within the social, operating as a standard of normality even when expressed pathologically. More seriously it ignores the way in which the blame for the fall into a pathological heterosexuality is often attached to the figure of the woman. However, where cinematic pleasure is concerned, I would argue that the blending of erotic obsession with murderous design is a fatally seductive combination. *Swoon* as an essay in cinematic persuasion is well aware of this. The film's intention is not to let us off the hook. As Kalin continues:

We refused to let you leave Leopold and Loeb, so you're with them the whole time, and so that you are forced to identify with them, whether you wanted to or not. You become compliant to a certain degree and you can imagine some kind of identification and projection with them. (Bevan, 1992: 13)

This enforced identification leaves us questioning our own desires: 'It's a very prohibitive kind of thing to talk about this very messy, murky relationship. I think it's to do with imagination and desire and these kind of things that don't fall out along a kind of political agenda' (Bevan, 1992: 13). *Swoon*'s seductive link between sex and death is interesting in the light of Lynda Hart's reading of this dynamic where she figures the combination in terms of a white male supremacist construction of white heterosexual desire: 'sex = death is a fantasy formation of a heterosexual masculine imaginary; when it makes an appearance, the trace of the "lesbian" is often recuperable' (Hart, 1994: 116). As I describe in chapter one, however, while I agree with Hart in arguing that the femme fatale is a primarily white construction, and her translation into lesbian has to be registered on these grounds,[28] still I do not believe that the lesbian trace is ever fully recuperable to this heterosexual imaginary. Sex and death, lesbianism and criminality, reworked through a dynamic of abjection which is grounded in, but which seeks to reappropriate, the heterosexual, can still operate through the prism of a lesbian-focused desire as well as through the homophobic. For unlike Hart, I believe that the trace of the lesbian continues to inform and translate the dominant in a way that secures a mutual dis-ease. What is more, I know from my own passionate readings that this relies upon a romanticisation of the abject which is profoundly productive of my own cinematic fantasies. Hence, and in the words of *Heavenly Creatures'* Juliet Hulme, I would maintain: 'Cheer up, all the best people have bad chests and bone diseases. It's all so frightfully romantic.'

And indeed *Heavenly Creatures* is as complicated an articulation of sex and death as Tom Kalin's *Swoon*, sharing the latter's blend of fascination and repulsion. As with Leopold and Loeb, we are so drawn into the passion and beauty of the relationship between Pauline and Juliet (and the voyeuristic pleasures in observing this beauty on screen; see figure 1) and yet so shocked by the denouement that as an audience we are constantly torn between desire and disavowal. In fact I would argue that *Heavenly Creatures* is so powerful because it is a film where pathology and desire are in perfect equilibrium, the characters so lovely, and so perverse, figuratively angels of death.[29] The film also of course utilises some conventional empathetic devices: the actresses are beautiful, easy on the eye, their love star-crossed. Innocent love spoiled through the intrusion of dirty-minded adults is, in cinematic terms, a love rendered all the more precious because it must fight for life against the odds (in the knowledge that, as the film's articulate narrator Pauline Parker writes in her diary, 'only the best people fight against all obstacles in the pursuit of happiness'). The film also employs some notable clichés of lesbian representation, for instance the blonde femme, the beautiful Kate Winslet, since fêted by the media pundits, and the more articulate and thus blameworthy 'butch' Pauline (played by Melanie Lynskey), less physically appealing to straight audiences and accordingly less publicised.

1   Heavenly creatures: Juliet Hulme (Kate Winslet) and Pauline Parker (Melanie Lynskey) in *Heavenly Creatures*, 1994

In reflecting upon the film I am less interested in the pros and cons of its production, or the motivation for the girls' criminal behaviour, or indeed even whether they can be considered lesbian or not, than in the fascination it affords me, the viewer, in looking on. It is in my lesbian look, caught in the warp between desire and lack, between visual abundance and the frustration of sight, that my fascination with the text lies. The cinema is of course famous for offering us everything (vivid colours, appropriate music and lighting, an intimate look into other people's lives, a larger than life experience) and delivering nothing (since our fascination is predicated upon a desire that can never be realised). What interests me is, to what extent is my lesbian look shaped by this promise of abundance succeeded by disappointment? To what extent does this tension between desire and lack operate as my own perverse pleasure in looking?

One scene in *Heavenly Creatures* strikes me as particularly representative of this tension. It is the scene where Pauline and Juliet sit facing each other in the bath. The camera cuts from one pair of eyes to the other, and then frames the girls at middle distance. It then cuts to the evil Dr Hulme, Juliet's father, who is seen spying on the two. The scene is accompanied by Pauline's eloquent voice-over which defines the crux of the film and the moment at which the girls' love is first visibly played out to the audience on the screen. The voice-over reads as a hymn of defiance, even as it is to be imminently curtailed by the actions of Dr Hulme, the figure whom, ironically, the girls consider to be their closest ally. In all of these senses the scene seems caught in the warp between the realisation of desire and the recognition of its failure:

It is indeed a miracle one must feel, that two such heavenly creatures are real. Hatred burning bright in the brown eyes with enemies fuel; icy scorn glittering in the grey eyes, contemptuous and cruel. And why are men such fools? They will not realise the wisdom that is hidden behind those strange eyes. And these wonderful creatures are you and I.

As with many films, I, the viewer, am given a privileged view – I see Dr Hulme where the characters do not. I see them framed together where they see only each other. At the same time, I am positioned outside their look, not the object of their desiring gaze, always positioned outside the frame. Wanting to look on *and* be party to the look, I am left outside looking on, as much of a voyeur as Dr Hulme, caught looking and yet forever excluded from the intimacy of their exchange. Still I continue to look on regardless, in the belief that, if I just look hard enough, my look will be satisfied in the end. The realisation that in looking on (seeing it all) one is forever excluded is, by some perverse and awful logic, as painful to watch as the agonising death of Pauline's mother which we ought to turn away from but continue to watch anyway.

I do not argue that this is a tension specific to lesbian desire. In many ways it is reflective of looking relations within the cinema in general. I do wonder to what extent my lesbian look works most productively through the contemplation of a desire which is always foreclosed, a desire which, in its perverse pleasure in looking on, seems in contradiction to the desire for positive images espoused elsewhere.

The film *Butterfly Kiss*, released the same year as *Heavenly Creatures*, exploits the tension between desire and repulsion to an even greater degree. Fascination and repulsion certainly vie in contemplation of the wounded body of the strange martyr Eunice. A film which traces the relationship between the dysfunctional Eunice, roaming the motorways in futile pursuit of a lost and possibly imaginary love, and the strangely canny Miriam (Saskia Reeves), it is a love story which remains hermetically sealed within a world of 'monochrome motorways ... locales emptied of society, blank urban spaces filled with fantasies, sex and violence' (Campbell, 1995: 35, see figure 2). Staging scenes of unsettling sadism, the film describes a desire that proliferates on the tension between 'love and risk' (Campbell, 1995: 35). In so doing, it tests

2 Killers on the rampage: Eunice (Amanda Plummer) and Miriam (Saskia Reeves) in *Butterfly Kiss*, 1994

the viewer's tolerance and sympathies as Eunice lunges from one violent encounter to the next. It is in its ending that the film moves, however, where Miriam, at Eunice's behest, kills her beloved, ensuring that the bond between them edges, in Bea Campbell's words, 'inexorably towards an intimate apocalypse' (Campbell, 1995: 35). It's a romantic and of course silly fantasy but seductive none the less.

Vito Russo situates the demonisation of the pathological homosexual, into which I would insert the contemporary vogue in lesbian psycho-killers, alongside the growth in gay and lesbian rights in the 1970s.[30] Increased visibility implied increased threat, which had to be countered by increasingly vicious representation. Susan Faludi appropriates this argument in critiquing the resurgence of pathological women films in the 1980s, a response, she argues, to the increasing visibility of the professional woman.[31] As I have noted, recent debates came to a head in 1992 with GLAAD and Queer Nation's boycott of *Basic Instinct* in the United States. For these groups, *Basic Instinct*: 'encapsulates the way that Hollywood has always depicted lesbians as either man-hating or wanting to be men. All the characters who are lesbian or bisexual are homicidal' (McClellan, 1992: 89). It is impossible to say for sure whether the recent, indeed ongoing, vogue in lesbian killers does link in with male heterosexual anxieties. What does seem clear is that the reception of such films cannot be determined at the outset. Hence, the reception of *Basic Instinct* in Britain, contrary to its demonisation by US activists, has tended to reflect the complexity of much contemporary thinking on lesbian representation and its reproduction by lesbian audiences. Here, for example, is Cherry Smyth, talking about one seat of contention, the famous crotch shot:

> I found that scene really hot. She's saying, 'I'm going to get you with my pussy.' That's great. It made me laugh – Sharon Stone was so sexy and powerful. I didn't find it threatening. But a man beside me didn't laugh at all – perhaps he was straight. (Or perhaps he was a politically correct male trying to figure out what exactly his reaction should be). (McClellan, 1992: 91)[32]

Smyth's remarks invert the habitual understanding of cinematic reception as a process over which men dominate. Here the man is threatened while the lesbian laughs, a fitting and satisfying reversal of a hitherto predictable relation.

Finally, to a movie which is about none of these things, but which plays on the tension between them all, *Fried Green Tomatoes at the Whistle Stop Café*, a quiet, heart-warming, platonic movie about the power of friendship and the triumph of good over bad. It is also a film about death and a film suffused with an eroticism as sticky as the honey that Idgie feeds Ruth in the field over lunch. For *Fried Green Tomatoes* begins with a death and ends with a death (it also plays on the reader's emotions with the fake death of Ruth and Idgie's son, Buddy). The movie begins, for most of the audience I attended the film with anyway, in tears. Tears for the death of the beautiful and foolish Buddy, tears for the quiet loss suffered by Ruth, and anguish for the tears of the broken-hearted Idgie. Love replaces tears, with the slowly burgeoning romance of Ruth and Idgie sealing the loss of Buddy in a mutual pact of love and remembrance.

The filmic diegesis also revolves around a death, that of Frank Bennet, supposedly murdered by Idgie in defence of Ruth and her child. The lesbian (albeit represented in covert Hollywood form) usurps the responsibilities and rights of husband, judiciary and state, wilfully deceiving the Georgia detective Curtis Snopes, and feeding him the dead body of the man he seeks for many years after. Or so it would seem. In fact as we learn, Idgie is guilty of Frank's death only as an accessory after the fact. Still, it's an awful lot of death for a movie that's been billed as pastoral romance.

And of course there is one more death which rocks and stuns the cinema audience and leaves us asking why, that is the death of Ruth. Life is good for the women. Buddy is safe, Idgie and Big

George are acquitted of murder, the café is prospering. Unexpectedly, Ruth takes ill and dies: 'There are angels masquerading as people walking around this planet and your mom's the greatest one of these' says Idgie to Ruth's son Buddy, but we, the lesbians in the audience, know there is another moral. For with death comes immortality. With love comes loss. With loss comes memory. In looking we experience, vicariously, the nostalgia for a love rendered all the more precious through loss. Hence Idgie's words to Ruth, 'I'll always love you, the bee charmer', become iconic of a text that articulates its greatest display of lesbian love in death.[33] As Bea Campbell notes of *Butterfly Kiss*'s Miriam: 'she bears witness and she mourns' (Campbell, 1995: 35). This same epitaph could read for Ruth. For as the words of card and gravestone combine 'Ruth, Forever' they make clear the strange abjections that render complete our affections. In the words of Francis Coppola (not the most apt choice I admit, but), 'love never dies'![34]

vi Appropriating the glamour of the mainstream: the fatal desire for the heterosexual scene

The fact that the love that never dies is by and large white and middle-class is rarely commented on but remains, as I have argued in support of Lynda Hart, a feature of the racist configurations that inform the dominant cinema at the level of both production and reception. What has also gone unremarked is the way in which lesbian cinematic appropriations often manifest what I will describe as the fatal desire for the heterosexual scene.

The history of lesbian cinematic representation has long been criticised for its heterosexist agenda. In what sense might this scene be reappropriated in order to render clear its operation as an abject, but fascinating and compulsive, point of return for the lesbian-identified viewer?

Many of the films discussed in this chapter are films which, though they represent same-sex desire to one degree or another, also disappoint the viewer in recuperating this to some kind of heterosexual resolution. The films I have discussed, and the ones I am about to consider, are all films which engender frustrations, as well as pleasures for the lesbian viewer. Of course it is not saying anything new to note that much of the 'lesbian' desire articulated on the screen treads a very fine line between lesboeroticism and lesbophobia, the first often recuperated to the last. Still, I would argue that such scenes are not without their own abject pleasures. Indeed, it is in reading these films, not despite, but because of, their heterosexual recuperation, that we really begin to get to the foundations of the lesbian abject.

In a reading of Freud's 'Mourning and melancholia' (1917), Judith Butler argues that melancholia operates through the incorporation of various desired, but lost, objects by the subject: 'incorporation – a kind of psychic miming – is a response to, and a refusal of loss' (Butler, 1991: 26). Butler then relates this dynamic to the incorporation of various gendered possibilities in which 'Gender as the site of such psychic mimes is thus constituted by the variously gendered Others who have been loved and lost, where the loss is suspended by a melancholic and imaginary incorporation of those Others into the psyche' (Butler, 1991: 27). Central, for the lesbian and gay subject, to this notion of loss and incorporation is the site of the heterosexual (the site of the abjected homosexual is no less central for the configuration of heterosexuality, though it operates with a different emphasis in being structured in terms of the domination of the former by the latter). Hence, for the lesbian, heterosexuality operates as the site of oppression and refusal, but also as the site of psychic coherence, the place where one's sexuality confirms the symbolic order, rather than being positioned in opposition to it. In refusing heterosexuality the lesbian leaves the charmed circle. The lesbian body is thus, I would argue, configured on the site of the pain engendered by the loss of one's position in the symbolic order, a loss which engenders a melancholia which, at the same time, makes visible and real one's lesbian identity.[35] The abject desire for the lost heterosexual is thus, ironically, necessary to the articulation of a lesbian identity. The desire for and incorporation of the lost heterosexual scene to a lesbian agenda is, however, one of the many appropriative pleasures that the mainstream cinema affords the lesbian-identified viewer.

One of the truisms about lesbian representation in the cinema is that, wherever lesbians appear outside of the feminist avant-garde, they do so as a function of male voyeurism. Be it through the mainstream sleaze of Paul Verhoeven's *Basic Instinct* or the left-of-centre agonistics of John Sayle's *Lianna*, lesbians are there for two reasons, one, to provide an interesting slant on an old story,[36] or two, because two women are better than one. *Bitter Moon* (Roman Polanski, 1992, Fr) is a good example of a film which employs lesbianism as interesting plot twist. The film charts the relationships of two couples, the mad, bad and dangerous Oscar and Mimi and the staid and unlaid English couple Nigel and Fiona, who are all thrown together on a European cruise. The film centres on and (through a series of tedious flashbacks) recalls the love affair between Oscar and Mimi who, locked in a bizarre and violent relationship, resolve to play out their last game on Nigel and Fiona. Oscar seduces Nigel with his scatological conversation,[37] while his wife, though appearing to pursue Nigel, is in fact intent on seducing Fiona (something we don't discover until the shock denouement!). Fiona, having kept her distance, finally concedes and plunges into a passionate clinch with Mimi. Following a night of sapphic passion (which we do not see), Oscar kills Mimi while she's sleeping next to Fiona then promptly kills himself, less, we are supposed to believe, out of jealous pique than as the latest and last ruse of their sick and twisted game. The film is typical Polanski territory therefore and contains its fair quota of embarrassing dialogue and hilariously bad heterosexual S/M scenes. It is also typical in its attempted heterosexual recuperation with its sexy ladies, its voyeuring men and melodramatic death, following which Nigel and Fiona find each other again amidst the pain and anguish of newfound knowledge and wisdom. In many senses, then, the film is an execrable production, but the fact that I enjoyed it enormously when I saw it seems justification enough to give it space in my account.

The recuperation of the plot to a compulsory heterosexual dyad ensures that the 'lesbian' is excluded, on the one hand through Mimi's murder and on the other through the reconciliation of Fiona with Nigel. In addition, one could be forgiven for thinking that Mimi and Fiona are merely playing around, enacting the ultimate betrayal as ultimate tease (in Mimi's case) and revenge (in Fiona's) against their philandering husbands. One does not, however, have to see it this way. Indeed, if one takes Yvonne Tasker's theorisation of film as a series of partial sightings seriously, then what one does see comes as something of a pleasant diversion. Indeed, the sight of Fiona and Mimi getting it together on the dancefloor of a boat that may well be sinking but for the moment is all that they are aware of, represents the only instance of, I won't say pure, but certainly unadulterated (by pretentious conversation at the very least) eroticism on the screen so far. It is certainly a moment of ball-breaking conviction for Nigel, who, thinking that he has finally made it with Mimi, has a few frames earlier attempted to seduce her, unaware that his wife is looking on: 'I love you', he none too originally announces. 'No you don't. You love a fantasy, a ship-board adventure', replies Mimi. 'But I love you.' 'That's why you can never have me' (a nice example of Lacanian reversal, there!). Fiona, on the other hand, finally comes into her own: 'I have never seen my husband in action with another woman before' she caustically announces.

'Call that action', retorts the ever acerbic Oscar, 'I don't think he was getting anywhere.' Fiona (watching Mimi on the dance floor): 'That's a shame.' The camera, focusing upon her gaze, watches her smile and switches to a front focus as she moves on to the dancefloor, with Nigel aghast in the background. The focus then moves away from the men and on to the women, whose gaze is now exclusive to each other (though still open to the voyeuristic gaze of the lesbian, or otherwise invested, viewer).

The 'lesbian' subtext of *Bitter Moon* works covertly, informing, shaping even the narrative progression, coming upon the audience unawares. The fact that the scene is equally recuperable to a heterosexual voyeurism does not detract from my arguments. Indeed, as Danae Clark points out in a reading of 'gay window advertising',[38] lesbian audiences are adept at negotiating the tensions between a straight and a subcultural reading:

> because lesbians (as members of a heterosexist culture) have been taught to read the heterosexual possibilities of representations, the 'straight' reading is never entirely erased or displaced. Lesbian readers, in other words, know they are not the primary audience for mainstream advertising. (Clark, 1991: 187)

Indeed, I would even go so far as to argue that the desire to read as lesbian proliferates upon this tension.

For this tension was particularly operative in the 'lesbian' films of my youth. Now I suspect I am not alone in admitting to having had a massive crush on the actress Meryl Streep through much of my adolescence which at the time seemed a natural consequence of my lust for strong, independent, but ever so maternal cinematic women (see figure 3). *Silkwood* was a film which played a powerful role in my nascent lesbian development. Needless to say, when I heard she was playing Karen Silkwood alongside Cher playing her lesbian friend Dolly, I was thrilled. Not because lesbianism was going to be represented through or by the body of Cher but because Karen, or rather Meryl, would be touched by its implications. Though generally situated within a more liberal standard of Hollywood representation of lesbianism (part of the *Lianna* school of liberal tolerance), the film *Silkwood* has been criticised by Andrea Weiss, who notes the infantilisation of Dolly in her relations with Karen and others.[39] Weiss's argument is a pertinent one. Nevertheless, in line with my present concerns, her argument is irrelevant, since for me it is not Dolly (Cher) but Karen (Meryl) who is the lesbian focus of the film. My argument is this: in a film such as *Silkwood*, why should the 'lesbian' character be the focus of lesbian desire and/or identification, why

3 Meryl Streep as Karen Silkwood, object of desire both on and off screen, in *Silkwood*, 1983

should desire be grounded in recognition or representation? Might it not rather find its cathexis, its lesbian look, in the character of the straight woman?

The other characters, male as well as female, in fact act as catalysts in the representation and visualisation of Karen (Meryl). So long as both Drew (Karen's boyfriend) and Dolly love Karen, the more the object of my desire is in focus. The more they are shown loving her, the more of her we see. Both men and women, Dolly and Drew operate as ciphers, licensing the look of the lesbian audience. Of course it is disappointing that Karen does not love Dolly back. And yes, as Weiss argues, Dolly is placed in the traditionally passive role of the 'wishing woman' (Weiss, 1991: 53) but my point is, aren't we all? Is it not exactly in Dolly's abjection in the face of her (our) impossible love, that we all find something to identify with? Likewise, is it not in Drew's loss of Karen through death that we also share? Karen is endlessly pursued in the film and endlessly lost. Just like my desire for Meryl.[40]

Walk on the Wild Side, a much earlier film, articulates the, by now, habitual relation between the grotesque dyke (albeit in this case played by the fabulous Barbara Stanwyck) and the fascinating and beautiful straight woman (played here by the French actress Capucine – rumoured, like Stanwyck herself, to be lesbian). Accordingly it renders the lesbian looking relation I theorise above all the more clear. Hallie Gerard (Capucine) is a sculptor, discovered living in poverty by Jo (Stanwyck) and brought to New Orleans to sculpt while working in Jo's brothel. The film visualises Jo's lesbianism through that classic denotation of sexual repression, sadomasochistic violence. She is good to Hallie but only so long as she bows to her greater will. Finally, Hallie is found by her old lover Dove Linkhorn and the fight is then staged (literally by the end of the film) over Hallie's dead body. Vito Russo understands Jo's villainy to be fundamental to her lesbianism, arguing:

> Stanwyck's Jo was the opposite to MacLaine's Martha, a villain, not a victim. Jo's acceptance of her own lesbianism is part of her villainy. Any decent woman would kill herself ... rather than open a whorehouse and prey on girls. (Russo, 1981: 143–4)

It is this combination of power and its abuse which sets up the dynamic of fascination and repulsion in relation to a character such as Jo. As 'the lesbian' in the film she is both me and not me. I am forced to identify with her as it were, by association, and yet resent the implication forged within the lesbophobic constraints of the film that to be lesbian is to be consumed by bitterness and a love that finds its ultimate expression in hatred. Jo operates for me then as a character both desired (in being played by Stanwyck in full bitchy flow) and disavowed (look what she's turned her into). What I was most fascinated by in watching this film, however, was the way in which the straight woman can act as a foil for the scopic desires of the lesbian viewer. Straight-identified characters in the cinema operate as the abject to the lesbian viewer's subject and are accordingly treated by lesbian audiences with a mixture of suspicion and fascination, of desire and the dis-

4   Looking lesbian: Jo (Barbara Stanwyck) and Hallie (Capucine) in *Walk on the Wild Side*, 1962

avowal of that desire.[41] This, I believe, structures our relation to the visible 'lesbian' in the film rather differently.

Contrary to the mass of lesbian-invested critical thinking on this matter, I believe that it is just as likely to be the 'straight' woman as her 'lesbian' counterpart who is the focus of lesbian interest in such films. What this means is that the 'lesbian' desire which, manifested in violence or abjection, we look upon and repudiate, at least allows us justification for our pleasure in looking on and desiring the (heterosexually identified) object of desire, Hallie. As an audience or individual viewer, we can 'look around' the unprepossessing figure of the evil lesbian (we can also love her for her sheer power and dynamism as I suggest we love all baddies as I argued above), channelling her transgressive ability to look (predicated upon her perverse and violent desire), into one's own voyeuristic pleasure in looking on.[42] She gives us, in other words, the licence to look without (in disavowing our relation to her evil machinations) implicating ourselves in the deviance of her look. We use her in this sense as the heterosexual employs the closet in D. A. Miller's account, where we continue to look on at the figure of the heterosexually identified Hallie, by disavowing any association with what we most desire, the lesbian implications of Jo's (as our) look (see figure 4).[43] Such films testify to am omnipresent, though seldom articulated, lesbian fantasy of appropriation, namely the desire to have and to hold, to steal away the heterosexually identified woman from the site of compulsory heterosexuality.

In their iteration of the attempted lesbian seduction of the non-lesbian such films, even though they rest upon an immediate or eventual diegetic failure or recuperation, nevertheless visualise a powerful lesbian desire. For the viewer, seeing it all and appropriating regardless, it does not ultimately matter whether the lesbian on screen gets the girl or not, what matters is that we, the audience, think we might if we just look long enough. In appropriating these moments, regardless of their diegetic recuperation to heterosexuality, they operate as stolen moments, all the more tantalising for their unlicensed nature. Thus, ironically (and somewhat perversely), the more heterosexual the recuperation, but appropriable the image, the better.

Each of the films I have examined in this chapter disappoints in one way or another. Nevertheless, I would argue that it is precisely in their refusal to 'go all the way' that they are so powerful. In relation to this I am struck by a comment of Judith Butler's, where she argues that it is precisely the instability of the category *lesbian* that makes it so interesting. Thus she observes when discussing the identity politics of performing lesbianism on the academic stage: 'it is precisely the pleasure produced by the instability of those categories which sustains the various erotic practices that make me a candidate for the category to begin with' (Butler, 1991: 14). I would like to take up Butler's point in order to argue that it is precisely the instability of the film texts discussed by me in this chapter, texts which offer up neither a positive image of lesbianism nor a coherent account of heterosexuality (except as a system of anxious and tellingly obvious recuperation), that renders them for me so pleasurable, so interesting, and ultimately so appropriable to individual spectatorial desire. These films do not confirm lesbian desire as such. Nor do they confirm heterosexual desire as such. Though there is generally a recuperation to an ostensible heterosexuality, this is, if not actually undermined, then always compromised by the anxiety revealed therein. And of course, by what remains excessive to the terms of recuperation. As Butler argues:

That heterosexuality is always in the act of elaborating itself is evidence that it is perpetually at risk, that is, that it 'knows' its own possibility of becoming undone: hence its compulsion to repeat which is at once a foreclosure of that which threatens its coherence. That it can never eradicate that risk attests to its profound dependency on the homosexuality that it seeks fully to eradicate and never can or that it seeks to make second, but which is always already there as a prior possibility. (Butler, 1991: 23)

Hence, in these films heterosexuality and homosexuality remain tied to each other in a mutually constitutive and deconstructive relation.

Far from being to the disadvantage of the viewer's enjoyment, however, I would argue that this makes of the cinema a veritable textual and sexual dreamscape, if not a free, then a freer space for the play of lesbian imagination, fantasy and desire. In the case of such texts, less is definitely more, their particular pleasure being discovered in the work the viewer has to do to fill in the gaps, change the emphases.

These are the images which, in the history of my cinematic viewership, have meant something to me. Readers may, if they wish, insert their own examples into the general paradigm. As I have argued, none of these images is *ipso facto* transgressive; the pleasure I continue to find in them is transgressive only in so far as it works against the dominant cultural insistence that lesbianism is a sin without pleasure (rather than pleasurable because sinful!).

Nostalgia is a way of reviewing the past through selective memory, one which remembers the good times and translates the bad times into a different light. Nostalgia is then a function of the present, a reaction to it and in many senses a disavowal of it. In this sense at least, nostalgia is somewhat regressive in its implications. Whilst detailing what I have elected to term a nostalgia for abjection in this chapter, however, I remain convinced that no less nostalgic in its intentions is the lesbian desire for positive images, a desire which, burdened by expectation, will never be realised. In structuring disappointment into its narrative pleasures, at the very least I believe that a nostalgia for abjection works against the inevitable failure of the lesbian utopian project.

This chapter is not a manifesto for viewing. These readings are examples of personal survival strategies rather than a more general philosophy of action. However, in the face of the prejudice that continues to inform mainstream film-making and that will not disappear by fiat, such strategies engender a cinematic pleasure that operates as in one sense a liveable alternative and in another sense as the triumph of the libidinous over the libellous.

Notes

1 That an iconic lesbian status continues to proliferate around Catherine Deneuve despite the actress's famed lesbophobia (for example her recent successful attempt to prohibit the use of her name by US lesbian magazine *Deneuve*) is one of the ironies of cultural appropriation. I would also argue that the popularity with lesbians of actresses such as Susan Sarandon and *Single White Female*'s Jennifer Jason Leigh impacts positively upon their portrayal of 'evil dykes', setting up a tension between desire and disavowal.

2 Concerning my use of the term *icon* in this chapter and the two that succeed it, it should be recalled, in the light of my use of the Lacanian configuration of desire as premised on lack, that in religious orthodoxy an icon is a window on to what is (of necessity) unseen, unknowable and out of reach. This appropriation of the approximation to godliness to the Hollywood star system might seem profoundly inappropriate to some. My thanks, notwithstanding, to Jane Howcroft for this definition.

3 I employ the term *psycho* in its cinematic sense, discouraging any association between the cinematic representation of psychopathology and the everyday experience of this condition.

4 By this I mean the assimilation of lesbian lifestyle into the middle classes, the romantic argument for same-sex marriage (though I believe the economic and political arguments made in support of this stand), the media construction of lesbian chic at the expense of lesbian politics, and the bid for positive images of lesbians in the mainstream.

5 A term I have appropriated from Calhoun (1995: 18).

6 I employ the term *queer* since Trammel is constructed as bisexual and Gumb suffers some kind of sex/gender dysphoria. They are more fittingly described as queer rather than obviously lesbian or gay, though with Gumb's characterisation in particular the stereotypical significations of homosexuality (clothing, jewellery, a poodle named Precious) are notoriously and perniciously deployed.

7 See for example Merck (1986) and de Lauretis (1990).

8 Part of Channel Four's *Out* series, screened in 1992.

9 Jehan Agrama, quoted on *Out*, 1 July 1992.

10 Certainly, one of my friends fancied her!

11 Where 'We are appalled at the callousness of their crime, yet charmed by Leopold's passion for Loeb' (*Weekend Guardian*, 15 August 1992). Unfortunately, I have no record of the author.

12 Doty figures reading queerly through 'mass culture' (Doty, 1993: xii), as well as through subculture. Reading queerly is not, in other words, confined to the marginalised. It is, however, accompanied by a certain amount of disavowal when effected within the mainstream. I use the term, as I noted in the preface, in order to convey a sense of lesbian identity as inclusive of other identificatory and desirous possi-

bilities. I am aware that the term has a contested history in both lesbian and gay circles.
13 See Foucault (1979: 101).
14 Indeed, she describes such films as 'thriving on ambiguity' (Tasker, 1993: 91).
15 It operates in this sense much like John Fiske's 'points of purchase' (Fiske, 1988: 247), where readers isolate and make sense of cultural forms in a way that affords them pleasure, ignoring that which contradicts their aim.
16 In exploiting these connections, lesbian readers are, in Danae Clark's words, 'privy to the inside jokes that create an experience of pleasure and solidarity with other lesbians "in the know"' (Clark, 1991: 188). This was certainly the experience with my cinematic viewings of *Fried Green Tomatoes*, which both times turned into a game of spot the dyke both on and off screen.
17 It might also be noted that when I theorised this film as an example of multiple audience reception in a film theory class, my largely heterosexually identified students, once armed with the meaning of this visual coding, could not help but read the text as lesbian.
18 A term coined by B. Ruby Rich (1992).
19 Naturally, one cannot propose a relation between sex and death without invoking the spectre of AIDS and other life-threatening sexually transmitted diseases. The reduction of this association to the level of sexual metaphor or romantic fantasy is certainly accompanied for me by a profound moral dilemma, reading, at the very least, as a species of colonisation, an inappropriate appropriation. At the same time, I recognise that the proliferation of AIDS discourse as metaphor remains a not unironic feature of the popular, medical and scientific cultures (see for example, Hanson, 1991).
20 I do wonder, in fact, whether there isn't something about a sexual identity born under the shadow of homophobia (a shadow which proliferates a sense of denial, disavowal and shame) that responds to the tragic in film. Whilst my personal aim is to eradicate the shame I feel at being a lesbian as far as possible from my life, I recognise in my own situation a certain poignancy in living as a lesbian within a homophobic society, a poignancy which at least allows me to empathise with the covert desires of others and with the occasional perversities of a love born out of denial, disavowal and abjection. In making this point I recognise the influence of Eve Sedgwick's preliminary articulations around the impact of shame on the developing queer personality (see Sedgwick, 1993).
21 Amongst these I would include the lesbian feminist classic *I, Vampire*, Jewelle Gomez's *The Gilda Stories*, and the lesbian short *Because the Dawn* (Amy Goldstein, 1988, US) as well as a large history of mainstream representations recently appropriated to a perverse logics of reading. See Case (1992).
22 See Faderman (1985: 277–94).
23 The preponderance of incest narratives in popular cultural depictions of same-sex desire read for example the recent *Sister my Sister* as well as the fantasised sorority of *Single White Female* – is an interesting and yet entirely predictable trope. Incest is of course useful as a way of figuring a lesbian desire which, since Freud, is assumed to be founded in narcissism – one looks for what one most desires, that is, oneself, in the figure of she who reflects back that self.

24 For an account of revenge as gendered see Carol Clover's account of the *Lex Talionis* in Clover (1992: 114–65).
25 These films are marketed as severe warnings as to what could happen to women who let another woman into their house. The very excessiveness of such films can now be read as a species of camp.
26 See Faludi (1992: 114).
27 In arguing this I disagree with the aspect of Lynda Hart's reading of the film, where she describes Hedy as being the opposite of Allie at the start (see Hart, 1994: 114–15). Hedy is just enough like Allie to appeal to her desire for the same, but not too alike to represent a rival for Sam's (or other men's) affections.
28 My feeling is, in agreement with Hart, that the relation between sex and death is by and large grounded in the exclusion of non-white women as erotic subjects (or indeed objects) of desire.
29 Where, as Elisabeth Bronfen notes, 'beauty is defined in contrast to destruction' (Bronfen, 1992: 5).
30 See Russo (1981: 181–246).
31 See Faludi (1992: 112–21).
32 For another favourable lesbian reading of *Basic Instinct* see Tasker (1994: 173–5).
33 I realise that to argue for the importance of a good death to a lesbian cinematic erotics (even to one that embraces the abject) is profoundly pessimistic and even regressive. At the same time, it is a profoundly romantic one. For an extensive account of the politics and poetics of female death, see Bronfen (1992).
34 For Kristeva the dead woman signifies 'jouissance as nostalgia, within reach but lost for ever' (Bronfen, 1992: 98).
35 If, that is, we follow Butler's reading of Freud, in arguing that the 'libidinal investment in pain is precisely what delineates a body part as part' (Butler, 1992: 134–5).
36 See Merck (1986: 166).
37 Needless to say, the homoerotic implications of their relationship are never articulated, despite the fact that Oscar's conversation continually oversteps the bounds of polite discourse.
38 The technique by which mainstream advertisers appeal to a gay or, increasingly, lesbian audience in a way that is not perceptible to a heterosexually identified audience.
39 See Weiss (1992: 56-63). Whilst I accept Weiss' point, I would argue that the combination of licit and illicit desire that results from the displacement of lesbian sexuality on to the maternal-erotic is reflective of a certain nostalgia amongst post-oedipal subjects for a fantasised return to the pre-oedipal. Whilst this is in one sense a regressive desire, I do not believe, like de Lauretis (1994), that such desire need determine the model of lesbian subjectivity espoused. We should also recall that a child–mother relation has operated as a coded form of lesbianism at certain times within cinematic history (see Dyer, 1990: 40-2) and thus its significance should not be underestimated.
40 My conflation of star with character (all the more problematic in terms of the factual origins of *Silkwood*'s story) is deliberate. For an examination of the potential for violence in the appropriation of star by fan, see chapter five.
41 In the sense that the straight-identified woman is usually configured

as femme. The ways in which the lesbian femme negotiates this issue are considered in chapter three.

42 I do worry about the erasure of the mannish lesbian from this scene. A function of what I described in the preface as a self-consolidation of the other, this reduction of the mannish lesbian to cipher seems fraught with dangers.

43 'Yet how might a desire to see what one is afraid to look at ever be gratified? Or how might a fear of what one can't stop desiring ever be allayed? The classic solution to both questions, of course, lies in the closet' (Miller, 1991: 131–2). The irony of this translation from homophobic disavowal to lesbian displacement does not escape me.

5 Stars and their proclivities

i Gossip

Gossip surveys the field through a peephole, but sees a great deal; its perspective shows the world from a different angle. (Meyer-Spacks, 1985: 263)

Boldly claiming to 'tell the facts and name the names' in July 1955 *Confidential* magazine embarked on telling the 'untold story of Marlene Dietrich.' The scandal sheet may have shocked the general public by its disclosures, but for many lesbians it only confirmed what they had long suspected. Rumour and gossip constitute the unrecorded history of gay subculture. (Weiss, 1992: 30)

I don't assume that all gay men or all women are very skilled at the nonce-taxonomic work represented by gossip, but it does make sense to suppose that our distinctive needs are peculiarly disserved by its devaluation. (Sedgwick, 1991: 23)

The academic profile of gossip has not been good. Seen as the province of women, and associated, in Eve Sedgwick's words, 'in European thought with servants [and] effeminate and gay men' (Sedgwick, 1991: 23), and hence not to be taken seriously, gossip is consistently devalued. As a result, very little has been written on it from an academic angle. One interesting recent example is John Forrester's reading of the psychoanalytic relation as premised upon multiple avenues of gossip from client to analyst, from client about analyst and about client between analysts. For Forrester, gossip underwrites the psychoanalytic contract, and is 'absolutely essential to the writing of the history of psychoanalysis' (Forrester, 1991: 183). At the same time, Forrester testifies to the problematic status of gossip on both an epistemic and a moral level:

> Knowledge had by gossip only barely maintains its claim on that word, sketching out the no man's land of fiction which equally constitutes the social knowledge by which we live. In addition, gossip only appears as such when there is a transgression of rules of discourse. Talking about someone who is not present is the rule, not the exception, in conversation: but that is not gossip. It only becomes gossip once talk implicitly or explicitly addresses moral questions concerning them, or moral questions raised by their actions. And of course to think of gossip as a form of moral discourse makes as much sense as talking of telepathy as a form of knowledge. (Forrester, 1991: 170)

Indeed, the lowered voice of the gossip communicating information which may be true, perchance is false, which is, whatever, as illicit as it is fascinating, testifies to the ambiguous moral status of the form.

For Patricia Meyer-Spacks, whose book *Gossip* is largely limited to the canon of English literary texts, gossip is confined to the private sphere, something to be indulged in moments of leisure as a means of forging intimacies within a couple or small group. Indeed, she observes, 'the privacy of the dyad or small group involved in this kind of talk largely determines its special tone' (Meyer-Spacks, 1985: 3). Meyer-Spacks does, however, admit that gossip may provide a: 'resource for the subordinated' (Meyer-Spacks, 1985: 5), observing that:

> An account of women in the muslim harem reports that they 'exchange experience and information and critically analyze ... the world of men. The general tone is one of satire, ridicule and disrespect for males and the ideals of the male world.' That's what I mean about the subordinated. (Meyer-Spacks, 1985: 5)

Still, she insists that the effect of such exchanges is to sustain the insularity of the group rather than effect change in the public sphere: 'The relationship such gossip expresses and sustains matters more than the information it promulgates: and in the sustaining of that relationship, interpretation counts more than the facts or pseudo-facts on which it works' (Meyer-Spacks, 1985: 6). This sense of the private nature of gossip is also present in Weiss, who argues for a double-layered knowledge, the official text and the lesbian and gay subtext. Unofficial knowledge as to the sexual orientation of stars remains private to the lesbian and gay community but informs its reception of the public heterotext. For Weiss, however, gossip of this sort also takes on the status of an unofficial history, a means of sustaining not only the private group but the public interventions of a subculture.

Though agreeing with Meyer-Spacks in so far as I believe that the gossip of the socially subordinated does possess communitarian effects, like Weiss, I will argue that homosexual rumour has a wider effect also. Legal theorist Rosemary J. Coombe, citing Spivak, argues for the political implications of gossip in the form of rumour:

> Rumor is elusive and transitive, anonymous, and without origin. It belongs to no one and is possessed by everyone. Endlessly in circulation, it has no identifiable source. This illegitimacy makes it accessible to insurgency, while its transitivity makes it a powerful tactic, one that Gayatri Spivak calls a truly subaltern means of communication. (Coombe, 1993: 421)

Coombe begins her article with an account of a piece of agitprop that sustains a more radical political dialectic than Meyer-Spacks can offer. She describes:

> Walking down the street one day in 1987, pedestrians were surprised to see a message flashing across an electronic bill board. 'Lesbians fly Air Canada' it repeatedly signalled. The next day the message was gone. A gay rights group broadcast the phrase, but their communication terminated abruptly when Air Canada threatened to apply for an injunction to stop the group from using its name. (Coombe, 1993: 411)

The sign, both affirmation and affront, sustains both a sense of lesbians as citizens and as an insurgent group willing to expose the heterosexist complacency of Canadian Airlines.[1] The fact that the sign was never in fact aired (lawyers advised the art group responsible of the likelihood of legal injunction) stresses the protean quality of the anecdotal which becomes a signifier of resistance even in the face of defeat. Even Coombe, retelling hearsay as fact, was temporarily fooled. Coombe is careful to stress the limitations of rumour, noting that:

> Although signifiers circulate in social fields, become inflected with new meanings, and are politically engaged in new articulations, the fields of discourse in which they figure as sites for identification shape and limit tactics of appropriation. Those in marginal groups will continually attempt to put signifiers into arenas of symbolic exchange – activities that do not contribute to capitalist production and accumulation – but they have fewer resources at their disposal than do those who maintain the exchange value of the sign. (Coombe, 1993: 417)

Here Coombe is referring specifically to a legal wrangle over the ownership of the title 'Olympic'. In 1981, when a non-profit-making lesbian and gay group, Arts and Athletics, tried to Promote a Gay Olympics, the United States Olympic Committee brought a suit to prevent the use of the name Olympic by the group (despite the fact that they confer this right on a number of other groups from the Paralympics to the police and even pets). The determination of mass corporate capital to retain signatory rights against those bodies of which it does not approve is, argues Coombe, clear: 'Trademark legislation thus enabled a public authority to exercise its authority over a signifier in a discriminatory manner – to prevent subordination from becoming translated into hegemonic articulation' (Coombe, 1993: 416).

It is this double-bind, between the protean effects and implications of gossip as a subcultural activity, and the attempts of dominant capitalist forces to control and legislate against its influence, that I will be pursuing in this chapter through the signifier of the Hollywood star. For me gossip operates as the clearest example of contemporary subcultural communication on both a national and an international scale. Be it rumour negotiated between friends, speculation in the minority (or even tabloid) press, or on the World Wide Web,[2] I will argue that gossip as to the alleged sexual orientation of Hollywood stars helps sustain, at the very least, a fantasy world of identifications and desires which operates alongside (since it is not completely set apart from what Hollywood would like us to do, that is, invest in stars), the official dissemination of the Hollywood heterotext.

ii Historically ours

Something that, through gossip, is commonplace knowledge within gay subculture is often completely unknown on the outside, and if not unknown, at least unspeakable. It is this insistence by the dominant culture on making homosexuality invisible and unspeakable that both requires and enables us to locate gay history in rumor, innuendo, fleeting gestures and coded language. (Weiss, 1992: 32)

Whilst the status of gossip remains, as I have argued above, at the very least problematic, it is clear that certain forms of licensed gossip proliferate within advanced western capitalist cultural networks. Information fed to chosen outlets by publicity agents and marketing executives has long been a staple of the Hollywood rumour mill, which attempts to promote its stars through a given set of social conventions. 'Proof' of a star's heterosexual liaisons is always news since it interpellates the star into the proper order of the symbolic. Still, rumour and gossip as to the sexual orientation of certain Hollywood stars persists regardless of the attempts of the Hollywood publicity machine (by which I mean agents, or formerly studios, press officers, syndicated newspapers) to limit the damage.

Of course, when venturing into the realm of filmic rumour it is worth drawing up a few distinctions between the various categories of historical subject. Historically, there have always been lesbian, gay or bisexual actors whose orientation has been available knowledge to those in the know. Greta Garbo, Tallulah Bankhead, Ethel Waters, Marlene Dietrich, Joan Crawford, Rudolph Valentino, James Dean and River Phoenix each remained hetero-iconic to the mainstream, while whisperings, innuendo and filmic allusion added fuel to the myth of their various homo-identifications. As Andrea Weiss notes, it has been the work of lesbian and gay archivists to read between the lines of the dominant text, piecing together the rumour and innuendo, deciphering the coded word or gesture, encouraging the homosexuality to speak through the text. In chapter six I will demonstrate the effects of such a reading through the star image of Hollywood actress Jodie Foster. The truth or otherwise of these rumours frequently goes with the stars to their grave. Still the ambiguity remains and, importantly, informs the receptive context of their films.[3]

Unlike this first category of stars, my second category never played on their reputation for sexual ambivalence but rather played against it. This category might include an actor like Rock Hudson, whose heterosexual identity remained in place as the result of a concerted press campaign to promote his heterosexuality in the face of speculation in the 1950s as to the meaning of his perpetual bachelor status. Hudson's marriage of convenience to Phyllis Gates, at a moment when, it has been suggested, he feared exposure as homosexual, presents one instance of such a promotion.

A third and, for our needs, final category of rumour is that which surrounds what we might call the desired homosexual. This category refers to those figures – Mae West, Bette Davis, Clark Gable, Vanessa Redgrave, Susan Sarandon, Sigourney Weaver, Jean Claude Van Damme – whom interested audiences virtually will to be homosexual since their filmic status is so easily recuperable into a certain lesbian or gay fantasy erotic.

All these categories are contentious – the burden of proof tending to lie with the desire of lesbians and gay men to believe such rumours. Often, indeed, the lesbian and gay community is criticised for its inappropriate appropriation of stars as lesbian and/or gay icons.[4] The accusation often implies that images of lesbians and gays are so rare and inadequate that we have to steal from heterosexual culture in order to affirm our own sad lives, justifying our existence through parasitic association (indeed, this assertion is frequently accompanied by the homophobic notion of homosexuality as contamination).[5]

This is not to argue that there is not a certain imperative to the promotion of and belief in the homosexuality of a given star. In fact, the tendency of a lesbian lifestyle magazine such as the British *Diva* is almost obsessively to place the question of a given star's sexuality in the realm of speculation, naming the possibility of their lesbianism and begging them to name themselves. There is then a desire to authenticate one's investment in a certain star and to have one's sexuality validated as it were by association. That I will be arguing in this chapter for the ultimate irrelevance of the confessional is not to say that I do not understand the desire, merely that in the end I believe that the notion of truth is irrelevant to the promotion of spectatorial fantasy.

This is not to forget for a moment that the tendency of the Hollywood market is towards the promotion of the integrity of the star as unambiguously heterosexual.

iii Marketing stars: the corroboration of the star image

The Hollywood studios went to great lengths to keep the star's image open to erotic contemplation by both men and women, not only requiring lesbian and gay male stars to remain in the closet for the sake of their careers, but also desperately creating the impression of heterosexual romance. (Weiss, 1992: 32)

The attempts of the star, and of the interests that support her, to retain ownership over the star image are often fierce. Where the star sign operates as a brandname or trademark whose reproduction needs to be secured within a specific discourse, 'Increasingly it seems that any publicly recognized characteristic will be legally recognized as having a commercial value that is likely to be diminished by its unauthorized or unremunerated appropriation by others' (Coombe 1992a: 367). Indeed, and as Coombe argues elsewhere, 'a celebrity may attempt to prevent the use of her image even where there is no competition between the parties, no evidence that the defendant intended to pass off his goods as those endorsed by the celebrity, and no evidence that the public was in any way confused by the use of the persona' (Coombe, 1992b: 1241).[6] For, as she continues: 'Celebrities ... have an interest in policing the use of their persona to ensure that they do not become tainted with associations that would prematurely tarnish the patina they might license to diverse enterprises' (Coombe, 1992a: 368). Tainted, for example, with the imputation of homosexuality. As a result, the star's responsibility to present an image which is in accordance with the promotion of a cultural and filmic fiction of compulsory heterosexuality demands the (sometimes fictional) authentification of heterosexuality. Indeed, I will argue shortly that this pertains even where the film's theme is homosexuality.

What Coombe does not talk about in her articles, probably since it occurred after the event of their writing, but what is most relevant to her arguments, is the contemporary practice of outing stars. Outing, the implication that a star is either gay, lesbian or bisexual, and the consequent demand that they should come out and admit this, goes right to the heart of the Hollywood heterotextual fiction since what is precisely being sold (out) is the myth of a star's unambiguous heterosexuality. Some of the aims and intentions, pros and cons, of outing will be taken up in part iv of this chapter and investigated further in relation to the outing of Jodie Foster, discussed in chapter six. For the moment, a brief excursion into theories of stardom.

Writing in 1957, Thomas Harris discussed the marketing of two very different stars, Grace Kelly and Marilyn Monroe. Harris's thesis is that the construction of stars works primarily through stereotyping: 'The star system is based on the premise that a star is accepted by the public in terms of a certain set of personality traits which permeate all of his or her film roles' (Harris, [1957] 1991: 40). The star persona encourages certain audience expectations which Harris argues will then be realised in the star vehicle or film. Extra-filmic information about the star is constructed so as to corroborate their star image. Hence, he argues: 'the carefully disseminated "lady" image of Grace Kelly is firmly grounded in her actual family background. As a product of wealth, genteel breeding and close family ties she became widely accepted as representative of man's ideal longings within the family structure' (Harris, [1957] 1991: 42). The star image of Monroe on the other hand is distinguished by her marketing as 'playmate' (Harris, [1957] 1991: 42) through a series of interviews and photo spreads that emphasise her approachability (at least in the fantasies of her projected male audiences). The complete marketing of image, argues Harris, ensured that 'the two stars were so successful in communicating a comprehensible image that both became national celebrities worthy of treatment in newspapers and news magazine departments other than those dealing with the cinema' (Harris, [1957] 1991: 43). An unfortunate by-product of this cohesive marketing was the occasional glitch in the star persona: for example Ingrid Bergman's betrayal of her 'St Joan' image in bearing an illegitimate child by Roberto Rossellini put into crisis, at least temporarily, the lustre of her star image.

On reconsidering Harris's essay some forty years on, however, one would have to conclude that perhaps time has altered the emphases, or rather that perhaps Harris over-emphasises the correlation between image and reception a little. For, as Richard Dyer (1991) notes, the relation between 'star' and 'image' is more fascinatingly complex than Harris describes. Rather than securing an authentic connection between star and star persona, Dyer theorises an endlessly proliferating relation of images that sustain one another in a constructed fiction of 'authenticity'. As example he notes, if the studio images of Joan Crawford seem inauthentic, 'distorted (deauthenticated) by the manipulation of the filmmaking or photographic process' (Dyer, 1991: 136), then we can always turn to the homestyle photographs of Joan 'doing the chores ... [or] cuddling baby Christina' (Dyer, 1991: 136). If these images also seem too contrived then we can look to the 'candid camera shot of her without her makeup, or uncover a snapshot of her scowling at Christina' (Dyer, 1991: 136). One image succeeds another in an 'infinite regress by means of which one more authentic image displaces another. But then they are all part of the star image, each one anchoring the whole thing in an essential, uncovered authenticity' (Dyer, 1991: 136). That this contrived authenticity might then be further displaced by media not so firmly associated with the official Hollywood publicity machine (for example the scandal press, the unauthorised biography) is testimony, Dyer notes, to the suspicions provoked by Hollywood's too tight control of the star image. Even this information can be marketed, however, where a star's famed difference from their image can in turn be fêted as adding an intriguing edge of ambivalence to their image – the literary and televisual success of Christina Crawford's *Mommie Dearest* (Frank Perry, 1981, US) being a case in point.

The extent to which Hollywood will go in order to sustain the fiction of heterosexuality around its stars is of course demonstrated in the compulsory heterosexualisation of Rock Hudson. As Richard Meyer (1991) notes, Hudson's sexuality had been provoking speculation in the tabloid press for some time when in 1955 he married Phyllis Gates, the former secretary of his homosexual agent, Henry Willson. Argues Meyer, Hudson's star image had been implicitly threatened a number of times leading up to his marriage by magazines intent upon questioning, and then finally in the case of *Confidential* magazine (the same journal that had earlier tried to expose Marlene Dietrich), upon detailing the real reasons behind his confirmed bachelor status. His subsequent marriage was, argues Meyer, a ruse, a smokescreen constructed by his gay agent designed to promote the fiction of heterosexuality for an industry which would tolerate nothing else in its stars:

> Although descriptions of the relation between Hudson and Gates vary, it is clear that Willson, an openly gay man within Hollywood circles, masterminded both the match and the wedding, making certain that photographers would be on hand to record such seemingly intimate moments as the couple in their wedding-night hotel room, the drinking of champagne on the conjugal bed(s), the sharing of joy long-distance, with the bride's mother. What lay behind this picture of nuptial bliss, then, was not only the explicit threat of homosexual exposure but Henry Willson's (gay) knowledge of how to construct an ideal heterosexuality for, and in, representation. (Meyer, 1991: 272)

This fiction of heterosexuality survived almost three decades longer than the marriage.

I would, along with others, argue that this compulsory heterosexualisation of the star image extends even to the promotion of lesbian subject matter. The disclaimers that accompanied a film such as *Desert Hearts* for example, wherein at least one of its stars, Patricia Charbonneau, made every attempt to distance herself from the character she plays in the film, are a case in point. As detailed by Teresa de Lauretis, Charbonneau 'took great pains to re-establish a proper, straight and feminine, persona, by giving interviews and appearing in the popular press photographed with her husband and child' (de Lauretis, 1990: 12). Her anxiety is no doubt a reflection of the fear of being typecast by a homophobic Hollywood. Still, the question must be posed, in what political context does her distancing in itself become homophobic? This process of re-othering the lesbian in representation is a common tactic for garnering (straight) public empathy, as Penny Florence notes with reference to the BBC sapphfest *Portrait of a Marriage*, where the actresses' 'discomfort with the love scenes was sympathetically portrayed' (Florence, 1995: 124) in interviews. An instance of the world text imposing on the filmic image, the habitual de-lesbianising of the images of the women who star in films with an overt lesbian content reflects the cultural anxiety that attaches itself to images of lesbianism, even in performance.[7]

The double standard whereby heterosexuals will supposedly remain unconvinced by a 'known' gay man or lesbian playing a heterosexually identified character, but non-heterosexual audiences are presumed to be able to identify unproblematically with a 'known' heterosexual playing a lesbian or gay man is obvious but none the less persistent. The anxiety that accompanies any imputation of homosexuality ensures that a star's sexuality remains fixed within a heterosexual economy, at least at the level of production and marketing, even, as Hudson's case demonstrates, to the point of perjury. The effect is to present, within the mainstream culture at least, a narrative fiction of coherent heterosexual identity, which contrasts ironically with the eternal potential ambiguity of the filmic space.

In the face of this ideology of compulsory heterosexuality, it seems clear that extra-filmic gossip can inform a strategy of audience resistance in the face of the otherwise compulsory heterosexualisation of the star. As Rosemary Coombe argues indeed, such strategies become 'expressions of solidarity and legitimate social difference arising in the nascent struggles of subaltern groups to construct alternative (if not oppositional) social identities' (Coombe, 1992b: 1247).

iv **Invisibly visible**

What an apparent coup, then, for lesbian and gay visibility, when in 1991 an anonymous activist group, Outpost, billed posters around New York City 'outing' well-known Hollywood stars. Michelangelo Signorile, one of the chief exponents of outing, defines it as 'revealing the homosexuality of closeted gay public figures' (Signorile, 1994: xiii).[8] For Signorile, outing is primarily about resetting the balance:

> My interest in outing has ... been to equalize the discussion of homosexuality and heterosexuality in the media as a way of breaking down the closet. Everyday the media discusses aspects of public figures' heterosexuality when these facts are irrelevant to a news story whether or not the subjects want the facts reported and no matter how private they might be. But most of the 'responsible' media refuse to reveal a public figure's homosexuality, even when relevant – except, of course, when such revelations play into their own homophobic agenda. They thereby set themselves up as the enforcers of the closet, holding the key and opening the door when it is to their advantage. (Signorile, 1994: xv)

While I share Signorile's frustration and sympathise with his arguments when put in these terms, the response to outing by the mainstream media has been largely to reflect and build upon the very hypocrisy and homophobia which Signorile accuses them of.[9] Indeed, as Eve Sedgwick notes,

> To the fine antennae of public attention, the freshness of every drama of (especially involuntary) gay uncovering seems if anything heightened in surprise and delectability, rather than staled by the increas-

ingly intense atmosphere of public articulations of and about the love that is famous for daring not to speak its name. (Sedgwick, 1991: 67)

According to some of its adherents, however, outing is not merely about visibility but, responsibility. As Gabriel Rotello, editor of the now defunct *Outweek* argues, public figures 'have to recognise that they are members of an oppressed minority and that membership carries with it intrinsic responsibilities' (Heller, 1991: 13). What such responsibilities entail for a star is firstly to come out, to visualise pride in one's lesbian, gay or bisexual identity, and secondly to turn visibility into action in order to construct more representative roles for lesbians and gay men in Hollywood. How anyone is to achieve this in the face of an 'unbelievably homophobic' (Heller, 1991: 13) Hollywood remains unclear. Few stars get to identify themselves through as elegant a vehicle as Percy Adlon's *Salmonberries* which allowed k. d. lang to come out finally and eloquently.[10] My hunch is that if we insist upon a star's responsibility in a prescriptive way we do them an injustice. For their responsibility as actors is surely to play characters that entertain and convince. If, to a lesbian audience, this precludes certain kinds of characters, then I for one am not interested. For as outing fixes sexuality into the 'absolutely' queer or heterosexual (and yes I know it's a pun on the vodka adverts but the implication's still there), rather than questioning the heterosexist separation of sexual identity into binary positions, so it seems strangely old–fashioned.

More seriously, the fetishisation of the individual star, though a function of the Hollywood publicity machine, and though obviously a temptation even to an academic piece such as this, seems fundamentally misplaced. For exactly how much (rhetorical, never mind literal) power does a given star really have to refocus the multiple forces of homophobia? As lesbian journalist Cindy Carr comments: 'I'm still waiting for the news of Malcolm Forbes' homosexuality to improve the quality of my life' (Heller, 1991: 13). Not only this, but what is to say that a given star's admission of homosexuality would not disappoint in other ways? As Terry Brown argues in an article about the cultural representation of the actress Jodie Foster, outing activist Michelangelo Signorile's question '"Jodie, are you a dyke?" demands a verification that is ... impossible to verify' (Brown, 1994: 238). Indeed, quoting Judith Butler, she notes: '*Outness* can only produce a new opacity; and *the closet* produces a promise of a disclosure that can, by definition, never come' (Butler, 1991: 16). The fact that any imputation of homosexuality is almost always succeeded by silence or outright denial serves to inhibit audience speculation further where often a promise is replaced by a denial. I would also add, recalling the arguments of chapter four, that what we lose by the imperative to revelation is the sense of the shared secret, the 'in' joke, of having access to a cultural knowledge that most straight-identified subjects are blind to, a function of the closet which I would argue is a condition both of our oppression and of our 'liberation'.

While the power to out Hollywood stars is testimony to the increased visibility and vocality of the contemporary lesbian and gay scene, as outing results in simplistic equations and political prescriptiveness I feel that it has proved to be counterproductive. For as a discourse it shows scant awareness of the complexity or the vagaries of reception. For no matter how many times Tom Selleck is designated 'absolutely queer', heterosexually identified women will still fancy him just as little girls and boys continue to scream for the very out and very vocal Jimmy Somerville. Likewise, however cagey a star is as to their sexual orientation, audiences will still invest into this silence the meaning they most long to read. In this sense it is clear that desire has more to do with the one who desires than it does with the object of desire.

v Star images

What the public knew, or what the gay subculture knew, about these stars' 'real lives' cannot be separated from their star images. Whether these actresses were actually lesbian or bisexual is less relevant than how their star personae are perceived by lesbian audiences. (Weiss, 1992: 32–3)

As Rosemary Coombe asks, 'Who authors the celebrity? Where does the identity receive its authorization?' (Coombe, 1992a: 365). Her answer is that, despite, regardless of or even as a result of attempts to legislate the star image, the restrictions placed upon its representation and rearticulation in the commercial sphere, the star remains an open and contested signifier, encouraging a proliferation of unlicensed images: 'The celebrity image is a cultural lode of multiple meanings, mined for its symbolic resonances and, simultaneously, a floating signifier, invested with libidinal energies, social longings and political aspirations' (Coombe, 1992a: 365). For celebrity is not merely the organization of certain traits: it demands the corroboration of these traits by an audience. As Coombe notes, paraphrasing Richard Dyer: 'the star image is authored by its consumers as well as its producers; the audience makes the celebrity image the unique phenomenon that it is' (Coombe, 1992a: 369).[11] How anachronistic then are the legislative attempts to concretise this relation. As Coombe argues, this renders the current legal understanding of cultural artefacts as somehow belonging to a particular person or dynasty, part of a fatal misrecognition. Describing cultural production as a form of bricolage, Coombe asks:

> How much does Elvis Costello owe to Buddy Holly, Prince to Jimi Hendrix, or Michael Jackson to Diana Ross? Take the image of Madonna, an icon whose meaning and value lie partially in its evocation and ironic reconfiguration of several twentieth century sex-goddesses. (Coombe, 1992a: 371)

It makes no sense to secure an author for these images. Culture is necessarily a syncretic form, proliferating meanings and encouraging appropriations both appropriate and inappropriate. Coombe does however note an ironic effect of the legislation of star images, that is that '[the law] produces fixed, stable identities authored by the celebrity subject, but simultaneously creates the possibility of places of transgression in which the signifier's fixity and the celebrity's authority may be contested and resisted' (Coombe, 1992a: 387). Prohibition encourages a reverse discourse of inappropriate display, a licence to play against the grain of the dominant text.[12] The law of course continues to uphold the rights of the ostensible owner. However, a fundamental instability remains in its dependence upon the notion of a single *authority*.

Audiences, in other words, are not so easily manipulated into a display of compulsory heterosexuality as stars are. Coombe recognises the particular resonance celebrity has for those who find themselves in one sense or another disenfranchised by the preoccupations of mainstream culture, where 'embodying the realization of widespread aspirations for public affirmation, [the celebrity image] is especially likely to attract the authorial energies of those in marginal groups for whom recognition, legitimacy and positively evaluated identity are compelling issues' (Coombe, 1992a: 378). Coombe (1992b) reads a number of such investments — gay male appropriations of female film stars, Sue Golding's reading of James Dean as lesbian hermaphrodite, and female 'trekkies'' appropriations of *Star Trek*'s Kirk and Spock to a sadomasochistic homoerotics — as examples of subcultural appropriations of dominant discourses. Coombe's examples make it clear that there is nothing to delimit such subcultural appropriations to lesbian or gay expression. The making queer of popular culture, as I noted in the last chapter, need not be limited to those who publicly identify as queer. It is, however, frequently premised upon the subcultural desire to infiltrate the dominant through one order or another, or, as Coombe puts it, the 'Inclin[ation] ... to contest hegemonic norms of gender [and other] identity' (Coombe, 1992b: 1259). Nor is there anything innately radical about these appropriations, though, again, as Coombe notes, the trekkies who issue their own fanzines are aware of the dangers of appropriation, treading a fine line between fantasy investments and copyright law.

Public fantasies of the order of the *Star Trek* fanzines are probably not in the majority of our experience. Private fantasies about stars on the other hand proliferate, though the forms they take may resonate uncomfortably with the avowed identifications of the fan. Stacey (1994) articulates two modes of spectatorial identification which can be loosely designated cinematic and extra-cinematic. For Stacey the first is characterised by 'processes of identification that involve fantasies about the relationship between the identity of the star and the identity of the spectator' (Stacey, 1994: 137). These identifications are filmic, since 'On the whole, these forms of identification relate to the cinematic context; in other words, they are processes that take place during the actual viewing of the film' (Stacey, 1994: 137). Conventionally, these are the modes of identification explored within film theory which tends to conflate the site of the cinematic experience with the experience of watching.

Stacey's second mode of identification, however, 'examines forms of recognition that involve practice as well as fantasy, in that spectators actually transform some aspect of their identity as a result of their relationship to their favourite star' (Stacey, 1994: 137). Stacey argues that these practices extend beyond the cinema, encompassing processes of aspiration and imitation that extend into everyday life. They include imitation of hair or dress style, then interpellation of oneself into the scene of the movie, and, in childhood, the acting out of scenes from movies (translated into an adult imitation of posture or stance).

I suspect we have all found ourselves fantasising beyond the bounds of the contextually cinematic, interpellating oneself into the cinematic diegesis, extracting the star from the heterosexual diegesis, setting up the film or a given scene differently, or fantasising a relationship with a star separate from, but inspired by, filmic or extra–filmic material such as star interviews or gossip. The relative silence about such practices is representative of both the difficulty and the potential embarrassment of articulating, or even admitting to, them in print (an embargo which I am not about to break!). Yet they remain, I would argue, integral to the cinematic experience.

The interesting aspect of such practices for me is where they manifest desires or identifications outside of a socially inscribed or validated context. What might it mean for a heterosexually identified female spectator to indulge in lesbian fantasies about Michelle Pfeiffer or Sigourney Weaver? What does it say about a lesbian-identified subject who cannot tell whether she wants to be, or have, James Dean, River Phoenix, or, as I discovered in a recent conversation with a friend, the beautiful Denzel Washington? I would hazard, very little within a public context. Still, the private indulgence in cross–gender, cross–sex or interracial fantasies seems worth investigation. Sue Golding (1991) testifies to a lesbian cultivation of James Dean as 'The almost–perfect lesbian hermaphrodite'.[13] The recent rumours as to the alleged homosexuality of Keanu Reeves, rather than diminishing his fanbase, expand it into a cross-over audience of gay men, lesbians and heterosexually identified women who, post *Speed* (Jan De Bont, 1995, US), really don't care whether he's gay or not. Everywhere the multiple appropriations of the subtext contrast ironically with the monotony of the dominant Hollywood heterotext.

It is this feature of the cinema as fantasy space for inappropriate identifications and desires which Judith Mayne testifies to in writing:

Film theory has been so bound by the heterosexual symmetry that supposedly governs Hollywood cinema that it has ignored the possibility, for instance, that one of the distinct pleasures of the cinema may well be a 'safe zone' in which homosexual as well as heterosexual desires can be fantasized and acted out. (Mayne, 1993: 97)

She continues: 'I am not speaking here of an innate capacity to "read against the grain," but rather of the way in which desire and pleasure in the cinema may well function to problematize the categories heterosexual versus homosexual' (Mayne, 1993: 97). There is nothing particularly radical about this function of the cinema. As Mayne notes, 'this "safety zone" can also be read as a displacement' (Mayne, 1993: 97), and she gives the example of the buddy movie, a conventionally safe zone for the exploration of homoerotic desire between men. One can leave the cinema then with one's basic assumptions unchallenged. Can we argue that such appropriations are definitely transgressive? No, of course not. At the same time, inappropriate appropriations work ironically against the supposed hegemony of the heterosexual text while demonstrating that its images of heterosexuality may not be as watertight as they appear.

Still, disappointment as well as desire renders the relation between fan and star sometimes explosive. Terry Brown takes the definition of *fan* from the Latin *fanaticus*, suggesting fanatic. The relation of star to fan is, argues Brown, through a reading of the (non-)relation between Jodie Foster and her obsessive follower John Hinckley,[14] a fundamentally violent one:

> Insofar as the celebrity 'possesses' the fan, then the celebrity becomes both demon and deity to the fan, as Jodie Foster became for John Hinckley. While John Hinckley's fanaticism may be considered pathological, psychotic in fact, it is nonetheless a playing out in the extreme of the relation between *any* fan and *any* celebrity ... in which the celebrity makes the fan's desire both possible and impossible, structures as it castrates. (Brown, 1994: 229)

For Brown, the fan's fantasy relation to her idol will hence always be premised upon a disappointment, a non–relation which however continues to proliferate a desire which will not be thwarted and, at its most extreme, crosses into psychoses. The examples of a number of famous stalkers, such as Jodie Foster's obsessive fan John Hinckley, John Lennon's killer Mark David Chapman and the haunting of *Cagney and Lacey* star Sharon Gless by an obsessive female fan, are inferred to be extreme examples of that which many of us have experienced at times in pursuit of a particular star.

Whilst I think it is a mistake to pathologise fandom by definition,[15] I would relate this violence to the dynamic which is set up between anticipation and disappointment, that is, the way in which the star sign both encourages and disappoints desire. Some pursue the star through the fetishisation of her star role, others through the fetishisation of the star 'herself'. There are perhaps fewer dangers in the first than the latter but both function as what I termed in the preface a species of self–consolidation on the body or image of another.

Whilst I believe Brown's points to be pertinent, and would have the dangers of over-identification with any star remain an ironic subtext to this piece, I would still maintain that there is a real space for appropriative fantasies to be recognised as a form of sustenance to the private life of the underrepresented. The theorists I have represented demonstrate a reading of culture as engendered by its consumers as much as by its producers. Indeed, the two terms do not make sense outside of a mutually constructive relation. This strategy of audience appropriation will be utilised in my readings of the films of Jodie Foster in chapter six.

Notes

1 Coombe notes: 'Readers who are not Canadian should be aware that at the time this message was conceived (prior to the deregulation of the airline industry), all Canadians flying within Canada "flew Air Canada." This archetypal "normal" Canadian activity was selected to demonstrate similarities in Canadian lesbians' everyday experiences that were too often overshadowed by fears of sexual difference' (Coombe, 1993: 411).

2 Many Hollywood stars now boast their own fan bases on the World Wide Web, the relative anonymity of the medium encouraging identifications and desires both appropriate and inappropriate.

3 Andrea Weiss's reading of Greta Garbo and Miriam Hansen's reading of Rudolph Valentino, both located in Gledhill (1991), are particularly good examples of this kind of reception.

4 Of course I do not mean to imply any essentialism by this term *community*, which can be identified most coherently in the eyes of our detractors than in the multiple and manifold forms it takes between lesbians, gay men and others.

5 In fact I would argue that the sense of affront experienced by stars who are not happy with their promotion to lesbian or gay iconic status emerges from a certain hiatus between the star's projected and perceived image. There is something about the lesbian or gay appropriation of certain stars that audiences pick up on and ironise. The appropriation of arch-homophobe Jeremy – *Top Gear* – Clarkson thus becomes intelligible not so much in terms of the homosexual 'community's' abject need for a role model, however inappropriate, nor in terms of the irresistibility of the 'hunk' himself, but in terms of the distance between Clarkson's own control of his machismo image and the reproduction and misappropriation of that image within a gay context. I would even go so far as to argue that the gay appropriation of 'nelly' Clarkson horrifies him since it testifies to something in his manner, visible to the gay men who celebrate him, that can be appropriated. The fact that Clarkson does not understand what this is, whereas his gay fans do, serves only to place the joke all the more firmly on him.

6 Needless to say, I had little chance of securing copyright for the reproduction of magazine images of Jodie Foster in this book, even in proffering a euphemistic account of its subject matter.

7 In a further revolution of the wheel, actress Jodie Foster was reported in 1996 to be suing Polygram for allegedly reneging on an oral contract for her to play the romantic lead in the upcoming *The Game*. Polygram alleges 'creative differences' but the papers are speculating about a possible link with the fact that rumours around Hollywood suggest that Foster is thinking about coming out. See *The Guardian*, 21 June 1996.

8 Though at the beginning outing was directed at closeted politicians who were actively homophobic, these days it seems to extend to any public figure.

9 A hypocrisy exposed in Britain by the activist duo Faggots Rooting Out Closets (FROCS) who tantalised the British media with promises to name names and subsequently presented the press with evidence of their own obsession in shape of blocked out faces covered with their own media print.

10 An act she confirmed in *Capital Gay*, June 1992.

11 She also notes that a star image is dependent upon a multiplicity of sources from writers, directors, agents and media to fan clubs, ex-lovers and the admiring audience. What she does not note is that many of these have a stake in promoting the compulsory heterosexuality of their star.

12 Indeed, for Fiske (1992), the very exclusion of subordinated subjects from the dominant culture renders this ripe for appropriation.

13 'I know you've seen the type: no tits, no cock, oozing with a kind of vulnerable "masculinity" and sheathed in a '50s style black leather motorcycle jacket. Or to put it slightly differently, it's James Dean, with a clit' (Golding, 1991: 198).

14 Hinckley was the man who in 1981 shot US president Ronald Reagan.

15 In an interesting reading of the critical mass on fandom, Joli Jenson (1992) warns against the temptation to view the fan as pathological by definition, noting that behaviour is always judged according to the social valuation attached to it. Hence, someone who collects Elvis memorabilia is a fan, someone who collects first editions of James Joyce novels is an aficionado even though both might invest as much energy and money as the other into the realisation of their desires.

6 Fostering the illusion

i Stars

> Whom she may or may not have slept with is strictly taboo. It is also what makes her so fascinating. (Kennedy, 1995: ix)

The alleged lesbianism of US actress Jodie Foster came to the fore with her outing by the anonymous Outpost collective in 1991. The image of Foster in Armani suit and bobbed hair with its career précis, 'Oscar winner, Yale graduate, Ex-Disney moppet, dyke', and above it the emblazoned phrase 'ABSOLUTELY QUEER' became in many ways symbolic of the issues surrounding outing. Foster's own pronouncements on related issues (she has never as far as I know directed conversation towards outing except allusively, and forbids people from raising the subject of her sexuality in interviews) have continued to fuel speculation around her sexual identity. Her characterisation of her role in *The Silence of the Lambs* as 'saviour of women in peril'[1] certainly added fuel to the fantasies, of her substantial lesbian fanbase as I will argue subsequently. Her reluctance to inscribe herself into the symbolic order of marriage and motherhood (or rather of motherhood within marriage)[2] has continued to provoke comment and speculation within the media. At the same time her continued re-heterosexualisation within films like *Sommersby* (Jon Amiel, 1993, US) and *Maverick* (Richard Donner, 1994, US) (the latter in league with arch-homophobe Mel Gibson, now one of Foster's best friends: 'He's a complicated but beautiful soul,' she says, 'I would do *anything* with Mel. I would do the phone book with Mel')[3] has hardly endeared her to sexual militants. Still, the resurfacing in the retrospective of sexual ambivalence in films like *Foxes* (Adrian Lyne, 1979, US), *Hotel New Hampshire* (Tony Richardson, 1984, US), *The Accused*, *The Silence of the Lambs* and *Nell* (Michael Apted, 1994, US) makes for an extremely complex and contradictory image, at least when compared to the run-of-the-mill antics of the average Hollywood star personality.

These are the elements of the Foster star personality that I want to examine here. This chapter is not, however intended to be an excavation of the truth behind the rumours, since, following Terry Brown, I will argue that a subject's sexuality is never finally recuperable to a notion of truth. As Brown argues: 'Jodie Foster's revelation, her coming out as either heterosexual or homosexual, would only set up expectations that would exceed the sign under which she placed herself' (Brown, 1994: 239). My focus will rather be on 'Jodie Foster inc.' and will examine the processing of the star by market and fans through a mixture of the extra-filmic (critical commentary, interviews, Foster's own remarks about her life and image) and the inter textuality of film to life (which the marketing of stars encourages when conveyed in official form and, as I described in chapter five, disapproves of when unlicensed). What I want to avoid in this chapter is the idle speculation, naive psychologising and dubious intentionalism that characterises much media debate about stars. I am, however, interested in the extra-filmic in so far as it reflects upon the circulation of the star image in the contemporary culture, chiefly in the workings of the Hollywood image machine as it was subsequently geared up to defend Foster, and in the cultural appropriations of the desiring audience, the culture of fandom, the photographs, autographs and extra-filmic discourses, that fantasise the lesbian in Foster. I do not want to succumb to the temptation to draw a facile comparison between art and life, to forge some naive teleology between Foster's screen roles and her real life, though I will imply some relation between the two in recognition of the way in which both star and audience attempt to make sense of a life lived on the screen.

ii The hetero-textual supplement

Foster's response to the allegations that she is a lesbian was a silence that she has frequently characterised as dignified: 'Protest is good, criticism is good, that's not against any American values, but anything else falls into the category of the undignified' (Szymanski, 1993: 32). Of course Foster's silence recognises the double-bind she is faced with. If she vociferously denies the imputation of lesbianism she might be characterised as homophobic; if she admits, the subsequent media flurry would represent a gross intrusion into the privacy she has long sought to establish and maintain. In the interpretation of others this dignified silence becomes something rather more belligerent, however. Here, for example, is her Yale roommate, Henrietta Conrad, declaring that Foster will not 'dignify those people with a response' (Heller, 1991: 13). The response of Foster's publicity manager in a contemporary discussion with *The Independent on Sunday* is also typical in its refusal to engage with the allegations: 'Outing ... is not something I want to talk about. No, I am not going to talk about it. Look, I am not ... no, I am not ... right, I'm hanging up the phone' (Heller, 1991: 12). The silence of Foster's publicity agent following the debacle of her outing was of course soon superseded by a publicity campaign whose intention was to attempt to re-heterosexualise Foster's image as unambivalently as possible. Here, the methods of image control detailed in chapter five come into their own with the planting of personal details, the rumours of heterosexual romance, the syndication of information and images to carefully chosen outlets all designed to promote the Foster star personality as unambiguously heterosexual.

Thus, following upon her outing, Foster's press campaign was virulent in its efforts to deny the imputation of lesbianism, concentrating in interviews upon her image as a 'regular girl' (Szymanski, 1993: 31), somewhat akin to the promotional re-heterosexualisation of Jason Donovan. This was reflected not so much in the roles Foster played – after all she's an actress and ought to be able to play whatever roles she wishes – as in the publicity and marketing that accompanied the film *Sommersby*.

Fêted as Foster's first romance, *Sommersby* was subject to endless speculation. The film's director, Jon Amiel, in typical pre-release hyperbole, vowed to 'steam up' Foster's image in the wake of her role as the relatively asexual Clarice Starling in *The Silence of the Lambs*, promising that the love scenes between Foster and her co-star Richard Gere would be 'hotter than hell'.[4] As far as audience attendance went, he seems to have succeeded, though, like most of the audience, I suspect, I was more impressed by Foster's impassioned speeches than by her passionate clinches. Still, the marketing angle on *Sommersby* was definitely towards the recuperation of Foster into happy healthy heterosexual femininity. *Woman's Own* magazine's proud trumpeting of the fact that 'in one very intimate scene, Jodie's character is left weeping after experiencing her first orgasm'

(Midwinter, 1993: 6) merely clinches the cultural reification of compulsory heterosexuality.

As demonstration of some of the lows to which the publicity machine will stoop, pre-screen publicity for *Sommersby* was accompanied by such (undignified) innuendo as Richard Gere's alleged inability to make love to his then wife Cindy Crawford, where 'The heart-throb admits the on-screen action killed the passion between him and supermodel Cindy Crawford' (Midwinter, 1993: 6).[5] Of course there are always the odd marketing headaches to sort out. Richard Gere's contention that 'During our love scenes I had to smile. I always thought of Jodie when she was growing up as a tomboy. Her voice is not that feminine. It's strong and definite. And she certainly doesn't look like someone who might need help in a fight' (Kennedy, 1995: 181) is hardly unambiguously flattering to his co-star or to the efforts of her publicity machine. Simultaneously Foster was refusing to fuel speculation by insisting 'Richard and I got along really well and there was no big off-screen relationship to hinder us – we were just friends. Our intimacy was on screen only, and there's nothing sordid about it' (Midwinter, 1993: 6).

That all of this heterosexual posturing did not succeed in quelling the rumours about either Foster or her co-star Richard Gere testifies to the speculation that continues to inform the reception of their films. Here critic Stuart Klawans underwrites his praise of the love scenes between Foster and Gere with an ironic negotiation of the multiple masquerades in play in *Sommersby*:

From Caracas to Tokyo, audiences will sigh and swoon and twitch in their seats as these two big stars go through the charade of hot sex. Never mind that a substantial body of rumour would lead you to doubt any real attraction. These two are troupers, and they deliver, within a surplus ... In *Sommersby* an imposture of a Hollywood film, about a man who's an imposter, you have two actors going through an imposture of arousal, and somehow it seems real. (Klawans, 1993: 316)

Echoing Richard Meyer's account of Rock Hudson, Klawans demonstrates the performance of heterosexuality on screen as a series of impostures, of star with star, of screen fantasy with supposedly lived reality, of text with an audience intent on believing in the authenticity of the screen passion regardless of the rumours (see figure 5). Equally as ironic to the lesbian-invested critic is the way in which homosexual rumour and speculation is felt to deauthenticate the presumably always sham lovemaking between stars on the screen (thus rendering heterosexuality all the more authentic for being acted out by actors who are always already presumed to be heterosexual).[6]

5   Performing sex: Laurel (Jodie Foster) and Jack Sommersby
    (Richard Gere) in *Sommersby*, 1993

Still, where words might encourage ambiguity, image could set the speculators right, and the pre-publicity photographs for *Sommersby* only too obviously seek to relocate Foster within a conventional heterosexual, and feminine, role. Indeed, Foster's publicity stills posed with Gere are a veritable essay in femininity. In one she lies across a chaise longue in a see-through lacy shirt, with her hand on Richard Gere's open-shirted chest. In another publicity still Foster is encased in a gold silk diaphanous cloth held from behind by a fully clothed Gere. Foster is placed in the conventional (that is subservient and vulnerable) feminine role to Gere's protective, and framing, masculinity. The innuendo is clear, this couple's on-screen passion has, or so the marketing executives would have you fantasise, translated into real life. Jodie Foster is back in the fold.

The *Sommersby* campaign was succeeded by numerous pictures of Foster in more lacy shirts, Foster in baby-blue cotton, even Foster as sex kitten on the front of the *Sunday Times Magazine*.[7] Such image-revamping may of course merely reflect a change of fashion consciousness. However, in the light of Foster's then recent outing, it seems hard not to read her compulsory reheterosexualisation as the product of a deep cultural anxiety.

In chapter five I described the meaning and inscription of star photographs, noting the way in which images of stars, rather than securing a singular authentic relation between star and persona, proliferate through a succession of images which both sustain one another in a narrative fiction of authenticity and replace each other in a never-ending bid to reflect the authentic star image. Photographs of Foster inhabit an equally contested space. For years lesbian friends and I have chuckled over Foster's contradictory sartorial statements. My favourite picture from the late 1970s shows the young Foster in tweed jacket and the hunting cap so favoured that she apparently wore it in the bath. The style and pose is classically butch, and the subcultural significations seem self-evident to a viewer tuned to recognise the coding. The image is also of course of Foster as an adolescent and its reproduction should be read in this context (after all, we all dread having photographs from our youth return upon us). It is, however, tempting to invoke this image in the light of two distinct visual codings of Foster in her contemporary imaging.

For in contradistinction to the ultra-feminine Foster of the publicity shoots, is the cultivation of images of Foster 'at rest'. In an interview for *OK!* magazine which is contemporary to the release of *The Silence of the Lambs*, for example, Foster is shown 'at home', shoeless, in brown Armani suit and grandad shirt. Though this of course goes unnoted in the interview (we are after all dealing with *OK!*), the visual coding is again patently, albeit elegantly, butch.

It is tempting to divide these images between the constructed, femme, image of the market and the 'authentic', personal preference of the star interview, though as Richard Dyer (1991) warns, we have to be aware of the way in which star images circulate within a medium of cultivated authenticity. The market is never far behind the image in other words, and usually one step ahead. Nevertheless, it seems clear that the iconography of the Foster star persona remains caught in a certain visual ambivalence. As Terry Brown (1994) describes, this visual ambivalence has been a feature of Foster's reception since childhood: critics have continually skirted around her appearance, avoiding, if possible, the connotation of tomboy or butch. As Brown notes:

What has been said about Jodie Foster publicly from the start of her career has been characterised by a peculiar code. Although reviewers never name it as such, Foster's performances as a child actor are marked by a tomboyish excess, an excess that is safe so long as she is a child ... Reviewers of Foster's performances as a child actor recognized the tomboy but called it something else. One reviewer of *Taxi Driver* [Martin Scorsese, 1976, US] called Foster 'an unusually physical actress,' while a reviewer of *Alice Doesn't Live Here Anymore*

[Martin Scorsese, 1974, US] said 'She looks like a boy and talks like a man.' (Brown, 1994: 232)

The cultural allowance, albeit already circumscribed by the Hollywood publicity machine, given to the child as tomboy is translated into a cultural anxiety at the vision of the young adult who still refuses to conform.[8] Like me, Brown notes the 'revisionist construction' (Brown, 1994: 241, note 2) of Foster by the media, where Foster is quite clearly, and presumably with her cooperation, translated from contentious figure into straight femme. That interviewers are aware of the contradictory configuration of gender in Foster's visual coding (or at least feel the need to make snide allusion to it), is clear from this *Tatler* interview with Foster:

At first glance Jodie Foster may look like a waitress but on closer inspection it is obvious that the crisp white shirt (later to be splattered with grilled salmon) has a beautiful shawl collar and that the trousers fit ms Foster's trim, compact body exquisitely. A classic, understated dresser who would probably die rather than wear anything too girly. Foster is doubtlessly wearing Armani, and his elegant, somewhat androgynous lines suit her. (D'Souza, 1994: 79)

More revealing perhaps about the interviewer (whose bitchiness seems to increase the clearer it seems to her that she and Foster are not going to make it as friends for life!) than about Foster, this description carefully treads the line between Armani androgyny and outright butch. In so doing it flirts with the notion of Foster's sexual orientation as 'open secret', a point I will elaborate below.

So the speculation about Foster continues regardless of the attempts of her publicity machine to represent her as *Absolutely het*. It is a speculation only fuelled, I would argue, by the obsessive return to the subject of her problematic sexual status in interviews. For it is in interviews that the spectre of lesbianism is continually raised if only to be disavowed. As Terry Brown points out, the configuration of Foster's sexual identity as an open secret presents an interesting analogy with the image of director Dorothy Arzner in the work of feminist film historians and others. As Judith Mayne describes in a reading of Arzner's representation by heterosexually identified feminists:

While virtually none of the feminist critics who analyze Arzner's work have discussed lesbianism, a curious syndrome is suggested by the use of 'accompanying illustrations.' The photograph on the covers of the pamphlet edited by Claire Johnston speaks rather literally what is unspoken in the written text, in a teasing kind of way. Johnston's and Cook's essays are reprinted in a recent collection of essays on feminist film theory, not one of which discusses erotic connections between women. Yet on the cover of the book is a photograph of Arzner and Rosalind Russel exchanging a meaningful look with more than a hint of female homoeroticism. One begins to suspect that the simultaneous evocation and dispelling of an erotic bond between women in Arzner's work is a structuring absence in feminist film theory. Like any good symptom it rather obsessively draws attention to itself. (Mayne, 1990: 107)

Indeed, remarks Mayne, this structuring absence operates as something in the nature of a fetish. That a visual comparison was constructed (consciously or not) between Foster and Arzner in the pre-release publicity for *Little Man Tate* (Jodie Foster, 1991, US) is noted by B. Ruby Rich (1991) in her retrospective of Foster's work. Thus she notes, in a publicity still for the film: 'Foster was positioned between the giant shadow figures of motion-picture cameras, the actress now emblematically the director ... in a pose that couldn't help but recall certain Dorothy Arzner poses' (Rich, 1991: 10). Rich, a well-known writer on lesbian films, rather puzzlingly makes the allusion without drawing attention to either Arzner's or Foster's alleged lesbianism. Her reticence proliferates what Brown terms 'an erotics of silence' (Brown, 1994: 237) around Foster's image.

Whatever the conscious or unconscious motivations of Foster's interviewers, it seems clear that the dynamic they set in motion establishes lesbianism as the open secret the spectre of which needs to be continually raised so as to be put to rest but which in its continual resurrection operates in the nature of a fetish, the discursive display of a compulsory heterosexuality that can't stop talking about its other. I do not intend to review the critical mass of Foster publicity here, choosing to isolate a few moments from her contemporary reception only. These are pieces, the Kennedy biography excepted, picked at random. Their very randomness of selection, however, rather makes the case that the media negotiation of the spectre of lesbianism operates as something of a collective obsession.

The most interesting critical strategy is that of over-identification with one's subject so that the very hint of lesbianism becomes a slight against oneself (at the very least implying that one might be tainted by association). We recognise a remarkable example of this in the latest Foster biography, Philippa Kennedy's *Jodie Foster: The Most Powerful Woman in Hollywood*. In a chapter rather unfortunately titled 'Sex and the single Jodie', Kennedy gamely defends her subject against the aspersions cast by those nasty homosexuals at Outpost: 'which has no address or telephone number [for obvious reasons, i.e. they don't want to get sued!] and is condemned by other gay organizations' (Kennedy, 1995: 170). As

Kennedy admits, however, 'The subject of Jodie's sexuality comes up frequently in Hollywood whenever her name is mentioned. People inevitably asked "is she gay?" when they learned I was writing the book' (Kennedy, 1995: 170). Unfortunately for Kennedy her book will remain without a resolution: 'The answer is that nobody knows, although the rumours are strong and won't go away' (Kennedy, 1995: 170). The task for Kennedy then is to negotiate the rumours, which she does by bringing them all up again. Thus she tells the story in which Foster and *The Accused* co-star Kelly McGillis are, first rumoured to be having a relationship, and are then linked in a 'jealous cat fight involving another [female] star' (Kennedy, 1995: 171) from which McGillis is reputed to have surfaced with a black eye. Having raised the spectre of this no doubt vicious rumour (and thereby surprising at least one reader, who had heard a different and far less pernicious version of the story), Kennedy then condemns it to the status of urban myth (somewhat of the order of the Richard Gere and the gerbil rumours). Kennedy is of course right to consign such narratives to the dustbin since they have their roots in a perniciously homophobic and lesbophobic discourse which conflates homosexuality with bestiality and represents lesbians as psychopathic bitches. Kennedy of course, does not consign the stories to the realm of homophobic mythology, but rather implicates those very homosexuals who are traduced by such a tale in its reproduction. Taking as writ *National Enquirer* gossip editor Mike Walker's contention that 'If you listen to the gay community in Hollywood they will tell you that everybody is gay. There is definitely a gay network in Hollywood, although I wouldn't go as far as to say they run the place' (Kennedy, 1995: 172), she implies a queer conspiracy to lesbianise Foster, as it were, by default! Here is expert witness Walker again: 'Jodie Foster does not act like she is gay. She really is a mystery woman. She is probably the most successful star at keeping her private life private' (Kennedy, 1995: 173).

In the face of her tired old clichés, however, Kennedy's protestations are rendered more and more absurd. Here's a classic:

Clearly Jodie Foster has become a fantasy figure to lesbians, and the lesbian commedienne Lea de Laria alluded to that fantasy when she was interviewed in a gay giveaway paper. She was asked by the interviewer if there was anything else she would like to touch on and replied: 'Yes Jodie Foster's vagina.' Mike Walker said: 'It's a kind of yearning among lesbians. You notice that she did not add "and believe me Jodie would love it." Lea De Laria must be fairly plugged into the Hollywood gay network and clearly she does not know if Foster is gay either.' (Kennedy, 1995: 174)

Arguably Kennedy's rhetoric of homosexual contamination is informed by the same homophobic anxiety as demonstrated by *Top Gear*'s Jeremy Clarkson's. The patent misunderstanding of the way in which de Laria's fantasy desire works as a strategy of self-consciously inappropriate appropriation is evident from Kennedy's by now flailing argument. As a biographer of course she's in a tight spot in trying to describe a subject who won't give anything away. Hence she concludes, rather lamely, that 'Whatever people may think, nobody knows for sure which way she swings, if at all. And one thing is certain, Jodie Foster is saying nothing' (Kennedy, 1995: 175).

At other times, it appears as though the lesbian fantasies of the otherwise heterosexually identified interviewer are somehow let loose by the spectre of Foster's own alleged orientation. Here Christa D'Souza fantasises Foster as an academic whose students would all be falling in love with her!

She enunciates her words like a teacher and her conversation is laced with words that are used only on American college campuses: 'reductive', 'valorise' and 'synergise' for example. And in a way it is a miracle Jodie Foster is in Hollywood, and not in the Semiotics department of some Ivy League college teaching some obscure but highly popular course on literary criticism as it applies to contemporary film, with students both male and female falling in love with her left, right and centre. (D'Souza, 1994: 80)

D'Souza expands this idea into something of a recurring fantasy, supplementing her comment with the (rather inappropriate) analogy to a remark made by President Reagan's would-be assassin, John Hinckley: '"From head to toe, every square inch of Jodie is what attracts me," and I know what he meant. If Jodie Foster had been a couple of forms ahead of me at school I would probably have had a crush on her too' (D'Souza, 1994: 79). A really quite bizarre piece, D'Souza's public fantasies certainly draw attention to the way in which the Foster image operates as a site of speculation and contest within the media market.

Naturally, and most cynically, interviewers' fascination with Foster, is engendered quite simply by the desire for a scoop, to be the one that Foster finally comes out to in print. The fact that if they broach the subject too clearly she might just throw them out is of course a peripheral concern and is perhaps part explanation for the proliferating negotiations around her sexual orientation. None the less, over and over again in these pieces lesbianism is both introduced and then laid to rest in a way which leaves it constantly on our minds. (At an earlier point in her article D'Souza describes the 'prurient' interest we have in 'calling Ms Foster's sexuality into question' (D'Souza, 1994: 78) as though sexuality is always heterosexual and lesbianism always situated elsewhere.) It seems clear that, though rendered off-stage and off-centre, lesbianism remains a site of anxiety and fascination which needs constantly to be articulated, if only to be disavowed. Of course, and viewed at its most cynical, all this makes for an excellent marketing ploy and, transposing Mandy Merck for a moment, it would seem that 'if lesbianism hadn't already existed [Foster's interviewers] would have had to invent it' (Merck, 1986: 166).

iii The desiring audience

In the last chapter I noted the way in which the viewer is encouraged to identify heterosexually with the on-screen and extra-filmic construction of the star, even where the subject matter represented is designated 'lesbian'. In both this chapter and the last I have argued that both intra- and extra-filmic discourse is utilised against the non-heterosexually identified viewer, encouraging a compulsory heterosexual identification whatever the scope of subject matter or extra-filmic knowledge about the star or stars performing. What I have also argued, however, is that an extra-filmic discourse may yet operate through the unofficial channels of rumour, gossip and innuendo to inform both the extra- and intra-filmic context of viewing. It is this argument that I now wish to expand through a contextualised reading of a few of the on- and off-screen performances of Jodie Foster.

In chapter five I drew attention to the ways in which, in the context of gossip, stars can be fitted into three historically situated categories of homosexuality. These were the 'known' homosexual, the disavowing homosexual and the desired homosexual. Prior to her outing Jodie Foster would probably (though not unambivalently) be numbered amongst the latter. Her outing and the gossip that accompanies it places her in category two. In not exactly admitting the rumours, but not actually denying them either, she is pushed towards category one. Whatever, as Hollywood's favourite child and as 'persona americana' (Rich, 1991: 7), Foster's outing goes right to the heart of the Hollywood star system.

As I have argued in this chapter, following Terry Brown, there is no essential or tangible truth to the ontology, teleology or epistemology of a subject's sexuality. This chapter does not intend to attempt somehow to establish the truth behind the Foster sexual persona. It is not in fact even interested in Foster the person (whoever she may be), but rather the way in which Foster the star is signified in the covert decisions of agents, marketing executives and the media, the subject of the last section, and in this section the ways in which this star persona is invested in by a desiring audience. The fact that Foster's alleged lesbianism can never be proved, and, I have argued, would remain unsatisfactory even if it were, makes very little difference to an audience that already fosters a lesbian fantasy identification in the star. As I argued in chapter three, filmic fantasy, desire and thus identification lie ultimately with the audience, not the text. It is of course a fantasy investment founded in allusion and marked by a certain sense of grasping at straws. In not having access to the unmediated Jodie Foster, all we, the desiring audience, possess is a series of enigmatic silences supplemented by choreographed promotional answers, and of course the films themselves. It is to these I will now turn, as I examine features of the Foster corpus, moments that become, through the weight of audience investment and/or critical speculation, iconic moments, moments of the hyper-realisation of something 'queer'. Playing the tomboy; designating herself, in the role of Clarice Starling, the 'saviour of women in peril'; failing to save her friend in *Foxes*; playing out lesbian desire in the pre-publicity for *Il Cosotto* (Sergio Citti, 1977, It); or on the screen in *Carny* (Robert Kaylor, 1980, US); exchanging the 'lesbian' look with Nastassja Kinski in a bear suit in *Hotel New Hampshire*; holding Kelly McGillis's hand in *The Accused* – each of these moments, once hyperbolised through the interplay of extra-filmic gossip about Foster's alleged lesbianism, interrupts the exchange of compulsory heterosexuality on screen, and, or so I will argue, in terms of the fantasy investments of the desiring audience at least, off-screen as well. For as Yvonne Tasker argues: 'The moments that are remembered, the images which an audience may take home from the cinematic experience, cannot be summed up within the terms of narrative resolution' (Tasker, 1993: 153).

In this section of the chapter therefore, I want to identify the specifics of a spectatorial pleasure argued to be available to the lesbian-identified viewer. I want to explore how a handful of films, with no obvious lesbian reference points, can be appropriated to a lesbian economy of desire as the direct result of extra-filmic information about its star or stars. This extra-filmic material circulates through such unofficial (and hence unsanctioned – one of its benefits as I argue in chapter five) sources as the tabloid press, but more importantly through subcultural gossip, speculation and rumour. What I suggest is that knowing that a particular actress is rumoured to be lesbian makes possible an appropriation of her films as lesbian texts, regardless of the possibilities the films themselves offer.

As I argued in section ii, there has always been speculation about Foster since her earliest days as a filmic tomboy. Constant media speculation about her low voice and boyish appearance has been supplemented by a pop psychological investigation of her family setup, her strong mother and absent father securing for the media a classic teleology between familial dysfunction and lesbianism. As Ruby Rich describes, Foster's on-screen families are marked by violent absences and strange insufficiencies:

The family is where little girls are made. In Foster's case the family that Hollywood created for her is particularly striking ... In film after film she plays a girl with an absent dad, a missing mom, hated parent or a divorce survivor, or even an orphan ... Whatever the reason, the independence of the Foster character was usually matched by a narrative self-sufficiency. (Rich, 1991: 8)

It is tempting then to read such absences into Foster's own background, particularly where her mother Brandy notes how the absence of the father from the family picture (Foster's father left the family home before she was born) meant that Foster never had to play daddy's little girl: 'Jodie was never a traditional looking little girl ... Maybe it comes from being raised without a father to say, "Turn around and show daddy how pretty you look"' (Miller, 1988: 30). Of course such a teleology is dubious to say the least. It is of relevance here, however, in so far as it informs the media construction of Foster as different.

Read within this discourse of thinly veiled heterosexual anxiety, Foster's choice and articulation of certain parts raise what one might describe as lesbian sensory detectors in her lesbian audience. The Foster heritage – a generation of little tomboys who grew up alongside her – these days translates into a dedicated following of thirty-something wannabes. For these her status as a lesbian icon seems stable. A newspaper advert calls for amateur lesbian film stars, securing attention with the promise 'Have sex with Jodie Foster'.[9] A film commissioned by Channel Four devotes itself to an examination of the status of Foster as lesbian icon. A *Pink Paper* personal: 'Thirty-something seeks k. d. lang or Jodie Foster lookalike, to drink wine, watch sunset and fall in love'. All these seem to confirm Foster's place within a conventional lesbian erotic.[10] So what are the iconic moments of the life lived on screen?

There is only one recorded moment in which Foster is publicly party to a flirtation with lesbianism off-screen. Philippa Kennedy tells of a moment in the pre-publicity for the 1977 film *Il Cosotto* in which Foster's co-star, Sydne Rome, when asked if the two stars would pose for a photograph together, infamously declared: 'Since we're living in a climate of feminism, it's better to photograph two women together – the worst they can say is that we're lesbians' (Kennedy, 1995: 53). The following day's pictures show Foster walking down a street with her arm around Rome, an image which, as Kennedy puts it, 'had [both] their publicists reaching for the smelling salts' (Kennedy, 1995: 53). The fact that Foster remains silent but visually incriminated by this exchange seems salient in the light of what Brown terms the open secret of her sexual imaging.

On screen, however, the imagery screams for appropriation. In conjunction, perhaps, with the dysfunctional family situations played out in many of Foster's screen roles goes a fearless independence. The adolescents Foster plays are always knowing before their time, and none more so than the character of Donna in *Carny*. *Carny* is the story of a travelling fair run by Patch and his friend Frankie. The seventeen-year-old Donna runs away from home and into the arms of Frankie (though, throughout the film she is played off between the two friends in predictable homosocial fashion). What I would term the film's iconic lesbian moment comes, however, towards the middle of the screen-time, when Donna is given work on her friend Greta's 'Pulla Gift' store. Greta is clear about Donna's particular appeal to the punters who visit the stall: 'The girls like you', she says, 'Go for 'em.' We then watch as Donna flirts with two blond femmes, engaging them in distinctly sexual banter: 'Pull a string, win a prize, win your date a prize,' she cries and, turning to the more forward of the two, ' Hi, why don't you give it a little tug. I know you're going to be lucky. Pull a string, take me home ... pull that real hard, there you go. Break my heart. Pull that one it's on me.' The innuendo is blatant, Donna with foot raised on the front of the stall, the physical proximity between her and her interlocutor deliberately reduced by the camera placed low and centre-left. Then Donna turns to the other girl: 'What about your friend?' she says, 'Your friend wanna play? Come on honey, give it a tug'. The hitherto silent friend's reply, 'We'll be in the parking lot', and Donna's acknowledgement, 'O.K.', conclude the exchange.

This scene is structured within the narrative as a financial scam. Donna is, in the words of Patch, 'a good hustler' and indeed at the conclusion of the scene we see her delivering the same words to a male punter. In addition, the scene is intercut with the voyeuristic gaze of Patch, who watches the performance from off-side. But (and it's a big but, but all the same), this moment can still be fantasised by the desiring audience as one of the rare moments that bespeaks Foster's (alleged) lesbianism on-

6   It was the bear suit: Franny (Jodie Foster) and Susie (Nastassja Kinski) in *Hotel New Hampshire*, 1984

screen, a moment that renders visible that which I describe in chapter four as the 'nostalgia for what has never been seen'.

What has never been seen remains just as invisible, hinted at through a gauze veil in fact in Tony Richardson's 1984 film *Hotel New Hampshire*. What *is* seen on screen is, however, the visual exchange of a lesbian look between Franny (Foster) and Susie, the woman who hides inside a bear suit for most of the film. Susie loves Franny and in a moment of rare intensity challenges her with a gaze which lasts almost ten seconds of screen time. This is of course a very long time in filmic terms, particularly as the look between the two women is foregrounded, framed by the camera, while the conversations of the others are merely over-played. It is, needless to say, a powerful, one could even argue iconic, moment, on the screen (see figure 6).

Of course these are only moments, and rare ones at that. The sum of these scenes is merely further food for speculation. Certainly, one cannot *claim* lesbianism from or through them. Also, of course, they are moments which are easily recuperated into the heterotextual resolution – in *Hotel New Hampshire* for example, both Franny and Susie end up married by the end of the film (needless to say, not to each other!). Nevertheless, I would argue that such moments continue to operate within the imaginative scene of the filmic space in order to fuel audience desire and fantasy wish-fulfilment. Certainly speculation about the relation between screen and life was rampant around the on-set and post-filmic reception of *The Accused*, and it is accordingly to this film that I will now turn.

In reviewing my piece on *The Accused*, first written in 1993, for inclusion in the book, I was tempted to drop it altogether. The argument three years on seemed slight, trite, even silly. I seemed, more clearly than ever, to be writing out of my own predilections only, committed to a practice that may have resonated within the darkness of the cinema but which on the page read as weak. Imagine my surprise then when, glancing at a collection I should have read two years before, I came across Barbara Johnson's reading of the film in her short piece 'Lesbian spectacles'. In this essay Johnson seeks to explain her lesbian investment in Nella Larsen's novel *Passing* over Toni Morrison's *Sula*, and *The Accused* over *Thelma and Louise*. Of the latter two she says:

> Thinking back to my initial reactions to the films, I remembered my very strong sense that I experienced *The Accused* as a lesbian plot while *Thelma and Louise* promised one but, for me, failed to deliver. My justifications for these reactions might run as follows: Thelma (Geena Davis) and Louise (Susan Sarandon) hardly ever stop to look at each other – they are either looking straight down the road or Thelma's eyes are wandering towards sexually interesting men and Louise is attempting to keep Thelma's sexual appetite contained ... In *The Accused* on the other hand, from the moment deputy district attorney Kathryn Murphy (Kelly McGillis) picks up rape victim Sarah Tobias (Jodie Foster) in her car ... the two women are intrigued by their differences and cannot leave each other alone ... They fill each other's screen as objects of fascination, ambivalence and transformation. (Johnson, 1993: 162)

Johnson then describes how she subsequently learnt of the rumours of an on-set relationship between the two stars of *The Accused* and speculates on the intertext of rumour to on-screen presence: 'Was this what I was seeing in the electricity between the two actresses? Or was their alleged affair itself an *interpretation* of what was happening on screen?' (Johnson, 1993: 165).

The Accused is a film about the prosecution of the perpetrators (whether by direct action or proxy) of a vicious gang rape.[11] It is also a film about the developing relation of trust between two women, a lawyer and her client. It is a relationship that negotiates the difficulties of class and education divides as well as ideological differences between the two women. A relationship whose filmic dynamics are in many ways conventional,[12] the relationship as it is portrayed on screen is not a lesbian one. I must insist upon this since I want to make clear that I am not arguing for some kind of lesbian continuum whereby women are accredited as lesbian by the very fact of being woman-identified. What I am arguing is that, by virtue only of the extra-filmic information and gossip we are given about its stars, we are able to access desire which is appropriated to a lesbian fantasy. What I want to show is how this extra-filmic gossip, innuendo and speculation can lesbianise the focus of a film like *The Accused* through the lesbianisation of a single scene which can then be used to inform the rest of the text. Thus I will argue that in the closing scenes of the film, and knowing what we think we know about the off-screen relationship of its two stars, we come upon the rarest of chances to fantasise the potential manifestation of actual same-sex desire on screen. The example I want to make comes towards the end of the film. Sarah Tobias (Jodie Foster) and Kathryn Murphy (Kelly McGillis) are left alone together. While they wait Sarah projects Kathryn's horoscope, a trope which has recurred throughout the film. They are seen at the table looking at their futures together, futures very different in their astrological predictions but which are momentarily united in the signature which Sarah confers as gift and thanks for Kathryn's help. The exchange of looks that characterises the shot and its frame of reference constitute an intimate moment between two women who are grateful to each other for what they have learnt, nothing more, nothing less. However, in the exchange, a bond is confirmed. It is a bond cemented by the successful consummation of the case where a look is again exchanged, the camera intercutting from one face to another, first Kathryn's then Sarah's, then back again. Following upon this is the time-lapsed coming together of the traditional narrative resolution, which here culminates in a barely glimpsed hand-clinch.

In making this argument I am well aware of the fact that this scene can be, and is usually, viewed without any lesbian subtext being apparent. All that I am arguing is that the lesbian-identified viewer, as unlicensed party to the look, desires its transposition from its safe context into the exhibition of 'actual' same-sex desire. What we invoke by the force of our desire to believe the gossip about Foster and McGillis is the tantalising possibility that they, the actresses, *are not pretending* (see figure 7).

I am aware that I could be accused of fetishising this moment, of giving it more weight than it deserves. I can only agree – the whole point of this reading is the way in which my desire as a lesbian-identified viewer gives it special significance. However, I would

7   Fantastic desires: Sarah Tobias (Jodie Foster) and Kathryn Murphy (Kelly McGillis) in *The Accused*, 1988

also retort, what moment can we not fetishise in a medium that relies upon the power of the reified sign, rendered even more accessible since the advent of the pause button on the domestic VCR?

Foster is also of course relevant to the concerns of this book in the way that her outing has become central to the debate about positive and negative imaging. Two main effects are desired of outing. Firstly, outing is about 'providing the gay community with role models'.[13] Secondly, it is meant to inform the star of their responsibility to the lesbian and gay community. Whether it performs either of these roles is of course subject to some debate. It does, however, explain why Foster was castigated for her role in *The Silence of the Lambs*. I do not want to get into the pros and cons of the film here, except to note that its director, Jonathan Demme, exhibited a very naive understanding of the way in which cultural stereotypes resonate with a homophobic audience.[14] Foster's own role as the independent Clarice Starling, 'Saviour of women in peril', seems on the other hand, irreproachable. The association is Foster's own and makes (or so we can fantasise!) a covert appeal to her lesbian audience.[15] Foster couches her own interpretation of the role in terms of its rewriting of the conventional narrative progression of the hero towards enlightenment through danger:

> There's a terrible disease in his country. He [the hero figure] has to leave and go into the forest of experience to find this panacea and to slay the dragon. And in the midst he runs into gnomes and demons

along the way and realises that his handicaps are his own failings and once he recognises those failings he finds the dragon, slays the dragon, brings back the panacea. *But* is the great hero, but will never be a citizen of his own country again, will always remain outside ... I wanted to play that hero because she was a woman.[16]

Certainly the role of Clarice Starling is one which tends to promote rather than inhibit identification for the lesbian viewer since it shows a woman who is out on her own, unhampered by ties to men or family. As Diane Hamer notes in correspondence about the film:

> Foster's role in *The Silence of the Lambs* [is] interesting because of the way she [is] not sexualised in the context of any man but is the protagonist who [drives] the narrative forward through the powers of her investigations. It [is] an exciting role and Clarice Starling a thrilling character because she is so unfeminine.[17]

As I see it, however, Clarice is not so much unfeminine as standing in an uneasy relationship to her own femininity. This unease, as Lector observes in his first encounter with Clarice, has as much to do with class as it does with gender. Indeed, it is perhaps in the intersection of the two that her discomfort lies. Here Lector dissects Clarice's past with ruthless precision:

> You know what you look like Starling with your good bag and your cheap shoes? You look like a rube. A well-scrubbed hustling rube with a little taste. Good nutrition's given you some bone, but you're not one generation from poor white trash are you agent Starling? ... You know how quickly the boys found you, all those tedious, sticky fumblings in the back seats of cars while you could only dream of getting out, getting anywhere, getting all the way to the FBI.

Lector's perspicacity is confirmed in Clarice's reply: 'You see a lot Dr Lector'. Of course Clarice is pursued by a number of men throughout the film, from the slimy Dr Chilton to, by implication, Lector himself, and in the denouement by the killer Jame Gumb. All of these men are posed as a threat either to her life or to her career, though in the course of the film she manages to elude them all. Her only meaningful relationship, apart from her encounters with her boss Crawford and her battle of wits with Lector, is with her friend and fellow trainee Ardelia Mapp. In the film the two women are shown working together at crucial stages of the investigation, with Mapp taking over the domestic support role usually reserved in filmic cliché for the sympathetic husband or boyfriend (or more usually, given the predominant maleness of the genre, the sympathetic wife or girlfriend). The film seems unconcerned by this, playing up where necessary the scenes between the friends, though it is never implied that their relationship is anything but innocent. The lack of an obvious romantic interest *is* a site of anxiety in the book, which first assures the reader that Starling is straight and then forges a rather facile relationship between Starling and the entomologist Pilcher. The patent unlikelihood of this event, given the characterisation of Starling up to this point, serves only to encourage disbelief – it is not, for instance, pursued in the film. None of this makes Starling a lesbian of course, but it does make her a character who is never comfortably recuperable to a heterosexual paradigm.[18] Interestingly, Foster's first film as director, *Little Man Tate* continues rather than dissipates this unease, skirting any hint of sexuality in a film where the (virtually compulsory) romantic interest is missing and the only romantic lines are spoken to a seven-year-old-boy (see figure 8).[19] The limitations of the role Foster takes on as Fred's mother do perhaps point to her difficulty in finding a satisfactory sexual niche in Hollywood in the light of her outing and the continuing speculation about her sexual orientation.

Such moments secure a teleology for Foster followers, becoming significant or heightened reflections in the Foster pantheon of characters. In a sense, they operate like other star tokens, photographs and autographs in particular, as contemporary totems that serve to fill the gulf between desire and lack. The associated, albeit specious, fantasy that these films may have meant something to Foster adds to the phantasmatic possibility that is Foster's own lesbian identification. The connections, which I must continue to emphasise are never more than spurious, are rendered all the more enticing where Foster herself argues that the parts she chooses may at times reflect on her self-image. Writes Rachel Abramowitz:

Foster, it seems, often chooses movies as a kind of therapy. 'What I've found is that the greatest terrain for me is to go find out what I am really afraid of, then go play it. I wasn't going to have somebody tell me that I had to only play what was safe, because I wasn't going to get anywhere doing that.' (Abramowitz, 1995: 65)

Her choice of role in *Five Corners* (Tony Bill, 1987, US),[20] *The Accused* and *The Silence of the Lambs*, which follow upon the John Hinckley episode (where Foster was stalked by the man who subsequently shot Ronald Reagan in order to gain her attention), is almost always described in terms of some kind of catharsis. Again a link between art and life is forged: 'it seems obvious in retrospect why Sarah's [Tobias, the figure Foster plays in *The Accused*] fear so quickly turned to anger at being victimized' (Abramowitz,

1995: 65). Here Foster and Tobias become one and the same character, united in their anger at a world which attempts to wrest control from them, the anger from Foster's own experiences being channelled into the events of the character. Her roles, within the teleology plotted by media critics and by Foster herself, become then a reassertion of the control she feels she lost at the time of the Hinckley episode. Thus again, in an interview with *Premiere* she describes Clarice Starling in *The Silence of the Lambs* as the nearest parallel to 'who she is in real life' (Abramowitz, 1995: 95). Hence:

> Clarice Starling is a woman with a mission to 'save the women she's been taught to disrespect. She needed to love them in order to respect them, to not find repulsive their commonness, their fatness, their anonymity. It's examining what she's so goddamned afraid of becoming that finally gives her the answer.' (Abramowitz, 1995 95)

Remarks such as this are a representation of Foster's well-known 'feminism', articulated in interviews and Oscar-acceptance speeches. Her film production company, which is concerned to encourage 'female driven projects' (Szymanski, 1993: 32), continues this vein.

Once more I must emphasise that the temptation to read Foster's films as metaphors of her own development is a strong, though I think nevertheless misplaced, one (just as we can never 'know' a subject's sexuality, so we can never really gain access to the 'real' motivation of the star where this is always mediated through market forces). Perhaps, however, we can fantasise for a while. After all, this is what the medium, in effect, demands. Within a fantasy dynamic, it is hard not to read a subtext into the choices Foster makes in her films. This has been particularly apparent with *Little Man Tate*, a film which is generally seen as a symbolic representation of Foster's own situation as something of a child prodigy. Hence it has been suggested that the story of Fred Tate is in fact semi-autobiographical. Terry Brown, for example, argues that the movie may be read figuratively as: 'a movie about growing up queer' (Brown, 1994: 233). She continues:

> Foster admits that *Little Man Tate* may have a 'biographical parallel' to her own childhood insofar as she was 'different' as a child because she was an actor. But in another sense Foster has projected her tomboy fantasy onto the boy in the movie while playing his tomboy mother, oddly desexualized and childishly playful. (Brown, 1994: 233)

Brown argues that what in fact rematerialises in the film is the tomboy child Foster used to be, rendered safely through 'the body of the eight year old boy in *Little Man Tate*' (Brown, 1994: 233).

8 Mother love: Dede Tate (Jodie Foster) and Fred Tate (Adam Hann-Bryd) in *Little Man Tate*, 1991

Certainly the transposition of Foster into 'queer' (but genius) boy child ('an unconscious reference to her lesbianism?'[21]) is interesting, though no more than speculative. More troubling (at least within the hypersexual conventions of Hollywood) is, as Brown suggests, Foster the director's desexualisation of her role as Dede Tate which, as Ruby Rich notes, 'desexualises Foster the actress just as rigorously, this time in the service of motherhood' (Rich, 1991: 10), as *The Silence of the Lambs* had Foster, the 'saviour of women in peril'.

The subtext returns with a vengeance in publicity around *Nell*, which *Premiere* magazine describes as the 'modern-day fable of a woman discovered living beyond the edge of civilization' (Abramowitz, 1995: 60). This may not mean much to the average reader, but is a recognised metaphor for any lesbian who might be fantasising a connection between her life and the Foster role. Indeed, the story of the wild child Nell, who teaches the world to accept her on her own terms, resonates with a utopian fantasy of self-individuation and sexual and social tolerance. Here the article's writer, Rachel Abramowitz:

Like *Little Man Tate*, *Nell* echoes a theme from Foster's well-chronicled life: the predicament of an innocent with exceptional gift who faces a kind of insidious corruption by well-meaning individuals. Nell succeeds in making the world accept her on her own terms. She doesn't learn English, but the doctors and the audience learn Nellish. (Abramowitz, 1995: 62)

Such textual analogies are further supplemented by Foster's own descriptions of her artistry, links that allow us to fantasise that, like Nell, Foster is looking for a soulmate, for her lost sister in arms. Here's Abramowitz again, describing Foster's conceptualisation of Nell's motivation and desires:

Mostly, she tried to tap into Nell's physicality. Foster worked with a movement teacher for the first time in her life, and devised Nell's curious gesture. It looks like a dance, one meant to be done with another person. But Nell does it alone, breathtakingly, in a kind of poem of loss.

'I said, What if another person were there? What would the gesture become?' She demonstrates 'Please come towards me – bringing them into you'. She's pulling the invisible partner forward. 'And them saying, "Please come back to me," and them pulling you back to them. And everytime I would do this I would cry.'

Foster suddenly seems filled with melancholy. 'I couldn't explain it. There was just something about that gesture that was so moving that I went, if this other person is not there, then I'm going to create them. I'm just going to make them up because it's the only thing that's allowing me to cope.' The thing that Nell is most informed by is that she has loved somebody, without barriers and without hesitation. (Abramowitz, 1995: 64)

This passage, a colloquial restatement of the Lacanian paradigm of romantic love (founded in the fiction of abundance, grounded in lack), is, for this lesbian reader at least, an equally colloquial metaphor for a lesbian love that cannot speak its name. As a fantasy scenario, this passage resonates with the individual's own sense of loss and also as a fantasised connotation of Foster's own possible lack, which can then be displaced by a vision of lesbian plenitude where we, the audience, are the one who can fill that emptiness, take the place of the dream-love, in order to perfect and unite the dance.

iv **Tokens of affection**

In reading in this way, it seems possible to treat the films like other star tokens and memorabilia. Just as committed fans buy autographs and signed photographs,[22] so the invested viewer buys into certain images, storing them up for future reference. As I argued in chapter five, the fact that, in writing about this, I contribute to the fetishisation of Foster the person (who, despite my insistence that she should be seen as separate from Foster the star, continues to be conflated with the latter) is perhaps equally an indictment of the violence of desire which structures the relation between star and fan.

On the other hand, as audiences to the Hollywood spectacle we are positively encouraged to make links between star and role, private life and public persona. Such associations are specifically contrived by the extra-filmic snippets afforded to us by the Hollywood publicity machine and rumour mill.

As I made clear in chapter five, the type of extra-filmic information available to fans and audience is circumscribed. As I also detailed in chapter five, however, rumour and gossip and innuendo form the unofficial subtext to much of the reception of stars, and it is here that lesbian fantasies may be let loose. Silly as they look on the pages of an academic text and inappropriate as they may be as configured against the star persona of Foster, such fantasies are central to the audience's cathection upon the star as desired object. And as I have argued in detailing possible appropriative strategies in chapters three and four, it is in our ability to make inappropriate connections and associations between text and extra-text that we get our own back, albeit in a limited manner, on the Hollywood marketing machine that seeks to define us through a compulsory heterosexuality regardless of the fantasy possibilities of the cinema in general.

Notes

1 *The Late Show Silence of the Lambs Special.* This was screened on BBC2 shortly after the release of the film in Britain. I did not, at the time, keep a reference of the date.

2 In recent interviews she has talked of rearing a child on her own (see Kennedy 1995: 164).

3 Haphazard cataloguer of popular culture that I am, I must confess to being unable to find the reference for this quote.

4 Interview with Amiel in *The Sunday Express*, 23rd August 1992.
5 In her recent biography of Jodie Foster, journalist Philippa Kennedy tells of another marketing attempt to link Foster to English actor Julian Sands: 'Her publicists tried to dream up an affair ... Together, conspicuously holding hands – something that Jodie would only do in public – they appeared at several post-award parties. But Jodie's mother Brandy was with them and nobody was really fooled. Headlines like "Jodie's a winner in love" appeared in newspapers and Jodie and Julian were said to be "inseparable" but it was hardly a romance made in heaven and had more to do with Pat Kingsley's publicity office – her organization, PMK, handles them both' (Kennedy, 1995: 175).
6 Media speculation about Foster's sexuality had quietened down a little by the time of the release of *Maverick* in 1994, though there was the occasional criticism directed at her as (inexplicably) 'unsuitable' (Kauffmann, 1994: 64) for the role. Generally, criticism was focused upon the lightweight character of the film in which Foster's character, Mrs Bransford, 'exists mostly to bicker with Brett [Maverick]' (Schickel, 1994: 60).
7 See *The Sunday Times Magazine*, 18 April 1993. Needless to say, I was unable to get permission to reprint any of these images, the marketing agents retaining as always tight hold on the star image of Foster.
8 Strangely enough, anxiety is as often directed at the depth of Foster's voice as it is at the 'ambivalence' of her look. I have mentioned Richard Gere's characterisation of Foster's voice as not 'that feminine' and Terry Brown's reference to Kathleen Carrol's remark that the child Foster 'Looks like a boy and talks like a man'. Here both the timbre of voice and, presumably, the points made with it, become sites of cultural anxiety. As with the characterisation of Jo Carstairs, multi-millionaire and close friend of Marlene Dietrich, as the 'baritone babe' (Weiss, 1992: 30), a deep voice operates as a contemporary connotation of lesbianism as surely as the physiological categories of Havelock Ellis in the 1920s.
9 Unreferenced newspaper advert left in my departmental pigeon-hole by an anonymous fan, March 1995.
10 Respectively, *Jodie: an Icon*, 1 September 1996, Channel Four and *The Pink Paper*, April 1992.
11 On its release the film was criticised by some for its depiction of a rape scene which, it was argued, played into the hands of the sadistically motivated (assumed to be male) voyeur. While I would agree with this argument, the ethics of filming rape sequences is not my focus in this piece. The ethics of appropriating to a lesbian fantasy erotic a film which treats the subject of rape does, however, continue to worry me.
12 In the sense that the film negotiates familiar dynamics of trust/mistrust, antagonism/support, crisis and resolution.
13 Gabriel Rotello quoted in Heller (1991: 13).
14 For an account of the various debates, both for and against, that proliferated around the film at its time of release, see Kennedy (1991: 49, 56). For an account of the outing of Foster as symbolic sacrifice, see Staiger (1993: 142–54).
15 'For me there was a personal issue which is, I wanted to play a woman who in some ways is probably the closest character to myself. You wouldn't think so, right, because she's so, West Virginian, but so close to me, somebody who for whatever reason in her character, even though it may be foolish, has a mission, and that is to save women and the women that she has to save are the women that rep-

resent a side of herself that she's afraid of; women who are too small, or too fat or too marginalised or not good enough or strong enough, or not important enough. And that's a hard fact for her to recognise, that they're as much a part of her as any other diploma that she may now have, that she has been too small and that that in fact is why her responsibility as a character ... is to save women and give them a voice, women who don't have a voice' (Foster, *The South Bank Show*, ITV, 12 March 1995). The film consolidates an earlier Foster role, that of Jeanie in *Foxes*. In this film, too, Foster is placed in the position of saviour of women in peril, though this time she fails to save her best friend, a hard-living teenager who ends up dead in a freak car accident by the end of the film. The film was, in the words of the then fifteen-year-old Foster: 'more me than any of the other films I've done' (Falk, 1991: 11).

16 Jodie Foster, *The South Bank Show*.
17 Diane Hamer, personal correspondence.
18 This argument is pursued to its logical (in)conclusion by David Sundelman, who, in an ironic counterpoint to Foster's own tracing of Starling's journey from self-hatred to self-perception, reads the narrative as inhibitive of Starling's sexual development (which, it should be noted, he figures through the trope of maternity, that is, of the film concluding with Starling being given a 'human lamb of her own to cradle' (Sundelman, 1993: 16). Hence, he argues: 'Except for the errant semen, Demme keeps sex away from his heroine; Starling seems like a cross between Little Red Ridinghood and Joan of Arc' (Sundelman, 1993: 16). Accordingly, for Sundelman, Starling, though ending the film as a hero, becomes 'both less and more than a woman' (Sundelman, 1993: 16). I would argue that it is the film's very lack of a compulsory heterosexual resolution which engenders the potential for lesbian appropriations of the film's heroine Starling.
19 In talking about her role, Foster describes Fred Tate, Dede's son, as 'the love of her life' (Foster, *The South Bank Show*). In interviews, of course, Foster often remarks upon the closeness of the bond established between the child of a single mother; hence her remark might just as well be read in this light.
20 In this she is pursued by an obsessive ex-boyfriend.
21 Hamer, personal correspondence.
22 Foster's autograph currently sells for about $130, currently beaten only by Madonna.

Afterword: The persistence of the specular

i Looking lesbian

The desire to see is a manifestation of the desire to be seen. (Phelan, 1993: 18)

Conventionally, the scopophilic relation which matches sight with sexual pleasure functions exclusively within the masculine line of vision. Looking belongs to men. Throughout this book I have argued, along with others, that looking, the right to look, to interpret that look, and, if one wishes, to employ that look to facilitate visual pleasure, can also be appropriated as a subcultural strategy that I have sought here to mark as lesbian.

This lesbian look is not always obvious in its directions. Its scope cannot be predicted upfront. Nor is it always directed at lesbians, conscious of its lesbianism, nor, indeed, need it always be articulated by lesbians alone. As Peggy Phelan notes, however, to see is manifested in the desire to be seen, and to 'look' lesbian secures a foothold for lesbians within a medium (the cinema) which has been characterised for us largely by absence, misrepresentation, lack. As an appropriative strategy, this look has been figured as one of visual abundance. This lesbian look has also been accompanied by a number of points of anxiety within the book.

There are in fact four main sites of anxiety in this book (anxieties which I hope will be read as productive rather than merely defensive). First, my fear that my argument for a lesbian nostalgia for abjection may be written out of a position of privilege which might resonate uncomfortably with cinemagoers who find their identities more visibly imperilled by dominant strategies of representation. That is, it is fine for me as a relatively well-heeled white, middle-class, academic, working in a job where I can confidently be out, to respond to the cult of abjection with glee, but it's a different story for the lesbian for whom such representations serve as a reminder of an only too well known reality. I believe this anxiety can be countered with a number of responses, amongst which are my trust in the imaginative possibilities of fantasy, my belief in the appropriative potential of translating the negative into the positive, and, finally, my conviction that most lesbian reception goes beyond an appropriation of the self-evidently positive anyway. It is then an anxiety accompanied by a confidence that I am not alone in my perverse readings of the abject.

The issue of whom my abject identifications and desires might unwittingly exclude is more serious and secures my second site of anxiety. As I observed in chapter one, Hollywood cinema works to erase, colonise and recuperate racial as well as sexual others. Appropriative strategies that are alive to a sexual context may not be as aware of a racial context. My fear is that, in testifying to the appropriative possibilities of the mainstream cinema, I have merely played into its dominant strategies. Indeed, coming to the end of this book, I worry that I have achieved little beyond noting the relative absence of a situated racial account from the mainstream Hollywood scene, an absence which is reflected in my own appropriative strategies, thus consolidating this absence. To be sure in the book I have attempted to testify to this absence as a species of exclusion and/or colonisation, noting the fetishisation of whiteness even within the non-white. More positively, I have given space to the appropriative possibilities theorised by researchers such as Jacqueline Bobo. Still, I worry that the very predictability of my own attempts to look lesbian perpetuate, whilst they seek to investigate, the colour-blindness of the Hollywood scene. To recall Friedberg: 'Identification can only be made through recognition, and all recognition is itself an implicit confirmation of an existing form' (Friedberg, 1982: 53). Though not, I hope I have begun to show, all-defining Friedberg's point certainly informs the appropriative possibilities articulated here.

Recalling my argument from chapter one, I do believe that it is easier to construct a white lesbian out of mainstream Hollywood images than a non-white woman of whatever orientation. This is not to argue that race is always configured on the plane of the visible. To recall Walker's point in chapter three, not all subjects who disidentify as white are visible as such. Nor, recalling the argument for appropriation in chapter four, am I arguing that significations of non-whiteness operate less effectively than signifiers of lesbianism. As Bobo makes clear, her black American respondents constantly read between the lines of the Hollywood master-text, and, as Michele Wallace argues, the black American women she attended the cinema with were more than capable of appropriating the white female stars of the Hollywood mainstream to a multi-racial context. Even so, I would argue, following Lynda Hart, that white 'lesbianism' is rendered constantly, albeit covertly, within the Hollywood mainstream in a way in which race is not, a fact which facilitates its appropriation by a desiring audience.

A third site of anxiety accumulates around what could be argued to be my hypostatisation of lesbian sexuality at the expense of other elements: class, race, nationality, age amongst others. Certainly the foregrounding of lesbian desire as a strategy for reading in this book can be argued to operate as something in the nature of a fetish. As I argued in chapter one, this is in part because the tendency of fantasy is to elide difference in the pursuit of sameness. Hence, whilst gender, race, class and other power inequalities do inform the type of appropriation secured, desire, when it does not proliferate upon these structural distinctions, will tend to elide the tensions between them in the pursuit of narrative coherence. That desire is always marked by what I have termed, following Spivak, a self-consolidation of the other remains a feature of the appropriative strategies I have described in this book. What this means is that such appropriations are always, to some extent or other, complicit with the dominant regimes from which they steal.

Looking back over my arguments, this seems a highly pessimistic, even conservative, conclusion to reach. Certainly it implies a view of culture founded upon a certain degree of stasis. Its alternative, to read into cinematic appropriations a subversiveness that I do not believe they hold, except perhaps for a short and situated moment, seems, however, merely naive.

The fourth site of anxiety is related to sight itself, namely the pre-eminence given to the look in my arguments. Is the look so crucial even in a medium which, like the cinema, seems to be structured around it? My answer is of course yes. Nevertheless it is accompanied by a sense that we are therefore constrained, within the specular imperative, to a desire which is predicated upon, mediated by and ultimately delimited within, the reified power of the image.

When lesbians begin to look and look lesbian, what is the

nature of this look? Do I, in appropriating the scopophilic function to my own desires, merely begin to look 'as a man'? For Mandy Merck (1993) the gaze is by definition voyeuristic: we are all then implicated in its objectifying purview. Sight is not then innocent, but how guilty is it? For Donna Haraway the universalising vision of the dominant is more than guilty where she observes 'The eyes have been used to signify a perverse capacity – honed to perfection in the history of science tied to militarism, capitalism, colonialism, and male supremacy – to distance the knowing subject from everybody and everything in the interests of unfettered power' (Haraway, 1991: 188). As a result, sight, vision has become 'a much maligned sensory system in feminist discourse' (Haraway, 1991: 188). Vision need not be implicated within these paralysing, domineering discourses by definition, however, since a partial or particularised vision can be a strategy for seeing in itself. In an oft-quoted passage Haraway observes:

I would like to suggest how our insisting metaphorically on the particularity and embodiment of vision ... allows us to construct a usable, but not an innocent, doctrine of objectivity. I want a feminist writing of the body that metaphorically emphasizes vision again, because we need to reclaim that sense to find our way through all the visualizing tricks and powers of modern sciences and technologies that have transformed the objectivity debates. (Haraway, 1991: 189–90)

Objectivity here becomes not the universalising will-to-knowledge that believes it can see it all, but the situated knowledge, the vision aware of its context and time and place, a vision which seeks to situate these elements within its conclusions:

The moral is simple: only partial perspective promises objective vision. This is an objective vision that initiates, rather than closes off, the problem of responsibility for the generativity of all visual practices. Partial perspective can be held accountable for both its promising and its destructive monsters ... In this way we might become answerable for what we learn how to see. (Haraway, 1991: 190)

How situated is my lesbian look? Certainly it is not unaware of its particularising vision, but does this render it innocent? I suspect not. Still I believe that it is finally no more guilty than the holistic point of view which argues that the voyeuring, the particularising, gaze is the objectifying gaze. To seek 'the whole person' is as limiting as the masculine search for the universal, since the pursuit of wholeness, like the pursuit of universality, is equally objectifying. Vision is by definition particularising. Seeing is rather a series of unfoldings. Better to be honest about one's guilty pleasures then.

In one sense I have argued that, where lesbians appropriate the scopophilic gaze, they do so not as a guarantee of masculinity but as a way of legislating a look which otherwise would remain censored from the line of vision. The possibility that looking lesbian is neither radical nor subversive but merely banal is an ongoing one. In that it is framed within the endless pursuit of desire and lack which structures both the Lacanian and pornographic scenes, I suggest that, as a strategy, looking lesbian is not without its ironies.

ii **Persistent desires and pleasurable frustrations**

I've been thrilled and deeply stirred by love pictures and love scenes. Usually when I see them, it seems that I'm the looker on and one of the lovers at the same time. I don't know how to describe it. (Quoted in Weiss, 1992: 26)

In this book I have focused on the act of reading as a lesbian, provisionally assuming that such a position is possible, but being quick to point out resistances to any attempt to delimit this act of reading to one thing over another. My argument has been that identification and desire need not be limited to certain film texts or characters designated 'positively lesbian' but is rather multiple and contradictory. It can colonise films with no obvious lesbian credentials and appropriate them to its own agenda. It can embrace good characters and bad characters where such distinctions no longer hold a self-evident meaning. It is not confined to gender. It may in fact find its expression focused on the inappropriate object of the male body (be this identified as homosexual or heterosexual). Nor can viewership, by implication, be confined to sexual identity, neither for lesbians nor for any other sexual constituency.

As the ultimate extension of my argument then, looking lesbian is not necessarily confined to lesbians. That a similarly chameleon understanding of identification and desire might also read for a heterosexually identified spectator remains an implicit possibility. This is not to say that the outcomes or implications of such a look are the same. Of course I am not talking here of the kind of heterosexual tourism which is familiar to us as a trope of, say, male heterosexual pornography (in which the representation of lesbianism is predicated upon the visual pleasure of men, which is not to say lesbian spectators cannot or do not find enjoyment in these images), but as a desire which pushes voyeurism out of its normative heterosexual focus and into a deviant and unhabitual same-sex relation. How this might disturb female heterosexual desire, pushing it out of a socially validated narcissism (the desire to be like) and into a same-sex erotic othering, remains the subject of another book.

On the one hand then I demonstrate how sexual identity is a factor in the motivation of cinematic desire while on the other I am arguing that expressions of desire are not confined to bespoken sexual identity. Although my argument shows how we can employ lesbian-invested desire as a positive strategy, it also suggests that we never have to delimit our desire to this, thereby upsetting the notion of a coherent sexual identity. Having made this point I want to emphasise that I am not arguing for a conceptualisation of identity as an endless utopian slippage. Identities are always situated. At the same time, identities are always subject to transformation and reformulation in the light of the impulses they receive. Within the narrative space of the cinema identities can be provoked, disturbed, resituated. This is part of the pleasure of recognition and surprise with which we engage with the filmic text.

No film text belongs to any one constituency. It seems as foolish to argue that any text is intrinsically lesbian as to argue that any text is intrinsically heterosexual, for this would deny the multiple possibilities of interpretation and appropriation that I as a lesbian rely upon in my reception of the films I see. Of course, as lesbians we will never agree on just which representations confirm our image of ourselves as good. However, as I hope I have begun to demonstrate here, as a lesbian reading against the grain of the hetero-textual, I have many potential viewing pleasures open to me. Why then delimit identification and desire to the positively representational? As B. Ruby Rich adjures, confronting the ideology of positive images head on: 'claim the heroes, claim the villains and don't mistake any of it for realness' (Rich, 1992: 44). The chief danger I see in the positive images debate is the temptation to confine lesbian representation to a single mode of spectatorial pleasure. The danger in this is that it becomes a profoundly isolationist strategy within a viewing world where we still have the chance to call everything our own. That this everything includes images that have formerly been argued to misrepresent lesbians is an intrinsic feature of an appropriative reading that seeks to turn the negative into a discourse of visual abundance. For, as I argued in chapter four, 'Invisibility, erasure, repression' (Weiss, 1992: 52) are as much the foundational features of my cinema as the discourse of positive imagery promoted elsewhere.

Bibliography

Abramowitz, R. (1995), Fearless, *Premiere*, January, 58–65.
Adorno, T. [1963] (1991), *The Culture Industry: Selected Essays on Mass Culture*, J. M. Bernstein (ed.), London: Routledge.
Allen, L. (1995), *Salmonberries*, consuming k d lang, in T. Wilton (ed.), *Immortal/Invisible: Lesbians and the Moving Image*, London: Routledge, 70–84.
Ardill, S. and O'Sullivan, S. (1995), Sex in the summer of '88, in T. Wilton (ed.), *Immortal/Invisible: Lesbians and the Moving Image*, London: Routledge, 85–91.
Barale, M. (1991), Below the belt: (un)covering *The Well of Loneliness*, in D. Fuss (ed.), *Inside/Out: Lesbian Theories, Gay Theories*, London: Routledge, 235–57.
Benjamin, W. [1936] (1970), *Illuminations*, London: Fontana.
Bernheimer, C. (ed.), (1985), *In Dora's Case: Freud, Hysteria, Feminism*, London: Virago.
Bevan, R. (1992), Psycho killer faggots?, *The Pink Paper*, 3 May, 13.
Bobo, J. (1995), *Black Women as Cultural Readers*, New York: Columbia University Press.
— (1991), Images of black people in the cinema, in A. Kuhn (ed.), *Women and Film: An International Guide*, New York: Ballantine Books, 43–6, 110–11, 332–3.
— (1993), Reading through the text: the black woman as audience, in M. Diawara (ed.), *Black American Cinema*, London: Routledge, 272–87.
Bogle, D. (1988), *Blacks in Film and Television: An Encyclopedia*, New York: Garland Publications.
— (1980), *Brown Sugar: Eight Years of America's Black Female Superstars*, New York: Harmony Books.
Bordwell, D. Staiger, J. and Thompson, K. (1985), *The Classical Hollywood Cinema: Film Style and Mode of Production to 1960*, London: Routledge.

Bordwell, D. and Thompson, K. (1993), *Film Art: An Introduction*, London: McGraw-Hill Inc.

Brennan, T. (1990), *Between Feminism and Psychoanalysis*, London: Routledge.

Bright, D. (1991), Dream girls, in T. Boffin and J. Fraser (eds), *Stolen Glances: Lesbians Take Photographs*, London: Pandora, 144–54.

Britton, A. (1978), For interpretation: notes against camp, *Gay Left*, 7, 8–16.

Bronfen, E. (1992), *Over Her Dead Body: Death, Femininity and the Aesthetic*, Manchester: Manchester University Press.

Brown, J. (1992), Sex, lies and penetration: a butch finally 'fesses up, in J. Nestle (ed.), *The Persistent Desire: A Femme–Butch Reader*, Boston: Alyson, 410–15.

Brown, T. (1994), The butch femme fatale, in L. Doan (ed.), *The Lesbian Postmodern*, New York: Columbia University Press, 229–43.

Budge, B. and Hamer, D. (eds) (1994), *The Good, the Bad and the Gorgeous: Popular Culture's Romance with Lesbianism*, London: Pandora.

Butler, J. (1993), *Bodies That Matter: On the Discursive Limits of Sex*, London: Routledge.

— (1990), *Gender Trouble: Feminism and the Subversion of Identity*, London: Routledge.

— (1991), Imitation and gender insubordination, in D. Fuss (ed.), *Inside/Out: Lesbian Theories, Gay Theories*, London: Routledge, 13–31.

— (1992) The lesbian phallus and the morphological imaginary, *Differences: A Journal of Feminist Cultural Studies*, 4:1, 133–71.

Byars, J. (1991), *All That Hollywood Allows: Re-reading Gender in 1950s Melodrama*, London: Routledge.

Calhoun, C. (1995), The gender closet: lesbian disappearance under the sign 'women', *Feminist Studies*, 21:1, 7–34.

Califia, P. (1988), *Macho Sluts*, Boston: Alyson.

— (1994), *Public Sex: The Culture of Radical Sex*, San Francisco, Cleis Press Inc.

Campbell, B. (1995), Kiss 'n' kill, *Diva*, August, 54–5.

Caprio, F. (1953), *Female Homosexuality*, New York: Grove.

Case, S.-E. (1988–9), Towards a butch–femme aesthetic, *Discourse: Journal for Theoretical Studies in Media and Culture*, 11:1, 55–73.

(1992), Tracking the vampire, *Differences: A Journal of Feminist Cultural Studies*, 3:2, 1–20.

Chomsky, N. (1989), *Necessary Illusions: Thought Control in Democratic Societies*, Boston: South End Press.

Chomsky, N. and Herman, E. S. (1988), *Manufacturing Consent: The Political Economy of the Mass Media*, New York: Random House.

Cixous, H. and Clément, C. (1986), *The Newly Born Woman*, tr. B. Wing, Manchester: Manchester University Press.

Clark, D. (1991), Commodity lesbianism, *Camera Obscura*, 25:7, 181–201.

Clover, C. (1992), *Men, Women and Chain Saws: Gender in the Modern Horror Film*, London: British Film Institute.

Coombe, R. J.(1992a), Author/izing the celebrity: publicity rights, postmodern politics, and unauthorized genders, *Carodza Arts and Entertainment Law Journal*, 10, 365–95.

— (1992b), Publicity rights and political aspiration: mass culture, gender identity, and democracy, *New England Law Review*, 26, 1221–80.

— (1993), Tactics of appropriation and the politics of recognition in late modern democracies, *Political Theory*, 21:3, 411–33.

Cowie, E. (1984), Fantasia, *M/F*, 9, 70–105.

Creed, B. (1995), Lesbian bodies: tribades, tomboys and tarts, in E. Grosz and E. Probyn (eds), *Sexy Bodies: The Strange Carnalities of Feminism*, London: Routledge, 86–103.

— (1993), *The Monstrous-Feminine: Film, Feminism, Psychoanalysis*, London: Routledge.

Cripps, T. (1977), *Slow Fade to Black*, Oxford: Oxford University Press.

Cucchiari, S. (1981), The origins of gender hierarchy, in S. B. Ortner and H. Whitehead (eds), *Sexual Meanings: The Cultural Construction of Gender and Sexuality*, Cambridge, Cambridge University Press, 31–79.

Davis, M. and Kennedy, E. L. (1993), *Boots of Leather, Slippers of Gold: The History of a Lesbian Community*, London: Routledge.

De Lauretis, T. (1990), Guerilla in the midst: women's cinema in the '80's, *Screen*, 31:1, 6–25.

— (1994), *The Practice of Love: Lesbian Sexuality and Perverse Desire*, Bloomington: Indiana University Press.

Deleuze, G. (1971), *Masochism: An Interpretation of Coldness and Cruelty*, New York: G. Braziller.

Doane, M. (1987), *The Desire to Desire: The Woman's Film of the 1940s*, London: Macmillan.

— (1980), Misrecognition and identity, *Cine-Tracts*, 11, 25–32.

Doty, A. (1993), *Making Things Perfectly Queer*, Minneapolis: University of Minnesota Press.

D'Souza, C. (1994), The prime of Miss Jodie Foster, *Tatler*, 289:7, 76–81.

Dunne, S. (1990), Voyages of the Valkyries: recent lesbian pornographic writing, *Feminist Review*, 34, 161–70.

Dyer, R. (1990), *Now You See It: Studies on Lesbian and Gay Film*, London: Routledge.

— (1991), *A Star is Born* and the construction of authenticity, in C. Gledhill (ed.), *Stardom: Industry of Desire*, London: Routledge, 132–40.

— (1988), White, *Screen*, 29:4, 44–64.

Ellis, H. (1925), *Studies in the Psychology of Sex, Volume II: Sexual Inversion*, Philadelphia: F. A. Davis Company.

Ellsworth, E. (1986), Illicit pleasures: feminist spectatorship and *Personal Best*, *Wide Angle*, 8:2, 45–56.

Faderman, L. (1985), *Surpassing the Love of Men: Romantic Friendship and Love Between Women from the Renaissance to the Present*, London: The Women's Press.

Falk, Q. (1991), Aiming for the top, *Flicks*, June, 11.

Faludi, S. (1992), *Backlash: The Undeclared War on Women*, London: Vintage.

Fanon, F. (1986), *Black Skin/White Masks*, tr. C. L. Markmann, London: Pluto.

Feinberg, L. (1992), Butch to butch: a love song, in J. Nestle (ed.), *The*

Persistent Desire: A Femme–Butch Reader, Boston: Alyson, 81–94.
— (1993), *Stone Butch Blues*, New York: Firebrand.
Feuer, J. (1989), Reading *Dynasty*: Television and reception theory, *South Atlantic Quarterly*, 88:2, 443–60.
Fiske, J. (1988), Critical responses and meaningful moments, *Critical Studies in Mass Communication*, 5, 246–51.
— (1992), The cultural economy of fandom, in L. Lewis (ed.), *The Adoring Audience: Fan Culture and Popular Media*, London: Routledge, 30–49.
— (1989), Moments of television: neither the text nor the audience, in H. Borchers, G. Kreutzner, E.-M. Warth and E. Seiter (eds), *Remote Control: Television, Audiences and Cultural Power*, London: Routledge, 56–78.
— (1989), *Understanding Popular Culture*, London: Unwin Hyman.
Florence, P. (1995), Portrait of a production, in T. Wilton (ed.), *Immortal/Invisible: Lesbians and the Moving Image*, London: Routledge, 115–30.
Forrester, J. (1991), Psychoanalysis: telepathy, gossip and/or science?, in J. Donald (ed.), *Psychoanalysis and Cultural Theory: Thresholds*, London: Macmillan, 169–87.
Foucault, M. (1979), *The History of Sexuality: An Introduction*, tr. R. Hurley, London: Random House Inc.
Freud, S. (1905), Fragment of an analysis of a case of hysteria, *The Standard Edition*, 7, tr. J. Strachey, London: The Hogarth Press, 125–245.
— (1914), On narcissism: an introduction, *The Standard Edition*, 11, tr. J. Strachey, London: The Hogarth Press, 67–114.
— (1923/4), Some psychical consequences of the anatomical distinction between the sexes, *The Standard Edition*, 7, tr. J. Strachey, London: The Hogarth Press, 243–58.
Friedberg, A. (1982), Identification and the star: a refusal of difference, *Star Signs: Papers From a Weekend Workshop*, London: British Film Institute, 42–56.
Frye, M. (1983), *The Politics of Reality*, New York: The Crossing Press.
Fuchs, C. (1993), The buddy politic, in S. Cohan and I. R. Hark (eds), *Screening the Male: Exploring Masculinities in Hollywood Cinema*, London: Routledge, 194–214.
Gaines, J. (1988), White privilege and looking relations: race and gender in feminist film theory, *Screen*, 29:4, 12–26.
Gallop, J. (1982), *Feminism and Psychoanalysis: The Daughter's Seduction*, London: Macmillan.
Gledhill, C. (ed.) (1991), *Stardom: industry of Desire*, London: Routledge.
Golding, S. (1991), James Dean: the almost-perfect lesbian hermaphrodite, in T. Boffin and J. Fraser (eds), *Stolen Glances: Lesbians Take Photographs*, London: Pandora, 197–202.
Graham, P. (1994), Looking lesbian: amazons and aliens in science fiction cinema, in B. Budge and D. Hamer (eds), *The Good, the Bad and the Gorgeous: Popular Culture's Romance With Lesbianism*, London: Pandora, 197–217.
Gripsrud, J. (1995), *The Dynasty Years: Hollywood Television and Critical Media Studies*, London: Routledge.

Grosz, E. (1991), Lesbian fetishism?, *Differences: A Journal of Feminist Cultural Studies*, 3:2, 39–54.

— (1995), *Space, Time, and Perversion*, London: Routledge.

Hansen, M. (1991), Pleasure, ambivalence, identification: Valentino and female spectatorship, in C. Gledhill (ed.), *Stardom: Industry of Desire*, London: Routledge, 259–82.

Hanson, E. (1991), Undead, in D. Fuss (ed.), *Inside/Out: Lesbian Theories, Gay Theories*, London: Routledge, 324–40.

Haraway, D. (1991), *Simians, Cyborgs and Women: The Reinvention of Nature*, London: Free Association Books.

Harris, T. [1957] (1991) The building of popular images: Grace Kelly and Marilyn Monroe, in C. Gledhill (ed.), *Stardom: Industry of Desire*, London: Routledge, 40–4.

Hart, L. (1994), *Fatal Women: Lesbian Sexuality and the Mark of Aggression*, London: Routledge.

Heller, Z. (1991), Outed, *The Independent on Sunday*, 16 June, 12–13.

Hollibaugh, A., Davis, M. and Nestle, J. (1992), The femme tapes, in J. Nestle (ed.), *The Persistent Desire: A Femme–Butch Reader*, Boston: Alyson, 254–67.

Holmlund, C. (1991), When is a lesbian not a lesbian?: the lesbian continuum and the mainstream femme film, *Camera Obscura*, 25/6, 144–178.

hooks, b. (1992), *Black Looks: Race and Representation*, Boston: Southend Press.

— (1993), The oppositional gaze, in M. Diawara (ed.), *Black American Cinema*, London: Routledge, 288–302.

Irigaray, L. (1985a), *Speculum of the Other Woman*, tr. G. Gill, Ithaca: Cornell University Press.

— (1985b), *This Sex Which is Not One*, tr. C. Porter, Ithaca: Cornell University Press.

Ishtar, A. (1992), Femme–dyke, in J. Nestle (ed.), *The Persistent Desire: A Femme–Butch Reader*, Boston: Alyson, 378–383.

Jeffreys, S. (1986), S/M: the erotic cult of fascism, *Lesbian Ethics*, 2:1, 65–82.

Jennings, R. (1995), Desire and design: Ripley undressed, in T. Wilton (ed.), *Immortal/Invisible: Lesbians and the Moving Image*, London: Routledge, 193–206.

Jenson, J. (1992), Fandom as pathology: the consequences of characterization, in L. Lewis (ed.), *The Adoring Audience: Fan Culture and Popular Media*, London: Routledge, 9–29.

Johnson, B. (1993), Lesbian spectacles: reading *Sula, Passing, Thelma and Louise* and *The Accused*, in R. Garber, J. Matlock and R. L. Walkowitz (eds), *Media Spectacles*, London: Routledge, 60–6.

Johnson, M. (1992), Butchy–femme, in J. Nestle (ed.), *The Persistent Desire: A Femme–Butch Reader*, Boston: Alyson, 395–98.

Kaplan, E. A. (1984), Is the gaze male?, in A. Snitow (ed.), *Powers of Desire: The Politics of Sexuality*, London: Virago, 321–37.

Kauffmann, S. (1994) Review of *Maverick*, *Newsweek*, 123:22, 64.

Kennedy, L. (1991), Writers on the *Lamb*, *The Village Voice*, 5 March, 49, 56.

Kennedy, P. (1995), *Jodie Foster: The Most Powerful Woman in Hollywood*, London: Macmillan.

Klawans, S. (1993), Motion pictures – reviews, *The Nation*, 256:9, 316–19.

Kristeva, J. (1982), *The Powers of Horror: An Essay in Abjection*, tr. L. S. Roudiez, New York: Columbia University Press.

Kuhn, A. (1988), *Cinema, Censorship and Sexuality 1909–25*, London: Routledge.

Lacan, J. (1977), *Ecrits: A Selection*, tr. A. Sheridan, New York: W. W. Norton.

— (1982), *Feminine Sexuality: Jacques Lacan and the école freudienne*, J. Mitchell and J. Rose (eds), tr. J. Rose, London: Macmillan.

— (1978), *Four Fundamental Concepts of Psycho-Analysis*, tr. A. Sheridan, New York: W. W. Norton.

Lamos, C. (1994), The postmodern lesbian position: *On Our Backs*, in L. Doan (ed.), *The Lesbian Postmodern*, New York: Columbia University Press, 85–103.

Laplanche, J. and Pontalis, J.-B. (1983), *The Language of Psycho-Analysis*, London: The Hogarth Press.

Lapsley, R. and Westlake, M. (1992), From *Casablanca* to *Pretty Woman*: the politics of romance, *Screen*, 33:1, 27–49.

Linden, R., Pagano, D., Russel, D. and Leigh Star, S. (eds), (1982), *Against Sadomasochism: A Radical Feminist Analysis*, San Francisco: Frog in the Well.

Mayne, J. (1993), *Cinema and Spectatorship*, London: Routledge.

— (1990), *The Woman at the Keyhole: Feminism and Women's Cinema*, Bloomington: Indiana University Press.

McClellan, J. (1992), Psycho drama, *The Face*, May, 89–92.

Memmi, A. (1965), *The Colonizer and the Colonized*, tr. H. Gee, New York: Orion.

Mercer, K. (1991), Skin head sex thing: racial difference and the homoerotic imaginary, in Bad Object-choices (eds), *How Do I Look? Queer Film and Video*, Seattle: Bay Press, 169–222.

Merck, M. (1993), *Desert Hearts*, in M. Gever, J. Greyson and P. Parmar (eds), *Queer Looks: Perspectives on Lesbian and Gay Film and Video*, London: Routledge, 377–82.

— [1984] (1986), *Lianna* and the lesbians of art cinema, in C. Brunsden (ed.), *Films For Women*, London: British Film Institute, 166–75.

Meyer, R. (1991), Rock Hudson's body, in D. Fuss (ed.), *Inside/Out: Lesbian Theories, Gay Theories*, London: Routledge, 259–88.

Meyer-Spacks, P. (1985), *Gossip*, New York: Alfred Knopf.

Midwinter, J. (1993), Love scenes with Jodie left me too tired for sex, *Woman's Own*, 26 April, 6–7.

Miller, D. A. (1991), Anal *Rope*, in D. Fuss (ed.), *Inside/Out: Lesbian Theories, Gay Theories*, London: Routledge, 119–41.

Miller, L. (1988), Victor of circumstances, *American Film*, 14:1, 26–31.

Minh-ha, T. (1986/7), Introduction, *Discourse*, 8, 3–9.

Mitchell, J. (1974), *Psychoanalysis and Feminism: A Radical Reassessment of Freudian Psychoanalysis*, London: Allen Lane.

Mulvey, L. (1975), Visual pleasure and narrative cinema, *Screen*, 16:3, 6–18.

Nestle, J. (1992), The femme question, in J. Nestle (ed.), *The Persistent*

Desire: A Femme–Butch Reader, Boston: Alyson, 138–46.

— (1987), *A Restricted Country*, London: Sheba.

Pearce, L. (1995), 'I' the reader: text, context and balance of power, in P. Florence and D. Reynolds (eds), *Feminist Subjects, Multi-Media Cultural Methodologies*, Manchester: Manchester University Press, 160–70.

Phelan, P. (1993), *Unmarked: The Politics of Performance*, London: Routledge.

Probyn, E. (1995), Queer belongings: the politics of departure, in E. Grosz and E. Probyn (eds), *Sexy Bodies: The Strange Carnalities of Feminism*, London: Routledge, 1–18.

Rand, E. (1995), *Barbie's Queer Accessories*, Durham: Duke University Press.

Rich, A. (1980), Compulsory heterosexuality and lesbian existence, *Signs: Journal of Women in Culture and Society*, 5:4, 631–60.

Rich, R. (1991), Nobody's handmaid, *Sight and Sound*, December, 7–10.

— (1992), A queer sensation, *The Village Voice*, 37:12, 41–4.

— (1993), When difference is (more than) skin deep, in M. Gever, J. Greyson and P. Parmar (eds), *Queer Looks: Perspectives on lesbian and Gay Film and Video*, London: Routledge, 318–39.

Robertson, J. (1989), *The Hidden Cinema: British Film Censorship in Action 1913–1975*, London: Routledge.

Rodowick, D. (1982), The difficulty of difference, *Wide Angle*, 5:1, 4–15.

Roof, J. (1991), *A Lure of Knowledge: Lesbian Sexuality and Theory*, New York: Columbia University Press.

Roy, C. (1993), Speaking in tongues, in A. Stein (ed.), *Sisters, Sexperts, Queers: Beyond the Lesbian Nation*, New York: Plume, 3–14.

Russo, V. (1981), *The Celluloid Closet: Homosexuality in the Movies*, New York: Harper and Row.

Schatz, T. (1993), The new Hollywood, in J. Collins, H. Radner and A. Preacher Collins (eds), *Film Theory Goes to the Movies*, London: Routledge, 8–36.

Schickel, R. (1994), Maverick, *Time*, 143:22, 60.

Sedgwick, E. (1991), *Epistemology of the Closet*, London: Harvester Wheatsheaf.

— (1993), Queer performativity, *Gay and Lesbian Quarterly*, 1:1, 1–16.

Signorile, M. (1994), *Queer in America: Sex, the Media and the Closets of Power*, London: Abacus.

Silverman, K. (1988), *The Acoustic Mirror*, Bloomington: Indiana University Press.

— (1980), Masochism and subjectivity, *Framework*, 12, 2–9.

Smyth, C. (1990), The pleasure threshold: looking at lesbian porn on film, *Feminist Review*, 34, 152–9.

Snitow. A. (1984), *Powers of Desire: The Politics of Sexuality*, London: Virago.

Spivak, G. C. (1988), *In Other Worlds: Essays in Cultural Politics*, London: Routledge.

Stacey, J. (1987), Desperately seeking difference, *Screen*, 28:1, 48–61.

— (1995), 'If you don't play, you can't win': *Desert Hearts* and the lesbian romance film, in T. Wilton (ed.), *Immortal/Invisible: Lesbians and the*

Moving Image, London: Routledge, 92–114.

— (1994), *Star Gazing: Hollywood Cinema and Female Spectatorship*, London: Routledge.

Staiger, J. (1993), Taboos and totems: cultural meanings of *The Silence of the Lambs*, in J. Collins, H. Radner and A. P. Collins (eds), *Film Theory Goes to the Movies*, London: Routledge, 142–54.

Stern, L. (1982), The body as evidence, *Screen*, 23, 38–60.

Storr, M. (1993), Psychoanalysis and lesbian desire: the trouble with female homosexuals, in J. Bristow (ed.), *Activating Theory: Lesbian, Gay, Bisexual politics*, London: Lawrence and Wishart, 53–69.

Studlar, G. (1992), *In the Realm of Pleasure: Von Sternberg, Dietrich and the Masochistic Aesthetic*, New York: Columbia University Press.

— (1984), Masochism and the perverse pleasures of the cinema, *Quarterly Review of Film Studies*, Fall, 267–82.

Sundelman, D. (1993), The demon therapist and other dangers: Jonathan Demme's 'The Silence of the Lambs', *Journal of Popular Film and television*, 21:1, 12–17.

Szymanski, M. (1993), I'm harder on myself than most people, *OK! Magazine*, June, 31–3.

Tasker, Y. (1996), Approaches to the new Hollywood, in J. Curran, D. Morley and V. Walkerdine (eds), *Cultural Studies and Communications*, London: Arnold, 213–28.

— (1994), Pussy galore: lesbian images and lesbian desire in the popular cinema, in B. Budge and D. Hamer (eds), *The Good, the Bad and the Gorgeous: Popular Culture's Romance with Lesbianism*, London: Pandora, 172–83.

— (1993), *Spectacular Bodies: Gender, Genre and the Action Cinema*, London: Routledge.

Vance, C. (ed.) (1992), *Pleasure and Danger: Exploring Female Sexuality*, London: Pandora.

Walker, L. (1993), How to recognize a lesbian: the politics of looking like what you are, *Signs*, 18:4, 866–90.

Wallace, M. (1990), *Invisibility Blues: From Pop to Theory*, London: Verso.

— (1993), Race, gender and psychoanalysis in forties film: *Lost Boundaries*, *Home of the Brave*, and *The Quiet One*, in M. Diawara (ed.), *Black American Cinema*, London: Routledge, 257–71.

Weiss, A. (1991), A queer feeling when I look at you: Hollywood stars and lesbian spectatorship in the 1930s, in C. Gledhill (ed.), *Stardom: Industry of Desire*, London: Routledge, 283–99.

— (1992), *Vampires and Violets: Lesbians in the Cinema*, London: Jonathan Cape.

Whatling, C. (1994), Fostering the illusion: stepping out with Jodie, in B. Budge and D. Hamer (eds), *The Good, the Bad and the Gorgeous: Popular Culture's Romance with Lesbianism*, London: Pandora, 184–95.

Willemen, P. (1995), The national, in L. Devereaux and R. Hillman (eds), *Fields of Vision: Essays in Film Studies, Visual Anthropology and Photography*, Berkeley: University of California Press, 21–34.

Williams, L. (1990), *Hard Core: Power, Pleasure and the 'Frenzy of the Visible'*, London: Pandora.

— (1989), Power, pleasure and perversion: sadomasochistic film pornography, *Representations*, 27, 37–65.

Wilson, E. (1983), I'll climb the stairway to heaven: lesbianism in the seventies, in S. Cartledge and J. Ryan (eds), *Sex and Love*, London: Virago, 180–95.

Wilton, T. (1995), On not being Lady Macbeth: some (troubled) thoughts on lesbian spectatorship, in T. Wilton (ed.), *Immortal/Invisible: Lesbians and the Moving Image*, London: Routledge, 143–62.

Wittig, M. (1992), *The Straight Mind and Other Essays*, Boston: Beacon Press.

Index

Note: 'n.' after a page reference indictates the number of a note on that page. Film titles are given in italic.

abject desire, 73, 78n.18
  contestatory viewership, 86–90
  deadly pleasures, 90–2
  desire for the heterosexual scene, 103–12
  eroticism of lesbian taboo, 92–6
  preliminaries, 79–86
  psycho-killer dykes and their lesbian fans, 97–103
Abramowitz, Rachel, 153, 154, 156
Accused, The
  Foster, Jodie, 135, 145, 149–51, 153–4
  Johnson's reading, 25, 30
  lesbian-identified readings, 18
  rumours, 142
  voyeurism, 25
action movies, 17–18
Addams Family Values, 95
Adlon, Percy, 1, 126
Adorno, Theodor, 11
Agrama, Jehan, 112n.9
AIDS, 113n.19
Air Canada, 118
Alarcón, Norma, 3
Aldrich, Robert, 1, 69
Alice Doesn't Live Here Anymore, 139–40
Alien trilogy

  identification and desire, 59
  lesbian-identified readings, 18
  monstrous-feminine, 16
  Ripley 2, 58–60
All About Eve, 62
Allen, Louise, 19, 26–7, 67–8
Allen, Woody, 57
Amiel, Jon, 134, 136
anaclisis
  femme-femme desire, 69, 71
  identification, 55
  Storr's writings, 42–3, 45
Another Way, 90
appropriation, 2–4
  audiences and texts, 11–14
  definition, 9n.4
  fantasising the dominant, 25–30
  fantasy appropriation, 22–5
  feminist readings of the dominant, 14–22
  lesbian psychoanalytic, 45–51
  limits of, 30–1
Apted, Michael, 135
Arrival of a Train at La Ciotat Station, The, 11
Arts and Athletics, 118–19
Arzner, Dorothy, 140–1
audiences and texts, 11–14
Audry, Jacqueline, 1
Avnet, John, 17

Index

Baker, Roy Ward, 79
Bankhead, Tallulah, 120
Barale, Michle Aina, 67
Barbie, 32n.9
Basic Instinct
  abject desires, 90, 101–2
  lesbian- and gay-identified pressure groups, response to, 83
  lesbian-identified readings, 18
  representation of lesbians, 79, 83
  voyeurism, 104
Because the Dawn, 113n.21
Benjamin, Walter, 11
Bergman, Ingrid, 122–3
Bevan, R., 97
Bigelow, Kathryn, 24
Bill, Tony, 153
Birth of a Nation, 20
Bitter Moon, 104–6
Blue Steel, 24
Bobo, Jacqueline, 19, 33n.24, 161, 162
  Color Purple, The, 14, 20–1, 32n.6
Bogle, D., 28
Bont, Jan De, 130
Bostonians, The, 2, 9n.2
Bright, Deborah, 57–8, 60, 75
Bringing Up Baby, 2
Britton, Andrew, 78n.19
Bronfen, Elisabeth, 114n.29
Brood, The, 16
Brown, Terry, 126, 131, 135, 138–40, 144, 154
Bulger, James, 31n.1
butch lesbians
  desire, 72–3
  for femmes, 65–6, 70
  identification and, 60, 63–4, 75
  visibility, 66–8, 74
Butler, David, 2
Butler, Judith
  appropriation, 4
  instability of lesbian category, 110
  melancholia, 104
  mimetism, 78n.17
  outness, 126
  psychoanalysis
    identity, 51n.2, 51n.4, 78n.18
    lesbian appropriations, 46, 47–50
  sexuality, 73
  visibility of heterosexuality, 111
Butterfly Kiss, 90, 100–1, 103
Byars, Jackie, 32n.6

Cagney and Lacey, 131
Calamity Jane, 2, 61
Calhoun, Cheshire, 67, 68, 74
Califia, Pat, 33n.18
Cameron, James, 18
Campbell, Bea, 101, 103
Caprio, Frank, 64–5
Capucine, 108, 109
Carny, 145, 147–8
Carr, Cindy, 126
Carrie, 16
Carrol, Kathleen, 140
Carstairs, Jo, 158n.8
Case, Sue-Ellen, 65, 66
castration complex, 37, 40, 41
censorship, 31n.1
Chabrol, Claude, 79
Chapman, Mark David, 131
Charbonneau, Patricia, 124
Cher, 106
Children's Hour, The, 79, 80, 90
Child's Play, 31n.1
Chomsky, Noam, 11
Citti, Sergio, 145
Cixous, Hélène, 52n.10
Clark, Danae, 106, 113n.16
Clarkson, Jeremy, 132n.5, 143
Clift, Montgomery, 2
Close, Glenn, 40
Clover, Carol
  audiences, 10n.7
  identification, 59
  Lex Talionis, 114n.24
  slasher/horror films, 14, 16–17
colonisation, erasure through, 26
Color Purple, The, 14, 20–1
coming out, 84, 87
Confidential magazine, 116, 123–4
Connelly, Mare, 20
Conrad, Henrietta, 136
contestatory viewership, 86–90
continuum, lesbian, 61, 150
Coombe, Rosemary J.
  gossip, 118, 119, 132n.1
  images of stars, 127–9
  marketing of stars, 121–2, 125
Coppola, Francis, 103

Cosmatos, George Pan, 88
Costello, Elvis, 128
covertness of lesbian representation, 9n.2
Cowie, Elizabeth, 23
Crawford, Christina, 123
Crawford, Cindy, 137
Crawford, Joan, 21, 120, 123
Creed, Barbara, 15–16, 79, 94
Cripps, T., 28
Cronenberg, David, 16

Dash, Julie, 77n.2
Davis, Bette, 120
Davis, Geena, 149
Davis, Madeline, 66
Day, Doris, 2
Dean, James, 120, 128, 130
death, cinematic, 80, 92, 102–3
  eroticism of the lesbian taboo, 93
  psycho-killers, 97–8
Deitch, Donna, 1, 77n.12
de Laria, Lea, 142, 143
de Lauretis, Teresa
  appropriation, 3
  audiences and texts, 12
  Charbonneau, Patricia, 124
  desire, 114n.39
  fantasy, 76
  and identification, 62–3, 78n.15, 78n.16
  femmes, 63–4, 70, 74
Deleuze, G., 18
Demme, Jonathan, 83, 151
De Mornay, Rebecca, 40
Deneuve, Catherine, 79, 112n.1
de Palma, Brian, 16
Desert Hearts, 1, 2
  aspirations, 85
  disclaimers, 124
  femmes, 70–1, 75, 77n.12
  representation of lesbians, 79, 84
  Stacey's writings, 90–1
desired homosexuals, 120
desires, *see* abject desire; fantastic desires; persistent desires
Desperately Seeking Susan, 62
Deville, Michel, 2
Diawara, Manthia, 20, 33n.14
Die Hard, 24
Dietrich, Marlene, 82, 116, 120, 158n.8
Diva, 121

Dmytryk, Edward, 79
Doane, Mary Ann, 55, 56–7
dominant
  fantasising the, 25–30
  feminist readings, 14–22
Donner, Richard, 134
Donovan, Jason, 136
Dora case, 43–4, 46, 52n.12
Doty, A., 86–7
Double Indemnity, 97
dreamscapes, sexual, 92–3
D'Souza, Christa, 140, 143–4
Durbin, Deanna, 61–2
Dyer, Richard
  blonde women, 67
  identification, 77n.2
  'star' and 'image', relation between, 123, 127, 139
  white perspective, 27, 28

Ellis, Havelock, 64, 158n.8
Ellsworth, Elizabeth, 32n.6
Entre Nous, 2, 75, 90
Ephron, Nora, 91
erotogenic zones, 48
exoticisation, cultural, 26
Extramuros, 79

Faderman, Lillian, 93
Faggots Rooting Out Closets (FROCS), 132n.9
Faludi, Susan, 101
fandom, 131
Fanon, Frantz, 4
fantastic desires
  all mixed up and nowhere to go, 71–6
  femme to femme, 63–71
  gauging the limits between identification and desire, 57–63
  identification, 53–7
fantasy appropriations, 22–5, 31
  of the dominant, 29–30
  of pain and anguish, 87
Farrow, Mia, 57
Fatal Attraction, 40, 95
fatal desire for the heterosexual scene, 103–12
Feinberg, Leslie, 66, 72–3
feminism
  appropriations, 14–22, 23
  femmes, 65

Index
179

Foster, Jodie, 154
psychoanalysis, 50
feminist sex wars, 33n.16
femmes
 desire 71–3, 74–5
  for femmes, 63–71
  and identification, 60, 75
 visibility, 74
fetishes, 25, 33n.22
 identity, 40–1
financial issues, 11, 32n.7, 33n.24
Fincher, David, 18
Fiske, John, 10n.7, 113n.15, 133n.12
Five Corners, 153
Flagg, Fanny, 89
Fleming, Victor, 20
Fliess, Wilhelm, 46
Florence, Penny, 124
Forbes, Malcolm, 126
Forrester, John, 116–17
Foster, Jodie, 19
 The Accused, 135, 142, 145, 149–51, 153–4
 Alice Doesn't Live Here Anymore, 140
 allegations of lesbianism, 134, 135–6
 Carny, 145, 147–8
 the desiring audience, 144–57
 Five Corners, 153
 Foxes, 135, 145, 159n.15
 Game, The, 132n.7
 heterotextual supplement, 135–44
 Hinckley, John, 131, 143, 153, 154
 Hotel New Hampshire, 135, 145, 148–9
 identification, 53
 Il Cosotto, 145, 147–8
 Little Man Tate, 141, 153, 154–5
 marketing, 132n.6
 Maverick, 134, 158n.6
 Nell, 135, 155–7
 outing, 126
 rumours, 120
 Silence of the Lambs, The, 58–9, 135, 151–3
  asexuality, 136
  role, 134, 145, 154, 155
 Sommersby, 134, 136–8
 Taxi Driver, 139

tokens of affection, 157
Foucault, Michel, 87
Fox, The, 69, 79
Foxes, 135, 145, 159n.15
Frankfurt school, 11
Freud, Sigmund, 51–2n.6
 castration complex, 51n.1
 fetishism, 25, 33n.22
 heterosexual imperative, 42–3, 52n.12
 identity, 37
 lesbian psychoanalytic appropriations, 46–8, 49, 50–1
 melancholia, 104
 narcissism and anaclisis, 42–3, 47–8, 55
Friedberg, Ann, 55, 161
Fried Green Tomatoes at the Whistle Stop Café, 17
 abject desire, 102–3
 contestatory viewership, 88–9
 death of Ruth, 80, 102–3
Frye, Marylin, 28–9, 34n.29

Gable, Clark, 120
Gaines, Jane, 34n.29, 52n.12
Gallop, J.
 heterosexual imperative, 42, 43–5
 identity, 37, 38–9, 51n.2
 lesbian psychoanalytic appropriations, 46, 47
Game, The, 132n.7
Garbo, Greta, 81, 120, 132n.3
Gates, Phyllis, 120, 123, 124
Gay and Lesbian Alliance Against Defamation (GLAAD), 83, 85, 101
Gere, Richard, 136–8, 142, 158n.8
Ghost, 34n.26
Gibson, Mel, 134
Gilda Stories, The, 21, 113n.21
Gless, Sharon, 131
Go Fish, 84
Goldberg, Whoopi, 34n.26
Golding, Sue, 128, 130
Goldstein, Amy, 113n.21
Gomez, Jewelle, 113n.21
Gone With the Wind, 20
gossip, 116–19
Gottfried, Martin, 63
Graham, Paula, 7, 8

Alien trilogy, 59–60
desire, 78n.16
fetishism, 25
Grant, Cary, 2
Green Pastures, The, 20
Griffith, D. W., 20
Gripsrud, Jostein, 10n.7, 12, 31n.2, 31n.5
Grosz, Elizabeth, 33n.22, 50

Hamer, Diane, 152
Hand That Rocks the Cradle, The, 40, 95
Hann-Bryd, Adam, 155
Hansen, Miriam, 132n.3
Hanson, Curtis, 40
Haraway, Donna, 163
Harris, Thomas, 122–3
Hart, Lynda
  racial fantasies, 27–8, 162
  sex and death, link between, 97–8
  Single White Female, 96, 114n.27
Hawks, Howard, 2
Hayworth, Rita, 21
Heavenly Creatures, 90, 98–100
Hendrix, Jimi, 128
Hepburn, Katharine, 2, 57
Hinckley, John, 131, 143, 153, 154
Holland, Tom, 31n.1
Hollibaugh, Amber, 66
Holly, Buddy, 128
Holmlund, Christine, 71, 74–5
Home Movie, 1
hooks, bell, 19–20, 22, 33n.25
Hooper, Tobe, 17
horror, 15–17
Hotel New Hampshire, 135, 145, 148–9
Hudson, Rock, 120, 123–4, 125, 137
Hunger, The, 79

I, Vampire, 113n.21
icons, 84–5, 112n.2
identification, 53–7
  and desire, limits between, 57–63
identity, 35–41, 165
Il Cosotto, 145, 146
Illusions, 77n.2
incests, 113n.23
Innenwelt, 56
Irigaray, L., 44

Ishtar, Arlene, 72, 73
I've Heard the Mermaids Singing, 77n.12, 84
Ivory, James, 2

Jackson, Glenda, 57
Jackson, Michael, 128
Jackson, Peter, 90
Jeffreys, Sheila, 33n.16
Jennings, Ros, 18, 78n.16
Jenson, Joli, 133n.15
Johnson, Barbara, 25, 149
Johnson, Mykel, 73, 74
Johnston, Claire, 140
Julia, 2, 9n.2

Kalin, Tom, 86, 97, 98
Kaplan, E. A., 86
Kaplan, Jonathan, 18
Kaylor, Robert, 145
Keighley, William, 20
Kelly, Grace, 122
Kennedy, Philippa, 134, 141–3, 146–7, 158.5
Killing of Sister George, The, 1, 69, 79, 84
Kingsley, Pat, 158n.5
Kinski, Natassja, 145, 148
Klawans, Stuart, 137
Kristeva, J., 44–5, 81, 96, 114n.34
Kurys, Diane, 2

Lacanian psychoanalysis, 50–1
  heterosexual imperative, 41–3, 45
  identification, 54
  identity, 35–40
  lesbian appropriations, 48, 49
Lamos, C., 71
lang, k. d., 19, 126
language, 37–8
Laplanche, J., 33n.15
Lapsley, R., 39
Larsen, Nella, 149
Lectrice, La, 2
Leigh, Jennifer Jason, 112n.1
Leigh Star, S., 33n.16
Lennon, John, 131
lesbian, definition, 5–6
Les Biches, 79
Lianna, 1, 77n.12
  femmes, 75

representation of lesbians, 84
voyeurism, 104
Linden, R., 33n.16
Little Man Tate, 141, 153, 154–5
looking lesbian, 160–4
Lumire, Auguste, 11
Lumire, Louis, 11
Lumley, Joanna, 2
Lutz, John, 96
Lyne, Adrian, 40, 95, 135
Lynskey, Melanie, 98, 99
Lyon, Phyllis, 65

Madonna, 128, 159n.22
Maidens in Uniform, 1, 86
Makk, Karoly, 90
Mamoulian, Rouben, 81
Mankiewicz, Joseph L., 62
Mapplethorpe, Robert, 29
marketing stars, 121–5
Martin, Del, 65
masochism, 18
maternal-erotic, 114n.39
Maverick, 134, 158n.6
Mayne, Judith
  Arzner, Dorothy, 140–1
  audiences, 10n.7
  colonisation, erasure through, 33–4n.26
  contestatory viewership, 87, 89, 90
  fantasy, 130
McCallum, David, 2
McClellan, J., 101
McGillis, Kelly, 142, 145, 149–51
McLaughlin, Sheila, 23, 62–3
McTiernan, John, 24
Meckler, Nancy, 90
Medusa, 16
melancholia, 104
Memmi, Albert, 4
Mercer, Kobena, 29
Merck, Mandy, 144, 163
Meyer, Richard, 123–4, 137
Meyer-Spacks, Patricia, 116, 117, 118
Miller, D. A., 110, 115n.43
mimetism, 78n.17
Minh-ha, Trinh T., 3
Mio, Mio, 2
Mommie Dearest, 123
Monroe, Marilyn, 122
monstrous-feminine, 15–16

Morocco, 79, 82
Morrison, Toni, 149
Mulvey, Laura, 41, 55

narcissism
  femme-femme desire, 69, 71
  Freud's writings, 47–8
  identification, 55, 56, 60, 61
  incest, 113n.23
  Storr's writings, 42–3, 45
Nell, 135, 155–7
Nestle, Joan, 63, 64, 65, 66
Newman, Paul, 79
new queer cinema, 91–2
Nichols, Mike, 2
nostalgia, *see* abject desire

Olivia, 1
Olympics, 118–19
outing of stars, 122, 125–7
  Foster, Jodie, 134, 136, 138, 144, 151
Outpost, 125, 134, 141
OutRage!, 83
Outweek, 126
over-identification, 56–7
Oxenburg, Jan, 1

Pagano, D., 33n.16
Parton, Dolly, 81
Pearce, Lynne, 88
Perry, Frank, 123
persistent desires, 164–5
Personal Best, 1
  abject desire, 90
  appropriation, 32n.6
  femmes, 75
  representation of lesbians, 84
Pfeiffer, Michelle, 130
phallus, 37, 48–50
Phelan, Peggy, 29, 39, 160
Phoenix, River, 120, 130
Picazo, Miguel, 79
Plummer, Amanda, 101
Point Break, 24–5
Polanski, Roman, 104, 105
Pontalis, J.-B., 33n.15
pornography, 14, 15
Portrait of a Marriage, 124
Postman Always Rings Twice, The, 21
pressure groups, 83
Prince, 128

psychic and the social, relationship between, 23–4
psychoanalysis, 8
  heterosexual imperative, 41–5
  identification, 54–5
  identity, 35–41
  lesbian appropriations, 45–51
psycho-killers, 97–103
Purple Rose of Cairo, The, 57

Queen Christina, 81
Queer Nation, 83, 85

race
  Allen's writings, 26–7, 68
  Bobo's writings, 20–1
  Frye's writings, 28–9
  Hare's writings, 27–8
  hooks's writings, 19–20
  psychoanalysis, 52n.12
  representation, 67, 161–2
  Wallace's writings, 21–2
Rachel, Rachel, 79
racism, 26, 103
Rambo, 88
Rand, Erica, 32n.9
Reagan, Ronald, 133n.14, 143, 153
Redgrave, Vanessa, 2, 57, 74, 120
  appropriation, 9n.4
  The Bostonians, 9n.2
  Julia, 9n.2
Reeves, Keanu, 24–5, 130
Reeves, Saskia, 100, 101
Rich, Adrienne, 61
Rich, B. Ruby, 19, 141, 146, 155, 165
Richardson, Tony, 135, 148
Rodowick, David, 36, 40
Rome, Sydne, 146–7
Roof, Judith, 46–7
Rose, Jacqueline, 35–6
Ross, Diana, 128
Rossellini, Roberto, 123
Rotello, Gabriel, 126
Roy, Camille, 92
Royalle, Candida, 15
Rozema, Patricia, 77n.12, 84
rumour, 118, 119–20
Russel, D., 33n.16
Russel, Rosalind, 141
Russo, Vito, 81, 93,101, 108

Rydell, Mark, 69

sadism, 18
Sagan, Leontine, 1, 86
Salmonberries, 1, 126
  Allen's reading, 19, 67–8
  racial difference, 26
Sands, Julian, 158n.5
Sapphire and Steel, 2
Sarandon, Susan, 79, 112n.1, 120, 149
Sayle, John, 1, 77n.12, 104
Schroeder, Barbet, 28
Scorsese, Martin, 139, 140
Scott, Ridley, 16, 18
Scott, Tony, 79
Sedgwick, Eve, 87, 113n.20, 116, 125–6
Segal, George, 57
Seidelman, Susan, 62
Selleck, Tom, 127
sexual dreamscapes, 92–3
shame, 113n.20
She Must Be Seeing Things, 23, 62–3, 70, 74
Showgirls, 78n.20
signified and signifier, 37–8
Signorile, Michelangelo, 125, 126
Silence of the Lambs, The
  Foster, Jodie, 135, 151–3
  asexuality, 136
  role, 134, 145, 154, 155
  identification and desire, 58–9
  lesbian- and gay-identified pressure groups, response to, 83
Silkwood, 2, 106–8, 114n.40
Silverman, Kaja, 36, 38, 40, 41
Single White Female, 28, 79, 90, 94–6
Sister my Sister, 90, 113n.23
Sleepless in Seattle, 91
Smyth, Cherry, 85, 102
Snitow, A., 33n.18
social and the psychic, relationship between, 23–4
Somerville, Jimmy, 127
Sommersby, 134, 136–8
Sonnenfeld, Barry, 95
Speed, 130
Spielberg, Steven, 14, 21
Spivak, Gayatri Chakravorty, 4, 118, 162

Stacey, Jackie
  identification, 54, 55, 129
  and desire, 61–2, 63
  lesbian popular romance, 90–1
  new queer cinema, 91–2
stalkers, 131
Stanwyck, Barbara, 80, 108, 109
stars and their proclivities
  gossip, 116–19
  historically ours, 119–21
  images, 127–31
  invisibly visible, 125–7
  marketing, 121–5
Star Trek, 128, 129
Sternberg, Josef von, 79
Stewart, James, 2
Stone, Sharon, 102
Storr, Merl, 36–7, 42–3, 44, 45
Streep, Meryl, 2, 106–8
Studlar, Gaylyn, 18
subjectivity, 36, 38, 56
Sundelman, David, 159n.18
Swoon, 86, 97–8

taboo, eroticism of the lesbian, 82, 89, 92–6
Tasker, Yvonne
  action movies, 14, 17–18
  ambiguities, 18
  audiences, 10n.7
  colonisation, erasure through, 34n.26
  desire, 78n.16
  the desiring audience, 145
  fantasy, 22–3
  lesbian films, nature of, 18
  multiple ideological readings, 88
  partial sightings, film as a series of, 105
Taxi Driver, 139
Texas Chainsaw Massacre, 17
texts and audiences, 11–14
Thelma and Louise, 2, 18, 149
Towne, Robert, 1
Tracy, Spencer, 57
Turner, Lana, 21

Umwelt, 56

Valentino, Rudolph, 120, 132n.3

Vampire Lovers, 79
vampires, 16, 69, 93–4, 95
Vance, C., 33n.18
Van Damme, Jean Claude, 120
Verhoeven, Paul, 18, 78n.20, 104
voyeurism, 25, 41, 104, 164

Walker, Alice, 21
Walker, Lisa, 66, 73
Walker, Mike, 142
Walk on the Wild Side, 79–80, 108–10
Wallace, Michele, 21–2, 162
Washington, Denzel, 130
Waters, Ethel, 120
Weaver, Lois, 70
Weaver, Sigourney, 2, 58–60, 120, 130
Weiss, Andrea, 10n.8
  butches and femmes, 67, 69
  Garbo, Greta, 132n.3
  gossip, 116, 117, 118, 119, 120
  identification and desire, 60, 164
  image of stars, 121, 127
  lesbians and cinema relation between, 82
  Morocco, 82
  racial differences, 26
  Silkwood, 106, 108
  vampires, 94, 95
well-of-loneliness effect, 82
West, Mae, 120
Westlake, M., 39
We've Been Framed, 84
When Night is Falling, 77 n.12, 84
Willemen, Paul, 9n.6
Williams, Linda, 14, 15, 23
Willson, Henry, 123, 124
Wilton, Tamsin, 6, 86
Winslet, Kate, 98, 99
Winterbottom, Michael, 90
World Wide Web, 119
Wyler, William, 79

Zinnemann, Fred, 2
Zucker, Jerry, 34n.26